WHO WAS JACK RUBY?

WHO WAS JACK RUBY?

by
Seth Kantor

Everest House

ISBN # 0-89696-004-8

Library of Congress Catalog Card No. 78-54078

Printed in the United States of America

Author's Note

HOUSTON, Nov. 21—The story of President and Mrs. Kennedy's "non-political" trip to Texas is chock full of bad timing and highly political backfires.

That's the beginning of the news article I wrote as correspondent for Scripps-Howard newspapers on a Thursday night, several hours after the White House correspondents reached Texas from Washington with the Kennedy traveling party. That article was running on the front pages of a number of Scripps-Howard papers— from *The New York World-Telegram & Sun* to *The Denver Rocky Mountain News*—as we made our way the next day through downtown Dallas in the presidential motorcade. When the shots went off, the reporter across the aisle from me in the press bus was banging out a story on his portable typewriter. He was working from an advance text of the speech Mr. Kennedy was to give in a few minutes at the Dallas Trade Mart. The reporter scarcely looked up. He thought the noises were no more than backfire.

Fifteen years later the backfire of that moment continues to be heard in the land. And even the House Select Committee on Assassinations, set up to probe the murder of President Kennedy that day in Dallas, was stricken with its own internal backfire in 1977, as its chairman Henry B. Gonzalez and staff director Richard A. Sprague feuded in a power struggle that destroyed each other's roles in the probe, and nearly destroyed the committee.

An hour after the shooting of President Kennedy I encountered Jack Ruby at Parkland Hospital. Ruby was someone I had known at the start of the Kennedy administration, when I had been a reporter on a Dallas newspaper. He sought me out at Parkland, called me by name and, later from jail, wrote me a warm, personal note. But he also later denied that he had been inside Parkland Hospital at that critical time. As a result, the Warren Commission questioned both Ruby and me in June, 1964, about the Parkland encounter. In the end, page 336 of the Warren Report declared that "Kantor probably did not see Ruby at Parkland Hospital. . . ." That helped make it more comfortable for the Warren Commission to conclude Jack Ruby was no conspirator in the murder of the President's accused assassin, Lee Harvey Oswald—a murder which took place a few feet from where I stood in the police station basement, two days after the Parkland encounter.

Now, however, after reading this book, Burt W. Griffin, the Warren Commission attorney who developed those conclusions about Jack Ruby for the Warren Report, has changed his mind about Ruby not appearing at Parkland soon after the President had been brought there. Griffin, who since has become a judge in Ohio, now says "the greater weight of the evidence" indicates I did see Ruby at Parkland.

Judge Griffin's reversed opinion is one breakthrough, but there are other conclusions in the Warren Report that can and should be reversed, hopefully by the House Assassinations Committee during its mandate in the 95th Congress to find the truth before the end of 1978, when the committee's work is to be done.

After the Warren Report was issued in late 1964, I put away all the personal notes and records that had come from the final trip of President Kennedy until the day when I could write a book with the right kind of historic perspective on the assassination—a book which might dispute essential Warren Commission conclusions on Ruby's activities in the weekend leading up to his shooting of Oswald, and show how the Commission failed to explore certain obvious avenues that might have led to other conclusions.

But historic perspective aside, there was no way I could have written such a book and continued my duties as a White House news correspondent covering the Johnson administration. President Johnson had strong private feelings that there had been more to the assassination than had met the Commission's eye, but he insisted the investigation be over and done with, and public suspicions laid to rest. In those pre-Watergate years the nation's newspaper establishment failed to cross-examine the CIA, the FBI, the Warren Commission and government leaders on the assassination findings. By late 1974, following the whole Watergate drama, more government documents were available and the investigative climate was better than it had been at the time of the Warren Report 10 years earlier. I began what would become a lengthy process of research, starting with Commission records and files in the National Archives.

By mid-1976 I undertook a 6,200-mile journey by automobile into several states to conduct interviews with people who held pieces of the Ruby puzzle. The interviews stretched from the New York City office of Dr. John K. Lattimer, a prominent specialist at Columbia Presbyterian Hospital, to the Jasper, Texas, office of a well-known trial lawyer, Joe H. Tonahill. On Lattimer's wall is a framed picture of Ruby's cancerous prostate gland. On Tonahill's wall is a massive photograph of Jack Ruby shooting Lee Harvey Oswald. Between the two men, Lattimer and Tonahill, was a look at Ruby, inside-out. Between the two men was a sprawl of America separating them by distance and custom, where I found several people secluded or distrustful or unwilling to discuss Ruby's dealings. Among them were the widow of Tom Davis, the CIA-connected gun-runner; Harold Tannenbaum, the New Orleans strip-show booker; and former Dallas police detectives George E. Butler and Wilbur Jay Cutchshaw. Were these people guarded about who they saw and what they said because my questions were about the sinister world of Jack Ruby? Or were they withdrawn for other reasons? I tracked down Butler and Cutchshaw, for instance, in remote areas of Texas, behind locked fences, with unfriendly dogs for their outdoor alarms. I remained haunted by what C. A. (Pappy) Dolsen had told me privately a few days after Ruby had been arrested for Oswald's murder. Dolsen ran a talent booking agency in Dallas and he told me he had received three phone calls threatening him if he came forward to testify against Ruby at the murder trial. There was no way he would testify, he told me, or talk on the record.

Numerous others have never testified, either in court or before the Warren Commission. This book names some of them and it is hoped they yet will be asked by the House Assassinations Committee to bring out facts in the case against Jack Ruby that the Warren Commission failed to seek.

Seth Kantor,
Bethesda, Maryland.
Summer, 1978.

Acknowledgements

Mary Ferrell of Dallas has worked enthusiastically, tirelessly and selflessly over the years to aid investigators and serious researchers in the long, hard quest for facts about the Kennedy assassination. There is much of Mrs. Ferrell's devotion to that quest in this book. I am especially grateful to her, and to Sylvia Meagher, whose objective and critical *Accessories After the Fact* in 1967 opened the door for America to see that the Warren Commission had bungled its job. I am also grateful to six individuals in Dallas and Fort Worth who were of special help—Earl Golz, B. L. (Buster) McGregor, Bert N. Shipp, Wayne Thomas, Russ Thornton and Bob Trimble—as well as Mike Novotnak of the Chicago Crime Commission; Tim H. Ingram of the House Government Operations Committee; Ken Roselle, editor of *The Wise County Messenger,* Decatur, Texas; R. L. Strawberry of the State Department; and Allen E. Blanchard, Washington bureau chief of *The Detroit News,* for his patience and wise counsel. But more than anyone else, to Annie.

Contents

Author's Note v

Acknowledgments ix

CHAPTER 1: Los Foxes And El Songbird 1

CHAPTER 2: The Private Government Of Jack Ruby 17

CHAPTER 3: The Weekend 38

CHAPTER 4: A Stillness On The Fifth Floor 78

CHAPTER 5: Any Friend Of Needle-Nose Labriola 96

CHAPTER 6: Put That In Your Pipe And Smoke It 104

CHAPTER 7: In Search Of Class 113

CHAPTER 8: Cuba 127

CHAPTER 9: The Ring Of Bulls 142

CHAPTER 10: An Amicable Solution 152

CHAPTER 11: May Day 156

CHAPTER 12: Man's Best Friend 167

CHAPTER 13: The Truth, The Whole Truth And Other Fables 176

CHAPTER 14: Faster Than A Speeding Magic Bullet 185

CHAPTER 15: A Matter Of Conspiracy 203

Notes 221

Sources 233

Index 237

CHAPTER 1

Los Foxes &
El Songbird

June 7, 1964, was another one of those days for the top people on the Warren Commission. They were blowing it again. This time it was the Commission's interview with Jack Ruby and it was being done behind the backs of Leon D. Hubert Jr. and Burt W. Griffin, the two attorneys who had been running the Warren Commission's investigation of Ruby for six months, since the investigation had begun.

Relations were uncomfortable between the team of Hubert and Griffin and the Warren Commission's top management, which was U.S. Supreme Court Chief Justice Earl Warren, the chairman, and J. Lee Rankin, the general counsel and staff director. Warren and Rankin were impatient because the two staff attorneys kept trying to broaden the probe into Ruby's background, especially the Cuban angles, rather than simply shutting down their investigation. Instead, Hubert and Griffin had written a snappish, 11-page memorandum to Rankin on May 14, three weeks before the Ruby interview. The memorandum in effect said the Commission had done a lousy job so far in carrying out an adequate investigation in three major areas that Hubert and Griffin had been trying to explore:

Why had Ruby killed Lee Harvey Oswald, the accused slayer of President Kennedy? Was Ruby associated with Oswald in any way? Did Ruby have confederates in the murder of Oswald?

The two investigators felt stymied and wanted, as Hubert later recalled it, "to protect ourselves against any accusation later on that we had not gone far enough."[1] Rankin sizzled at the tone of the May 14 memorandum and Hubert was allowed to resign from an active role as designated chief of the Ruby investigation at a private luncheon meeting between the two on June 1. According to a formal note Hubert wrote Rankin later that day,[2] Hubert's understanding of the luncheon agreement was that he would be available to participate in the long-anticipated Commission interview of Ruby when a date was set for it. Hubert was then allowed to finish up some commitments, clean out his desk at Commission headquarters on the edge of Capitol Hill, close down his apartment and leave for his home in New Orleans on Saturday, June 6, without anyone hinting to him that secretive plans had been well established for the Commission to interview Ruby the very next day in Dallas.

Hubert's associate, Burt Griffin, remained fulltime on the Commission staff but was not asked to go to Dallas for the Ruby interview, because Griffin clearly was in Rankin's doghouse.

Griffin had gone down to Dallas three months earlier and, in the course of taking sworn testimony from several Dallas police, individually and privately, on the shooting of Oswald by Ruby in the Dallas police station basement, Griffin went off the record with one of them, telling Sergeant Patrick T. Dean he didn't believe him. Griffin didn't speak harshly to Dean but urged him to "tell the truth" for the good of the "national interest."

A former assistant U.S. attorney in Cleveland, Griffin was known to his colleagues as a vigorous interrogator of witnesses. And on March 24, 1964, Griffin accused the police sergeant of having made up information about what Ruby is supposed to have admitted shortly after shooting Oswald.

According to Dean, Ruby admitted planning on his own to kill Oswald as early as 35 hours before he actually pulled the trigger, which strengthened the prosecution's case of premeditated murder against Ruby. Ruby denied he ever made such a statement, and insisted that he shot Oswald on impulse.

Secondly, Sergeant Dean said Ruby admitted entering the police station basement by way of the Main Street ramp. The admission was made in front of Secret Service agent Forrest V. Sorrels, Dean said. Sorrels denied Ruby ever made such a statement in front of him.

Dean had been a key prosecution witness at Ruby's murder trial. His testimony played a major role in the sentencing of Ruby to die in the electric chair.

In a six-page memorandum to Rankin, written March 30, Griffin furnished his superior with a number of reasons to investigate Dean further. Griffin also said he had reason to suspect "that Ruby came in by another entrance to a point where Dean could have stopped him and that Dean, having been directly responsible for all basement security, is trying to conceal his dereliction of duty." Griffin advised Rankin in writing that there was reason to believe that Dean had told Ruby to say that he had entered the police station basement by way of the ramp.

Dean was furious. He went to Dallas District Attorney Henry Wade to complain about Griffin's charges. There was an exchange of excited phone calls between Dallas and Warren Commission headquarters in Washington.

"The situation was critical and tense," remembers Howard P. Willens, who was Rankin's deputy.[3] "My own judgment was that Burt Griffin was a very competent and aggressive investigator, and was right in pursuing it aggressively." Willens supported Griffin and believed that "no real punishment or sanction was appropriate."

But Rankin caved in under pressure from Texas officials to get Griffin off Dean's back. Rankin ordered the investigator to return to Washington. Sources close to Griffin say he was humiliated by his recall, and was left with a deep feeling of rejection that he still won't discuss.[4] Griffin was confined to Washington through April and May, and was still stuck there on June 7, the day others went to Dallas to meet with Ruby.

Some members of the Warren Commission staff were very much upset that Hubert and Griffin had been ignored. One of them, David W. Belin, talked privately of resigning.

"I was very upset," Belin recalls.[5] "After all, these were the two men on our staff who knew most about Jack Ruby's life. It was just wrong not to allow them to be in on the interview."

Hubert and Belin's wife talked with Belin and helped convince him not to walk out on the investigation. Hubert rationalized that even if he had gone to Dallas to interview Ruby, the questions would have been controlled by Warren and Rankin anyway.

For instance, Gerald R. Ford, the lone Republican House member appointed to the Warren Commission, was the only other Commission member besides the Chief Justice who traveled to Dallas that Sunday. Ford was particularly interested in questioning Ruby about his Cuba connections.

Ford waited patiently for more than two hours for a chance to start his line of questioning. He had just begun asking about the route of Ruby's 1959 trip to Cuba when Rankin interrupted, asking Ruby abruptly if he remembered being taken upstairs to a cell in the Dallas police station after he had shot Oswald.

"That is so small to remember, I guess it's automatic, you know,"

Ruby shrugged. Rankin was groping. He tried something else before Ford could pick up the Cuba thread of the questions again. "Did you have this gun a long while that you did the shooting with?" Rankin asked. Ruby answered, "Yes." Moments later, Warren appeared ready to close the interview.

"You can get more out of me," Ruby invited. "Let's not break up too soon."

Ford took over the questioning again, on details of Ruby's 1959 visit to Lewis J. McWillie in Havana. McWillie had run crime syndicate gambling operations in Texas and was identified in Dallas police criminal intelligence section records as a murderer. This time Warren firmly broke off Ford's questions and changed the subject.

"Ford never did finish his interrogation on Cuba. Warren blocked Ford out on it," recalls one of those present, Joe H. Tonahill, a Ruby attorney. "That was very impressive, I thought. Ford gave him a hard look, too. I was sitting right there and saw it happen."[6]

The Warren Commission entourage had arrived in Dallas without much advance word and Sheriff J. E. (Bill) Decker hurriedly provided the jury deliberation room in the county jail building for the Ruby interview.

When they filed into the room that June Sunday in 1964, Tonahill, a 300-pound lawyer, looked toward the air vent in the wall and wondered for a moment if an electronic listening device was planted in there to carry the "private" interview with Ruby to unseen eavesdroppers.

Tonahill and other Ruby defense lawyers already had spent months meeting with Ruby off and on in another room upstairs in the jailhouse—known casually as the "squeal room"—and Tonahill usually had bid an irreverent greeting to the air vent on his way in and out because he had reason to believe that room was bugged by Decker.

Ruby bit at his lower lip in nervous anticipation as he looked at those who had come to question him now. Besides the Commission members, Warren and Ford, there were the Commission counsel, Rankin, Joseph A. Ball and Arlen Specter. There were two attorneys, Leon Jaworski and Robert G. Storey, representing the official Texas state inquiry into the Kennedy assassination, which was directed by Texas Attorney General Waggoner Carr and which was being muzzled by authorities in Washington. There were Elmer W. Moore, a Secret Service agent; Jim Bowie, an assistant Dallas district attorney; Sheriff Decker; and Tonahill.

In the next three hours Ruby went into a rambling, often-irrelevant discourse on what he had done for two days before killing Oswald, and then lapsed into one of his real hangups. His Jewishness. He began to rant that Jews would be killed in massive numbers in retribution for his having killed Oswald. At times Ruby could be a hot-tempered, two-bit thug who brawled and bellowed in behalf of his Jewishness. On a scale of from 1 to 10, with 10 being a profoundly rational, philosophical approach to Judaism, Jack Ruby was a 1. In the hot swirl of emotion after he shot Lee Harvey Oswald, the former Jacob Rubenstein was reported to have blurted: "I did it to prove Jews have guts."

Despite the rambling, there was a theme that began to emerge after the first hour of the Ruby monologue to the Warren Commission on his actions before shooting Oswald. The theme was repeated several times, weaving through a lot of other thoughts. It was that Ruby was a desperate man, begging to be taken out of Texas to Washington, where he could talk to Warren without fearing for his life. Like Tonahill, Ruby was aware that the room could be bugged. Even if the room were cleared of the sheriff and others, Ruby felt he could not confide in Warren there.

Ruby asked eight times to be taken to Washington, growing almost frantic about it toward the end. After the fourth time, Warren said it could not be done. "There are a good many things involved in that, Mr. Ruby." The prisoner asked the highest judge in the land to explain that better.

"Well, the public attention that it would attract, and the people who would be around," said Warren. "We have no place there for you to be safe when we take you out, and we are not law enforcement officers, and it isn't our responsibility to go into anything of that kind. And it certainly couldn't be done on a moment's notice this way."

But it certainly *could* have been done in reasonably short order by the Warren Commission, with its blanket subpoena powers to bring any witness to Washington.

Instead, Warren obviously must have concluded that the witness either was an opportunist making a grandstand move, or else was some kind of nut.

As to Ruby as an opportunist, there is no doubt about it. He was. Ruby was fascinated in particular by Joseph M. Valachi, a convict transported from an Atlanta federal penitentiary cell to Washington, to tell what he knew. Valachi became an informer on Mafia activities after he was jailed on narcotics charges, and had a $100,000 gangland price on his head. After years as an obscure Mafia soldier, Valachi rose to national prominence, detailing La Cosa Nostra crime operations before a congressional panel in the autumn of 1963—the period leading directly into the day that Ruby shot Oswald. In fact that day, although it was November 24 and the place was Dallas, authorities found part of a two-and-a-half-month-old *New York Sunday Mirror* in Ruby's car.

On page 41 of that September 8 copy of the *Mirror* was a Drew Pearson column, written by Pearson's associate Jack Anderson, glamorizing the exploits of "stool pigeon Joseph Valachi, who has been spilling crime secrets to federal agents."

Valachi made big headlines that autumn as a heavily protected informer in Washington before the Senate Permanent Subcommittee on Investigations. When he was done, Valachi was given special advantages and continued special protection within the federal prison system. There is no doubt that Ruby was acutely aware that if he had been removed from Texas to Washington he would have entered a federal jurisdiction where he might have bargained his way as a songbird into safer custody.

But the fact that Ruby was an opportunist wouldn't have ruled him out as someone who had valid information to give. Actually, in his role as opportunist, Ruby had been a two-way informer between the police and the hoods on a number of levels—a double-agent among the chasers and the chasees. Ruby had been an FBI contact in 1959, before and after he took the enigmatic trip to Cuba that Gerald Ford questioned Ruby about in more detail than Warren cared to hear. Ruby's hidden relationship with the FBI was not made public by FBI Director J. Edgar Hoover until several years after the Warren Report was published. The Commission cooperated with the FBI to keep that relationship from being made public in 1964 when the Warren Report came out.

In view of the later disclosure that Ruby had been an FBI contact, what would Burt Griffin, now an Ohio judge, have done differently about the Commission's whole approach to Ruby, if the 1964 investigation could be replayed?

"I would look for *serious* implications, rather than psychotic implications, behind the fact that Ruby kept wanting to come and talk with Earl Warren alone," Griffin says. "I would have treated this whole thing as possibly the efforts of a serious man, rather than of a crazy man."[7]

It seems apparent that by turning their backs on Ruby, Warren and Rankin could have made one of the critical mistakes of the investigation.

Then Tonahill was asked if Ruby could have been a blackmailed hostage of Dallas officers who might have had something on him—which could have led to his wanting to get away from them.

"They might have been doing that. Blackmailing him. We don't know all the activities Ruby was engaged in," Tonahill replied, "and we don't know what type of reaction he could have had to certain accusations over trivial matters."

Tonahill said "the people Ruby was dealing with and running with made him a sitting duck for any kind of verbal accusation that the law enforcement people wanted to make against him, and it may be that he was scared, and that he could speak more freely in Washington than he could there."

Ruby seemed to be scared. In the excited way that he talked, using the strange word patterns of his upbringing in a West Side Chicago immigrant neighborhood, he pleaded, "I may not live tomorrow to give any further testimony ... and the only thing I want to get out to the public, and I can't say it here, is with authenticity, with sincerity of the truth of everything, and why my act was committed, but it can't be said here."

The words came in a jumble but Ruby couldn't have put it more clearly. He said he would tell *why my act was committed, but it can't be said here.* Who was he afraid of, and why?

Perhaps the answers to those two questions were just as clearly there in the tumult of everything else Ruby had to say that afternoon to the Warren Commission.

Once he was sworn in by the Chief Justice of the United States—a privilege usually reserved for presidents being inaugurated—witness Ruby launched into a 50-minute-long monologue, relating his version of where he had gone and what he had done in the hours after President Kennedy's murder on Friday, November 22, 1963.

Ruby then described an encounter he'd had in the early morning shadows of Saturday, November 23, with Harry N. Olsen, a Dallas police officer who was with one of Ruby's strippers. Olsen told Ruby that Oswald should be "cut inch by inch into ribbons" and praised Ruby as "the greatest guy in the world" according to Ruby.

When Olsen was questioned by the FBI, he acknowledged that the encounter had taken place but denied encouraging Ruby to murder Oswald, and told the FBI he "never liked Ruby." A month after the shooting of Oswald, Olsen abruptly left the police force under unclear circumstances, and left Dallas.

For months Ruby remained close-mouthed about his hour-long clandestine conversation with the Dallas policeman—a conversation that took place soon after Oswald's arraignment for the murder of another Dallas police officer, J. D. Tippit. Ruby never brought up the Olsen meeting when he underwent a series of interrogations by local authorities, the Secret Service, FBI agents and psychiatrists who reviewed his movements with him before his murder trial—when premeditated murder on his part was the central issue. The meeting between Ruby and Olsen involved the strong suggestion of premeditation.

Ruby's murder trial had been over for nearly three months at the time he testified before the Warren Commission in the Dallas county jail. He had been sentenced to death but that verdict was pending before the state appellate court, and Ruby's chances of getting a reduced term with eventual parole through a new trial seemed favorable.

"I don't want to evade any crime I'm guilty of," Ruby told Warren. Why then would he want to be removed from Texas in order to talk, if it weren't that Ruby feared for his life behind Texas bars? Ruby and his lawyers already feared that a guard placed outside his cell on a regular basis—sheriff's deputy Jess W. Stevenson—had been transmitting Ruby's confidences to Texas lawmen. Stevenson had gained Ruby's trust and eventually Ruby had cause to believe that others were able to eavesdrop on him through a miniature listening device in Stevenson's clothing.[8]

Pointedly, Ruby waited until he reached a crucial place deep in his testimony to ask for the first time that the Warren Commission remove him from Texas jurisdiction and place him in protective custody in Washington. It happened so abruptly that the Chief Justice was taken by surprise. "I beg your pardon?" said Warren, incredulously. "Is there any way of you getting me to Washington?" Ruby repeated what he just had said. "I don't think so," said Warren. "It is very important," said Ruby.

The exchange took place moments before Ruby disclosed that he had discussed with officer Olsen the fate that Oswald deserved. Here was a Dallas policeman who had a reputation on the force for being unstable,[9] meeting in the dark of night with Ruby, who had a gun with him—with no license to carry it—and a set of brass-knuckles in his car. Ruby's concept of Dallas was that "this is a homicidal town."[10] And Ruby was described by one of his own defense psychiatrists as "basically an extremely unstable man. This is an aggressive psychopath with definite antisocial feelings."[11]

Immediately after disclosing limited details of the Olsen encounter, Ruby asked again for asylum in Washington. He said that "unless you get me to Washington, you can't get a fair shake out of me." He was telling them that he was holding back information, perhaps on the Olsen encounter itself.

Since before and after a cancer-ridden Jack Ruby died as a prisoner in Dallas, January 3, 1967, serious writers and researchers have suggested that the role of that two-fisted, bullying nightclub operator in the events of November 22, 23, and 24, 1963, never was properly explained. Some feel he was a sinister enigma. Some think he was hired by agents of a group that plotted the President's murder. Some believe that group could include any of Ruby's contacts among the syndicate criminals, labor racketeers, rightwing Texas militants, or Ruby's anti-Castro connection.

One of those groups in particular, the syndicate criminals who had a documented past of buying off protection within the Dallas police department, needed only to push one of its buttons in the department to open the way for Ruby to be brought in. Historically the department "was rotten from top to bottom," recalled a retired Dallas police captain.[12] "Oh, there were some good cops. But, man, it was a dangerous place to work in. You never knew which side your boss or partner was on. There was plenty of money floating around. All you had to do was raise your hand."

Syndicate payoff-man Paul Rowland Jones, who made routine police bribes but then was convicted when his offers to buy a new Dallas sheriff were recorded, told the FBI[13] that Joseph F. Civello of Dallas would know about plans to provide protection in 1964 for Ruby in jail. If Civello would know about plans to protect Ruby, he would certainly know about plans *not* to protect Ruby in any Dallas jail. Civello operated Civello's

Fine Foods & Liquor Store, and also operated the Dallas Mafia. Civello controlled "all rackets in Dallas and the vicinity."[14]

It was one thing for a man like Civello to push a button in the Dallas police department, but it was not conceivable that any group constructing a plot first to kill President Kennedy and then Oswald would ever confide in Ruby as part of that plot.

Ruby was as his mother had been, an incessant talker, and as his drunken, wife-beating father had been, a loser. He was brash and mercurial and never would have been trusted with knowledge of any plot to silence Oswald that would cause him to wind up in the arms of the police—unless of course some of the police themselves were involved. They could control his mouth.

Among these police were men with gut-reaction motives. Some were convinced a trial wasn't required to prove that Oswald was a cop killer—the killer of officer Tippit—and some believed Oswald had fired into the Kennedy motorcade as an agent of a communist government.

The idea of doing away with Oswald certainly didn't originate with Ruby. Only minutes after the killing of Tippit, Oswald was arrested in the Texas Theatre and when he was brought outside there already were angry people gathered on the sidewalk, shouting, "Kill the son of a bitch," and, "Give him to us. We'll kill him." Such was the feeling in Ruby's *homicidal town.*

Some police were concerned about anonymous telephone threats of lynching, when it came time to transfer Oswald from the city jail to the county jail, a mile away. There was tenseness in the police department that a mob determined to get the prisoner might shoot any policeman in the way.

In order to exact their own revenge on Oswald before he was sent out into the streets or placed in the custody of another jurisdiction, a few Dallas police contemplated getting the job done themselves. Of course no Dallas policeman could murder Oswald overtly, and the most logical person in town to be brought in to perform the hit was Ruby, a violent man who carried concealed weapons routinely, a police informant who could gain access to the police station without question and who provided the police with regular favors. For instance, Ruby was reliably reported to have cosigned Dallas bank loans for certain police.[15] But, *incredibly*, the Warren Commission left the investigation of Ruby's reported cosignature on loans for police in the hands of the Dallas police department to check out. A check was made of four Dallas banks,[16] but *not* of the one, Merchants State Bank, where Ruby did his business regularly and had two accounts. Ruby also provided small cash loans to police on his own and gave them discounts at the bar at his Carousel Club.

The idea of murdering Oswald, who appeared to Ruby to be "smirky, smug, vindictive,"[17] appealed to Ruby as something that had a patriotic overtone. Ruby fully expected to be treated as a hero and to be out on bond on the streets of Dallas again a day after the shooting. He anticipated a large payoff in publicity dividends. He was, after all, 52 years old, paunchy and balding, and still in search of the elusive big financial kill that would pull him back from the brink of economic ruin he faced almost daily.

The day he shot Oswald, Ruby possessed a small claims court summons for having passed a bad check to a downtown department store. The worthless check he'd written was for $12.19.

"I have been used for a purpose," Ruby told Warren as their meeting in Dallas county jail drew near a close. But nobody in the interrogation room even bothered to ask him who had used him and what was the purpose.

Naturally Jack Ruby presented himself during his June 7, 1964, testimony in as wholesome a light as possible. He pictured himself as an angel of mercy tending to the needs of those in the front lines on the day President Kennedy was murdered. "I want to bring some sandwiches" to the hard-working cops, he recalled in the present tense of an angel from a Damon Runyon story. "I see [District Attorney] Henry Wade talking on the phone to someone. 'Do you want me to get him over here?' " Ruby recalled asking a young reporter. "I want to bring . . . sandwiches to [radio station] KLIF so they would have the sandwiches."

Ruby was not asked about his underworld connections, not even the specific ones that the excluded Hubert and Griffin had learned about in the tightly controlled atmosphere Warren and Rankin had established in the interrogation room. Ruby told Warren and Rankin that his knowledge of hoodlums was strictly second-hand: "I have read from stories of personalities that are notorious; that is the extent of my involvement in any criminal activity."

Rankin asked Ruby about "a story that you had a gun with you" late Friday night, November 22, 1963, when Ruby simply walked into the Dallas police showup room as Oswald was led in to clamoring reporters and cameramen. "Story" was a strange word for Rankin to use in that connection since it was Ruby himself who told two FBI men on December 21, 1963, that he was carrying the weapon in his trousers that night.

"I will be honest with you," said Ruby in his best I-want-to-come-clean manner. "I lied about it. It isn't so. I didn't have a gun. But in order to make my defense more accurate, in order to save [my] life, that is the reason that statement was made." Ruby was street-smart. He was telling Rankin he had found it convenient, as a hedge against charges of premeditation, to deceive federal investigators six months earlier—by telling the FBI he'd had the gun but hadn't used it on Oswald when he could have, two nights before he used it "impulsively" on Oswald.

As a reporter I was in the heavily crowded police showup room that Friday night when Oswald was led in. Ruby simply could not have gotten off a clean shot at Oswald from the position Ruby had in the rear of the room, where he stood on a table. Oswald was bunched in the midst of detectives and obscured by a herd of photographers nudging and elbowing each other in front of the puny prisoner. Between Ruby and his ultimate target were more photographers and a number of reporters standing on tables closer to Oswald. From where Ruby was, it would have taken a 60-millimeter mortar lob to put Oswald out of commission. But Ruby's answer was good enough for Rankin, who changed the subject.

Rankin next wanted to know how many times Ruby had gone to Cuba. Ruby lied by saying he went there once, even though transportation records show he was there twice in 1959, and CIA files report him there at least twice more after it became illegal for Americans to travel to Cuba. But Ruby immediately obscured his answer by adding that "I probably had two dates from meeting some young ladies I got to dancing with, because my dinners were served at the Tropicana," the Havana nightclub where Ruby's crime-syndicate buddy, McWillie, operated the gambling casino.

"One thing I forgot to tell you," Ruby then obscured the answer a giant step further, "you are bringing my mind back to a few things—the owners, the greatest that have been expelled from Cuba, are the Fox brothers. They own the Tropicana."

"Who are the Fox brothers?" asked Rankin, going off on Ruby's angle.

"Martin Fox and I can't think of the other name."

"Do you know where they are located now?"

"They are in Miami, Florida," said Ruby. "They know everything about McWillie, I heard; and know the officials." Ruby went on to say that "the Fox brothers came to Dallas—I don't know which one it was—to collect a debt [from] some man [who] gave some bad checks on a gambling debt and they came to see me."

Ruby then said he met at dinner in Dallas (apparently in 1959, in the period when Ruby was an FBI contact) with one of the Foxes, who was a heavyweight Cuban gambler with connections leading to Las Vegas and Miami mobsters. Also at the table with Ruby were two Dallas lawyers, who turned out to have even more questionable connections than the Cuban.

One was David C. McCord, who subsequently gave up his license to practice law rather than face disbarment proceedings when charged with involvement in a shady securities deal. Then, in July, 1976, McCord was arrested on numerous other charges, including conspiracy and mail fraud involved in a bogus silver mine investment scheme. Money from investors in several states, according to federal grand jury indictments, was shifted instead to the controversial Castle Bank & Trust Co. of the Bahamas, a favorite money drop for organized crime bosses.

The other lawyer was Alfred E. McLane. Probate court records in Dallas show that when McLane was killed in a March 16, 1960, two-car crash in New York City, he was general counsel for Rimrock Tidelands, Inc., a Louisiana-based oil exploration firm with extensive leases in several states.

Records on file at the Securities and Exchange Commission in Washington, D.C., disclose that on January 15, 1958, Rimrock Tidelands took control of Rimrock International, which it formed out of several foreign companies, including the Societa Olii Minerali, a Sicilian-based firm.

A man named Santo Sorge, a minor stockholder in the Sicilian firm, was placed in control of Rimrock International, with headquarters at 680 Fifth Avenue, New York City. According to the published record of narcotics hearings by Senator John L. McClellan's Permanent Investigating Subcommittee at the time, Sorge had become "one of the most important Mafia leaders [and] travels extensively between Italy and the United States in furtherance of ostensibly legitimate international ventures, which probably cover for liaison duties between highest ranking Mafiosi in the United States and Italy."

Sorge ultimately was deported from the United States as an undesirable, just as he had been expelled from France earlier.

Rimrock International, through Sorge's firm, held operating permits and licenses in two countries where the narcotics traffic, aimed for entry into the United States, was heavy—Turkey and France.

Ruby's friend McLane was a leading member of a prominent Dallas law firm. He had a national reputation in the federal courts for his legal expertise on the effect of nineteenth-century U.S.-Indian treaties on oil and gas leases on tribal lands. As a result, Earl Warren knew of him and when Ruby couldn't come up with McLane's first name, Warren immediately identified him: "Alfred was killed in a taxi in New York."

New York police department records show McLane flew to New York on the evening of March 16, 1960, checked into the Waldorf-Astoria and an hour later, at midnight, he was in a taxi with Loraine Redding, who listed herself with police as a 32-year-old fashion model. The cab was rammed by another car, which disappeared into the night. McLane was killed on the spot. No one else was hurt.

"Funny thing about McLane," one of his 29 former law partners told me in Dallas. "He sure was 'different.' He was a loner. He was driven with the obsession of getting money and in that end he was successful. But he hung out with promoters and there were concealed people in his life."

Among the concealed people were Jack Ruby and the Fox brothers. It seemed apparent to several of the nation's more serious students of the

Warren Commission's blunders that there were no Fox brothers—they were a figment of Ruby's foxy imagination; they really were the Lansky brothers and Ruby was protecting the clandestine interests of the Lanskys with such wheeler-dealers as McCord and McLane.

Instead of the Fox brothers, Martin and Pedro, as Ruby identified them with a great deal of uncertainty, it appeared to some to be the powerful Lanskys, Meyer and Jake. It made sense. After all, according to Lansky biographer Hank Messick, Meyer Lansky "has pulled the strings in every important move made by the national crime syndicate." With a personal fortune reputed to be $300 million, Meyer Lansky once boasted that "we are bigger than U.S. Steel." Messick says Lansky would be chairman of the board of the syndicate. That would place his brother, Jake, in the role of first vice-president, and Ruby as a branch office errand boy.

The Lanskys had an enormous investment in gambling operations in Havana and in high-ranking members of the Cuban government, starting with its dictator, Fulgencio Batista. Lansky got Cuban laws changed in the 1950s to provide him with matching funds from the dictatorship government and a waiver of corporate taxes so that he could build and control hotels and casinos—with a substantial skim of the gambling profits for Batista, who stored away millions in Swiss banks.

Ruby described the Fox brothers to the Warren Commission as "the greatest that have been expelled from Cuba." Meyer Lansky escaped just behind Batista when Fidel Castro charged into Havana in 1959. Jake Lansky was imprisoned for a month before Castro let him go. Other Lansky operatives were jailed and then ousted.

Santo Trafficante Jr., the Tampa, Florida, numbers racketeer, had become the most significant Lansky operative in Cuba, and was imprisoned by Castro. According to CIA files, Document No. 150-59, Ruby is reported to have visited Trafficante in a Havana prison in 1959.

The Fox brothers "own the Tropicana," Ruby told the Commission. The Lanskys had hidden control of the Tropicana in Las Vegas. "They are in Miami," Ruby said, which is where the Lanskys headed when they fled Cuba, and "they know everything about McWillie."

Before and after Ruby shot Oswald, in 1963 and 1964, McWillie was working as a pit boss in the Thunderbird Casino at Las Vegas. Lansky was a hidden partner in the Thunderbird, established years earlier, and McWillie could not have worked at the level he did in Havana without approval from the Lanskys, who virtually controlled visas for imported pit men and other Americans who ran the games under the syndicate's dark and watchful eye.

The Tropicana in Havana, supposedly the largest nightclub in the world at that time, was honeycombed with U.S. syndicate figures such as John (Johnny Williams) Guglielmo from Boston, protected by the Lanskys.

Ruby said Castro considered the Foxes to be "a bitter enemy." It has become fashionable among aficionados of the Warren Commission's investigation into Ruby to believe by now that Ruby was talking about the Lanskys all the time, and simply invented the Foxes as a cover name to protect his own dealings with them.

Michael Canfield and Alan J. Weberman, for instance, in their 1975 book, *Coup d'etat in America,* wrote that the Foxes were a contrivance of Ruby's underworld mentality.

In another 1975 book, *"They've Killed the President!"* author Robert Sam Anson lists the "Fox brothers" in quote marks and tells the reader: *See Lansky, Meyer.*

Others who claim to have researched the knowledge of professional gamblers say no Fox brothers are to be found in the long list of those involved in organized gambling. But a search in the back-room stacks at the Library of Congress, through several years of Miami city directories and Havana telephone books from the pre-Castro period, shows something else. A 1958 Havana phone book shows a Martin Fox with two residence telephone numbers listed. One of the numbers corresponded exactly with a special office number placed in an advertisement at the back of the phone book for the Tropicana. By 1962, a Martin Fox was living on Southwest 22nd Avenue Road in Miami, one block from a Pedro Fox. The search led at last to Pedro Fox's daughter in Miami in 1976. She was able to verify that Martin and Pedro, dead for several years now, were brothers who were Cuban nationals and operators of the Tropicana, just as Ruby had said.

The significance of all this marching up and down the hill about the Fox brothers is that Ruby was a rational man at the time of the Warren Commission's June 7, 1964, interview with him. He was telling them the truth, and begged to be taken out of Texas so he could tell them more. But no one listened, on one of the sorriest days in the Warren Commission's history.

The Commission left a lot of questions unasked as well as unanswered that day, creating the firmament on which a lot of reasonable but misguided conclusions such as the legend of the "nonexistent" Fox brothers could sprout and grow. If the legend went unchecked, it wouldn't be long before everyone absolutely believed Ruby had made up the Fox brothers and had really had dinner with one of the Lanskys.

Among the major unasked questions of Ruby, the day the Warren Commission met with him, was his connection with a mystery-man named Davis.

Hubert and Griffin had alerted Warren, Ford and the rest of the Commission members to the existence of Davis more than two months earlier, in a memorandum dated March 19, 1964. Not only did the Commission fail to let Hubert or Griffin ask Ruby anything, but their question about Davis was ignored. Their March 19 memorandum said, in part:

> Ruby has acknowledged independently that, prior to the time that Castro fell into disfavor in the United States, he had been interested in selling jeeps to Cuba. Ruby states that he contacted a man in Beaumont, Texas, whose name he recalled was Davis. The FBI has been unable to identify anyone engaged in the sale of arms to Cuba who might be identical with the person named Davis.

Notice how the subject darted quickly from jeeps to guns. Hubert and Griffin believed Davis could lead them to some of Ruby's more important business with Cuba.

The FBI never even could find a first name for Davis. But the CIA knew all about him and still does in a closed file, under the name of Thomas Eli Davis III; born: Aug. 27, 1936; died: Sept. 6, 1973.[18]

Ruby had told Robert Ray McKeown of Bashore, Texas, about Davis in 1959. McKeown was a known Cuban gun-runner who had been jailed in Texas for supplying Castro with munitions when Castro was building his revolution. More than four years later McKeown told the FBI about Davis as someone with whom Ruby had had dealings. But McKeown, who could turn his memory off and on conveniently, told the FBI he couldn't for the life of him remember Davis's first name.

Not long after Ruby was jailed for the murder of Oswald, his first lawyer, Tom Howard of Dallas, asked him if there were any names of people the prosecution could produce who could be damaging to Ruby's defense.

Unhesitatingly, Ruby came up with Davis, a tall, handsome, charming Texan who "could talk the maggots off a dead fish," as Davis's widow puts it, in her home on a cove of Corpus Christi Bay.

Ruby told Tom Howard he had been involved with Davis, who was a gun-runner entangled in anti-Castro efforts. Ruby also told Howard he intended to go into the gun-running business on a regular basis with Davis. This was at a time when Ruby and lawyer Howard thought they could beat a really serious murder penalty by pleading extreme patriotism as the reason for Ruby killing Oswald. Ruby hoped to be out of jail and into partnership with the mysterious Davis.

The CIA knew a great deal about Davis, who carried out his work with the skill of an underwater commando. He was a professional deep-sea diver who operated a boat on the Gulf of Mexico. He had become involved in training anti-Castro units at a hidden encampment in Florida and at another site in South America, according to knowledgeable sources in Texas.

Davis's young attractive widow works in a bank and her husband was a bank robber. It was typical of their marriage. "He was very uncommunicative," she said. "I worked. He played." On June 18, 1958, he took $1,000 at gunpoint from a teller in a Detroit bank; then changed his mind, threw the money onto the floor and was arrested by the time he reached his car, which contained several more guns. Davis talked his way out of that, to the extent that he got a five-year probated sentence.

While still serving his federal prison term on probation, Davis obtained a passport, No. D236764, issued January 31, 1963, through the State Department, which could not be done by a convict without some extraordinary help. But by then Davis had become involved in activities familiar to the CIA.[19]

Sometimes Davis freelanced on his passport. At the time of President Kennedy's assassination, for instance, Davis was in jail in Algiers, charged with running guns to the secret army terrorist movement then attempting to assassinate French Premiere Charles de Gaulle. Davis was quietly released from the Algerian jail and returned to the United States. Evidence shows Davis was freed from jail through the efforts of QJ/WIN, the code name given by the CIA to an unsavory foreign agent with a network of Mafia contacts. He specialized in recruiting and directing other criminals to handle CIA assignments. QJ/WIN worked on African and European projects.[20]

Ten years later, in September, 1973, according to Eldon Moyers, who then was sheriff of Wise County, Texas, Davis was stealing three-quarter-inch copper wire from an abandoned rock-crusher site in the county. In the darkness Davis cut his way into a power line which he thought no longer was juiced. He was electrocuted by 7,000 volts.

More than 400 miles away in San Patricio County, Texas, Davis's widow keeps to herself. She lives in a large clapboard house on a rural lane at the water's edge. Nearby is Devil's Elbow, where the heavily barnacled old Spanish galleons lie on the Gulf floor, an area where Davis did boat salvage work, when he worked.

She was his third wife. They had been married slightly more than two years and Davis was gone a lot of the time, rarely telling her anything about what he did, where he had been, or much of anything about his past—except he once told her he knew the man who killed the man who had killed the President.

"I don't know where he got his money," she said. "He probably was mixed up with the Mafia or something." And then she laughed. "I'm joking." But the laughter had a nervous edge and when it stopped, she said, "I don't rightly know."

Neither did the Warren Commission, and threw away its chance to ask.

CHAPTER 2

The Private Government Of Jack Ruby

The Warren Commission carefully constructed a chronicle of Jack Ruby's contacts over a several-month period leading into the weekend that John F. Kennedy and Lee Harvey Oswald were shot dead. It was a daily chronicle that alleged to show everything but focused on nothing. It gave the American public a pastel portrait of Ruby, withholding the sinister shadows and the hard lines in his face.

There was no effort to lead the American public astray with the chronicle, Commission sources have told me. It was supposed to be strictly an in-house working summary of Ruby's activities—a guide to FBI reports on Ruby; a means of categorizing those reports as a device to help Commission lawyers get a handle on Ruby's day-to-day movements. It wasn't even required as a Commission document, I was told. Yet it was published as Commission Exhibit No. 2344 on pages 317 through 322 in Book 25 of the Warren Commission volumes, for the public to see, and what the public saw there was an incomplete picture of Ruby.

The Warren Commission said it could "not establish a significant link between Ruby and organized crime."[1] The Commission acknowledged that when Ruby moved to Dallas from Chicago in 1947 he was linked with Paul Rowland Jones, the Chicago crime syndicate's payoff-man to the Dallas police.[2] The payoffs were channeled through the office of a Dallas criminal lawyer to the police. "But Ruby has disclaimed that he was associated with organized criminal activities," said the Warren Report, "and law enforcement agencies have confirmed that denial."[3]

But a far more accurate picture of Jack Ruby in the six months before he pulled the trigger is one that shows him having private, hotline phone conversations with the underworld at two crucial intervals.

The first of these intervals was in June, 1963, when a group of Chicago gangsters held a clandestine council in Dallas to plan the takeover of local gambling and prostitution operations.

The second interval covered the 11 days just before President Kennedy's assassination, when Ruby abruptly signed a power of attorney, giving up certain rights to control his own money. He also suddenly bought and installed a safe for the first time in his 16 years as a Dallas nightclub operator, to store extra amounts of money. For a man who always had operated his finances out of his pants pocket and in paper bags, the two wholly uncharacteristic money transactions by Ruby at a time when he was meeting furtively with a number of people steeped in underworld connections—including Paul Rowland Jones, the syndicate paymaster—is significant.

Yet the Warren Report never mentioned the power of attorney, the new safe in Ruby's office, or Ruby's late-1963 contacts with Jones, who showed up suddenly from out of state.

Actually, during those critical months before the Kennedy assassination, Ruby was heavily in debt. He had grown desperate for money. His debts to the federal government alone had risen to more than $39,000 in owed excise and income taxes.

There is ample evidence that Ruby turned to the mob for financial help and had it lined up by November 19—only two days before President Kennedy arrived in Texas. On November 19 Ruby suddenly told his tax attorney that "a friend," a never-identified friend, would provide him money to settle the long-standing tax debts.

The mob was Ruby's "friend." And Ruby could well have been paying off an IOU the day he was used to kill Lee Harvey Oswald. Remember: "I have been used for a purpose," the way Ruby expressed it to Chief Justice Warren in their June 7, 1964, session. It would not have been hard for the mob to maneuver Ruby through the ranks of a few negotiable police.

Paul Rowland Jones, according to an FBI report, said that "from his acquaintance with Ruby he doubted that [Ruby] would have become emotionally upset and killed Oswald on the spur of the moment. He felt Ruby would have done it for money. . . ."[4]

William J. Cox, the loan officer who personally handled Ruby's loans over a period of years at the Merchants State Bank, recalls that "Jack could be hot-headed, but he didn't strike me as an impulsive man."[5] An analysis of the two significant intervals in 1963 shows that Ruby's quest for money—the quick buck—put him in the position of shooting Oswald.

The first interval began on June 5, ironically a day when an annoyed John F. Kennedy was in Texas. The President had been watching missile firings at a White Sands test range site across the state line in New Mexico and had come to El Paso to spend the night. With him were Vice-President Lyndon B. Johnson, Texas Governor John B. Connally and Navy Secretary Fred Korth. The preoccupied President zoomed through the streets of El Paso in a closed car and a lot of people were unhappy because Kennedy could not be seen. Privately that day, though, Kennedy discussed coming back to Texas, probably in the fall, in order to make several public appearances aimed at repairing a bad split in the Democratic Party between conservative leader Connally and the liberal tiger, U.S. Senator Ralph W. Yarborough. The Kennedy-Johnson ticket had carried Texas in the 1960 presidential election only by a hair-width 46,233 votes. Yarborough was a strong Kennedy supporter who despised Johnson. Yarborough also was up for re-election in 1964 and, with Connally working against Yarborough, a troubled Kennedy figured there was no way he could take Texas again in 1964 without an early buildup of public party unity. Kennedy also was troubled about Korth, the Texas banker named Secretary of the Navy at Johnson's request, when Connally left the Pentagon to run for governor. Korth had been using his official Pentagon stationery to further some of his Fort Worth banking interests. He also was involved in the multi-billion-dollar TFX warplane contract scandal under dogged investigation by Senator McClellan's subcommittee. Kennedy would wait for the right moment and dump Korth, who had become a liability.

That same day in the Pentagon, at the Navy Discharge Review Board, Commander E. I. Carson wrote to Lee Harvey Oswald that Oswald's request to have his undesirable discharge from the Marine Corps changed was under review. Oswald originally had been given a dependency discharge, on grounds that his mother needed his financial support. But then the discharge had been changed to "undesirable," when Oswald defected to Russia.

Oswald was living in New Orleans now, where his Russian wife, Marina, was both pregnant and miserable. In a letter dated June 5 to her friend Ruth Paine in Irving, Texas, a Dallas suburb, Marina wrote in Russian that "Lee has made it plain he doesn't want to live with me. But he doesn't give me a divorce, rather insists that I go away to the Soviet

Union—which I certainly don't want to do." Marina said "a gloomy spirit . . . rules this house . . . . Very likely I will have to go to Russia after all. A pity . . . ."

And on that same day, Jack Ruby telephoned New Orleans from Dallas. It was a 28-minute call to a striptease joint, the French Opera House. After that phone call Ruby got in his car—left Dallas but did not actually turn up in New Orleans, so far as is known, until three nights later, June 8. There is no record of where he spent that time.

On June 5 the three men—Kennedy, Oswald, Ruby—appeared to be moving in their own directions. But their mutual destinies now were locked in place, moving in a slow, narrowing orbit toward a weekend nearly half a year away when all would be sucked into the same bloody vortex.

On June 6, an official in the Dallas district Internal Revenue Service office entered a notation on Jack Ruby's records that Ruby's tax attorney, Graham R. E. Koch, had telephoned to report that Ruby would settle his three-and-a-half-year-old accumulation of $39,129 in federal tax debts "as soon as arrangements can be made to borrow money . . . [and] will contact this office not later than June 14."

June 7, Chicago tough-guy Robert (Barney) Baker was paroled from Sandstone Prison. He was a massive henchman who pushed people around for James Riddle Hoffa, head of the Teamsters Union. Ruby would soon be looking for help from Baker.

By June 8, a Saturday, a large group of Chicago racketeers began to show up at Ruby's Carousel and at two other nearby strip-show clubs, according to a confidential report to Dallas Police Chief Jesse E. Curry by Lieutenant Robert L. May Jr., who had been head of the vice squad. May's report, written June 16, said that out-of-state syndicate representatives and some area mobsters held a series of meetings that began on June 9, aimed at setting up syndicate-controlled prostitution and bookmaking operations in Dallas.[6] The plan was to bring in hired killers to muscle out the independent Dallas pimps and bookies. By Sunday, June 9, May said one of the nation's top vice lords was flown in for the meetings, landing in a private plane at a small airport south of Dallas. Ruby placed phone calls on June 10 and 13 to a restaurant between Dallas and Fort Worth, where some of the hoods were meeting.[7] If they were going to rearrange any of the action in Dallas he would want a piece of it. Ruby also found it useful for his own purposes, in dealing with a range of police agencies, to find out what he could about movements in the underworld. For instance, later in the summer of 1963, Ruby met privately with two Chicago detectives, Riccio R. Cisco and E. S. Kalinowski. The three had dinner together in Dallas, and Ruby told them as much as he wanted to about the pending involvement of the Chicago syndicate in the Dallas vice gutters. Ruby cherished his police contacts.

Ruby returned to Dallas from his New Orleans trip on June 9, determined to sign up Janet Adams Bonney Cuffari Smallwood Conforto (stage name: Jada), whom he had seen performing at Madame Francine's in New Orleans. Jada was 27, separated from her fourth husband and supercharged with an animalism she displayed in her act with a tiger rug. Ruby thought that was classy stuff and was willing to pay Jada twice as much as any of his other strippers was getting.

The next day, June 10, Ruby placed a 16-minute phone call to Edna, Texas, to Juanita Slusher Dale Phillips Sahakian (stage name: Candy Barr), who had been paroled from the Texas state prison in April on a marijuana possession sentence she had been serving since 1959. Candy Barr was 28 and separated from her third husband. Ruby had been contacting her steadily since April—five phone calls and a personal visit, but not to get her to resume her once-meteoric stripping career. She was under strict parole provisions not to strip again, at least until 1974, and she could not even visit Dallas under the terms of her release. Ruby had reason to be interested in underworld connections Candy Barr had made in prison and especially interested in her West Coast contacts. California mobster Mickey Cohen, king of the West Coast rackets, had been her boyfriend in a tempestuous affair before she had gone behind the walls.

Later that day, June 10, Ruby telephoned the unlisted West Coast number of convicted extortionist Rudy Eichenbaum. They talked for 20 minutes, according to phone company records. Eichenbaum had served his time and now was running an investments and loan business in the San Francisco area—with no employees, no listed business number in the phone book and from a house protected by a high barbed-wire fence and ferocious dogs. Ruby was looking for a way to settle his IRS tax debts.

But mob terms were too stiff for Ruby. If he defaulted on payments, for instance, the penalty was a lot more swift and painful than the penalties provided by the U.S. government. So Ruby set aside plans to borrow from the mob. Instead, his tax lawyer contacted the IRS with a proposal to settle Ruby's debts at about eight cents on the dollar. The IRS said it would think about it.

By the start of the second interval, November 11, Ruby's financial picture had grown more bleak. For one thing, Jada, the stripper from New Orleans, had been going amok on Ruby's Carousel stage. Ruby had to turn the lights out more than once because her act, more erotic than exotic, was so raunchy that Ruby expected authorities to shut the place down. Jada wasn't drawing the kind of business Ruby had anticipated and the two began to bellow at each other until Ruby stopped paying her and Jada hauled him into court on a peace bond. Secondly, Ruby was distraught over union regulations that he thought were stacked against him.

The union, the American Guild of Variety Artists (AGVA), had complaints that Ruby was working his entertainers too hard. In turn Ruby had tried and failed to get AGVA to stop Ruby's two hated competitors—Abe Weinstein, who ran the Colony Club next door, and Barney Weinstein, who ran the Theatre Lounge around the corner—from staging amateur nights. The clumsy, sometimes overly enthusiastic amateur strippers were drawing a lot of customers and, what was worse, the Weinsteins were getting by with entertainers they didn't have to pay for. Between the Weinstein brothers in their sporty cars, Jada's uncontrolled vulgarities, AGVA and the IRS, Ruby grew panicky for money and power.

On November 11, Ruby telephoned Chicago and talked with Jimmy Hoffa's sadistic, 370-pound professional bully, Barney Baker. That same day, Ruby telephoned Frank Goldstein at an unlisted San Francisco number. The two hadn't talked in more than 20 years. Goldstein later identified himself to the FBI as a professional gambler.

Also that same day Ruby met with Alexander Philip Gruber in Dallas. Alex Gruber and Ruby had boarded together in their Chicago days, when Gruber was using several aliases, was arrested a number of times and convicted as a grand-larcenist. Gruber was selling scrap metal in Los Angeles and running with Frank Matula, whom Hoffa had installed as a Teamsters official shortly after Matula got out of jail on perjury charges. Gruber also maintained known connections with hoodlums who worked with racketeer Mickey Cohen.

The next day, November 12, Ruby telephoned Cohen's favorite Texas pastime, Candy Barr, and talked to her for 14 minutes at her home in Edna. That same day, Paul Rowland Jones showed up *coincidentally* from Birmingham, Alabama. As a longtime operative for Chicago crime syndicate chiefs, Jones had taken a federal rap only once—when he was charged with conspiring to sell 60 pounds of Turkish opium—valued at $1 million—which had crossed the Mexican border into Texas at Piedra Negras. Jones also had worked with Ruby and Ruby's family over the course of time. Jones told the FBI he once had set up an arrangement for Hyman Rubenstein, Jack Ruby's brother in Chicago, to ship bootleg whiskey into Oklahoma. Jones said he knew that Ruby once had been "some kind of organizer for the Scrap Iron Workers Union in Chicago," and knew "the syndicate had an interest in this union." Jones said he presumed that this was Ruby's first connection with the syndicate.[8] On November 12 and 13, Jones met with Ruby, the former scrap-iron organizer, and with Gruber, the scrap-iron dealer. The three hadn't conferred since 1947, the year Ruby moved to Dallas. Gruber told the FBI that he was in Joplin, Missouri, in November, 1963, and just decided to drop in on Ruby "since Dallas, Texas, was about 100 miles from Joplin" (the distance is 360 miles).

At about this time Ruby telephoned Chicago thug Lenny (Leonard

Levine) Patrick, according to information the Warren Commission received from Hyman Rubenstein and from Ruby's sister, Eva Grant. Patrick was really bad news—a convicted bank robber, arrested numerous times on suspicion of being triggerman in several gangland killings. Using the mixed ethnic aliases of Joe Cohen and Pete Leonardi in his work, Patrick made his way to the ruling lower-class of Chicago's underworld as acknowledged gambling boss of the city's North Side (until October 22, 1975, when Patrick drew a four-year sentence for refusing to testify about protection money he had been paying a Chicago police lieutenant). Patrick and Ruby were old Chicago acquaintances.

The Warren Commission's chronicle of Ruby's contacts and actions during this mid-November period is marked not so much with inaccuracies but with the distortions of left-out particulars.

Here is an example of what the Commission said Ruby was doing, compared to what the Commission knew but left out:

The Ruby Chronicle

What the Commission Said	*What the Commission Failed to Say*
Nov. 11	Nov. 11
1 – Telephone call to Frank R. Goldstein, No. AT 2-7128 at San Francisco—wrong number.	1 – But then reaches Goldstein, a professional gambler, at Goldstein's correct number, JU 7-7674.
2 – Ruby called Barney Baker, Chicago ex-con and former Teamster organizer re "help" in fight with AGVA.	2 – Barney Baker tells authorities Ruby wants help in fight with AGVA but Baker also has told authorities he likes to tell "white lies."
3 – Alex Gruber visits Ruby.	3 – Dr. Ulevitch prescribes pills to calm Ruby's nerves. Ruby fills prescription immediately.
4 – Ruby came in to Dr. Ulevitch's office. Dr. Ulevitch saw and talked to Ruby who came in suffering from a bad cold.	
Nov. 12	Nov. 12
1 – William Edward Howard visited with Ruby at Stork Club in Dallas.	1 – William Edward Howard is manager of Stork Club. Ruby had visited him in 1959 in Miami, where Howard managed the Tropicana Club. Howard tells FBI Ruby always carries a gun.
2 – Paul R. Jones sees Ruby. Ruby complains competitors had become his enemies.	2 – Ex-convicts Paul R. Jones and Alex Gruber hold meetings with Ruby. They have come from out-of-town points after not visiting with Ruby in years.
	3 – Ruby telephones another ex-con, Candy Barr, in Edna, Tex.
Nov. 13	Nov. 13
1 – Ruby sends letter to (AGVA official) Faye re business troubles; includes breakdown of receipts.	1 – The Ruby-Gruber-Jones meetings continue.

Nov. 14

1 – Curtis Laverne Crafard saw Ruby at Carousel Club arguing with Earl Norman (approx. date).

Nov. 14

1 – Ruby calls Chicago gangland gunman Lenny Patrick (approx. date).
2 – Crafard sees Ruby pull gun on Norman.

Nov. 15

1 – B. A. Bates Jr. saw and talked to Ruby at Dal. Mng. News Bldg.
2 – Mary Martin saw and talked to Ruby at corner of Ervay & Bryan.
3 – Charles Straeght saw Ruby, Merchants State Bank.
4 – DPD Lt. George C. Arnett saw Ruby.
5 – Ruby receives letter from Bobby Faye.

Nov. 15

1 – These encounters with Bates, Martin, Straeght and Arnett were of minimal significance. They were chance meetings. For instance, Straeght was a barber who was transacting routine bank business. Faye's letter was a friendly acknowledgment.
2 – Ruby refilled the prescription to calm his nerves.
3 – Ruby began using a safe, which he planned to sink in concrete in his office (approx. date).

The Warren Commission's Ruby chronicle included an entry for November 16 that Ruby had been on a "rumored hunting party, ranch of Buck Sheaver." The hunting party was no rumor. But those on the hunting trip to South Texas said Ruby was not with them. In other words the Commission reported and then easily knocked down a rumor that Ruby had been out of Dallas on Saturday, November 16.

Meanwhile, the Commission's chronicle for Sunday, November 17, failed to include a reported trip made by Ruby to Las Vegas, even though the FBI spoke to witnesses who confirmed Ruby's presence in Las Vegas.[9]

Ruby's special Las Vegas connection was Lewis McWillie, the syndicate gambler Ruby had visited in Cuba in 1959. Ruby made a series of phone calls in 1963 to McWillie, who was closely associated with Meyer Lansky's hoodlum empire and was installed in Las Vegas as pit boss at the Thunderbird casino. On May 10, 1963, Ruby had a .38-caliber cal. Smith & Wesson Centennial revolver shipped to McWillie, according to the records of Dallas gun dealer Ray Brantley. Ruby didn't want his personal Las Vegas mission to become known, and Ralph Paul, a back-room business associate of Ruby's, told the Warren Commission that Ruby could be very secretive about his comings and goings. Ruby didn't want his club employees to know when he slipped out of town, in order to keep them from stealing his profits, Paul said.

Ruby often was secretive, it seemed to Graham Koch, his tax attorney. Koch recalls that Ruby "kept quite a bit of detail to himself, was distrustful of others and gave little important information."[10]

Two days after the Las Vegas trip Ruby turned up in Koch's office on November 19 and said he had a connection who would supply him money to settle his long-standing government tax problems. In turn, Ruby signed a power-of-attorney form in Koch's office, which entitled the lawyer to control much of Ruby's financial dealings with the government. The transaction was extraordinary for Ruby, who kept most of his money out of the bank so there could be no watch on the extent and use of his funds. Ruby said he feared the government would place liens on his bank account to obtain the tax money he owed.[11] Ruby's Carousel checking account that day, November 19, in the Merchants State Bank stood at $246.65, which was within a few dollars of what the account usually had in it. "Jack always carried a large roll of cash," remembers Bill Cox, then the loan officer at the bank.[12] "He would just come into the bank to make change for the club," said Cox, who vividly remembers Ruby standing in line at a teller's cage on the afternoon of November 22, after President Kennedy was slain.[13] "Jack was standing there crying and he had about $7,000 in cash on him the day of the assassination. He and I talked and I warned him that he'd be knocked in the head one day, carrying all that cash on him. I was concerned because it was common for Ruby to walk in and out of the bank with large amounts of money on him. Armed bandits watch patterns like that." But Ruby wasn't worried about what would happen out there on the street, where he could protect himself with the loaded, snub-nosed revolver, serial no. 2744, which he carried that afternoon. What he was worried about was leaving the $7,000 in the bank, where the federal government could get it.

Robert F. Kennedy was worried about what "The Private Government" was getting. That was his term for organized crime in the United States, which he said was controlled by the Cosa Nostra, "with an annual income of billions, resting on a base of human suffering and moral corruption."[14] Citing the high rate of crime syndicate murders in the United States, the boyish-appearing U.S. Attorney General ruthlessly went after Mafia leaders such as Salvatore Momo (Sam) Giancana, the Chicago crime boss who had some minor convictions but who had proved his real capabilities early in life by having beaten three different murder raps even while a teenager. Kennedy's attempt to imprison Giancana in 1962 on an illegal wiretap charge backfired on the Attorney General when it turned out that Giancana implausibly was being protected by the CIA. Unknown to Kennedy, until he was briefed May 7, 1962, by CIA General Counsel Lawrence Houston and Colonel Sheffield Edwards, director of the CIA's office of security, the CIA had put out a $150,000 contract on the life of Fidel Castro and had been using the services of a proven expert in assassination, Giancana. Kennedy was outraged. Houston later recalled that Kennedy's eyes grew steely and in a voice low and angry he said that "if you ever try to do business with organized crime again—with gangsters— you will let the Attorney General know."[15]

Kennedy still was furious two days later, May 9, when he met with FBI Director J. Edgar Hoover to discuss the subject of the illegal phone tap former FBI agent Robert A. Maheu had installed in Las Vegas at CIA expense for Giancana's private use. Hoover later wrote a memorandum for his file, stating Kennedy was upset for two reasons: First, because the CIA had put itself into a position where "it could not afford to have any action taken against Giancana or Maheu." Secondly, Hoover said that Kennedy "well knew . . . that the reason nothing had been done against Giancana was because of Giancana's close relationship with Frank Sinatra who, in turn, claimed to be a close friend of the Kennedy family. The Attorney General stated he realized this and it was for that reason that he was quite concerned when he received this information from the CIA about Giancana and Maheu."

The information the CIA did give Kennedy about Giancana was carefully limited, too. Having been given the CIA code name "Sam Gold," Giancana had been recruited by Mafia confederate John Rosselli[16] to participate, along with Florida racketeer Santo Trafficante Jr.,[17] in the top-secret project to rub out Castro. Known in CIA headquarters as Project ZR/RIFLE, its operations were a lot more current than Houston and Edwards had led the Attorney General to believe.[18] Subsequently, when Vice-President Johnson followed John F. Kennedy into the White House, Johnson discovered "we had been operating a damned Murder, Inc., in the Caribbean."[19]

ZR/RIFLE's outside contact was Maheu, the former FBI agent who Hoover felt had a bad reputation. Maheu became a private investigator in 1954 and had been involved in several sensitive, covert CIA activities on a freelance basis by the time the agency hired him at $500 a month late in the summer of 1960, the final months of the Eisenhower administration, to negotiate with the Mafia for a hit-man on the Castro job. Maheu, who was developing into billionaire Howard Hughes's chief Nevada operative, knew a great deal about Las Vegas gambling contacts and met with Rosselli to discuss the first steps of a professional killing.

Until mid-February, 1963, when the CIA decided to ditch the Mafia project, Rosselli appears to have been paid no contract fees by the CIA for his work. Both he and CIA representatives told the Senate Select Committee on Intelligence in 1975 executive hearings that he had paid his own travel and hotel bills, motivated strictly by "honor and dedication" as a patriotic American. Rosselli said he "never took a nickel, as long as it is for the government of the United States. This is the least I can do because I owe it a lot." But there was a generous payoff anyway. In 1971 the CIA surreptitiously went to the Immigration and Naturalization Service and successfully stalled deportation proceedings against Rosselli as an illegal alien.

Giancana's profit came quicker. Besides the phone tap, Giancana got the CIA to provide and install an electronic "bug" in a Las Vegas apartment, allowing him to monitor from Miami an affair his girlfriend, singer Phyllis McGuire, was having with another man. Trafficante had more long-range goals. Trafficante had plans to secure "gambling, prostitution and dope monopolies" in Cuba after the overthrow of Castro, according to CIA files.[20] He was dealing with a major figure in the Cuban exile movement to have Castro murdered in exchange for some sensitive electronic equipment and a $10,000 advance. The CIA provided both immediately, along with capsules to poison Castro at his favorite Havana restaurant, in March, 1961. But Maheu told the Senate Intelligence Committee, headed by Senator Frank Church of Idaho, in a closed door meeting[21] that the poison plan was not carried out because the "go signal" that would have touched it off never was transmitted.

Perhaps the signal was held up because another CIA doomed mission to overthrow Castro, the Bay of Pigs invasion of Cuba by U.S.-trained Cuban exiles, was only days away. It took place in April, 1961, not a full three months after John F. Kennedy became President and inherited the invasion plans which ended in almost instant disaster. The counter-revolutionary Cuban exiles had been led to believe by clandestine CIA and military advisers that they would have vital American jet air cover for the invasion. But the jets never showed up. Castro's Russian-made 122-mm howitzers barked unmolested and his B-26s sauntered at will over the battered invaders. Many bitter survivors believed it was the President's brother, Robert, who had counseled the White House not to commit the needed handful of jets because the action would have meant formal U.S. military intervention in what was supposed to be a Cuban matter. An even more bitter E. Howard Hunt Jr. of the CIA (who played a leading role in the Bay of Pigs invasion under the CIA code name of *Eduardo*, but who would become far better known 11 years later as a key figure in the Watergate break-in) wrote in a memoir that the Attorney General was instrumental in what Hunt saw as a post-invasion effort "to whitewash the New Frontier by heaping guilt on the CIA" for the badly planned invasion of Cuba.

Invading Cuba was not the war Robert Kennedy wanted. His war room at the Justice Department intended to bomb hell out of The Private Government. He couldn't have made the message any clearer to the Mafia when on April 4, 1961, less than two weeks before the Bay of Pigs disaster, the Attorney General had Carlos Marcello kidnapped.

Marcello operated a multibillion-dollar underworld empire from Florida to California, including Jack Ruby's Dallas. Short and tough, with a gruff voice, Marcello had amassed a hugh personal fortune at his home base, New Orleans, where he bought and sold politicians. But Robert Kennedy disdainfully ordered federal agents to grab Marcello, handcuff him and take him off in a black car, gangland style. Marcello was put on a special one-way jet flight to Guatemala and dumped in the Central American country, on grounds that he had lied about his place of birth on his immigration records. The extralegal action by the Attorney General didn't do any permanent damage to Marcello, but it was meant to show him who was going to be tougher. Kennedy made the point over and over. As Attorney General he got more indictments on members of America's crime industry than had any previous prosecutor, pursuing them relentlessly. Meyer Lansky, for instance, no longer was safe behind the bolted doors of that industry's executive suite. The Attorney General put together what was known inside the Justice Department as the OCD (Organized Crime Division) and was stalking Lansky's secret operations in the Bahamas and Las Vegas.

Both Lansky's "Kosher Nostra" and the hot-blooded Sicilian Cosa Nostra had ample reason to both fear and despise the younger Kennedy, as did Jimmy Hoffa. The Attorney General doggedly harassed Hoffa, certain that he could put the Teamsters president in prison and break the union's ironlike alliance with underworld thugs.[22] To nail Hoffa and others, Robert Kennedy went to Capitol Hill to seek tough legislation that would give his Justice Department broader power. He sought new laws to provide immunity for witnesses in crime investigations and to allow excessive wire-tapping privileges for law-enforcement agencies in search of evidence against the mob. Kennedy said that with legalized wire-tapping he could move in on three major metropolitan areas "where the major political leaders and figures in those communities are being corrupted, and are on the payroll of some of our bigtime gangsters and racketeers." In one of those communities, New Orleans, Carlos Marcello made his way back from exile in Guatemala, managed to beat a perjury rap in federal court and was determined to seek revenge against the Attorney General. "Don't worry about that little Bobby son-of-a-bitch. He's going to be taken care of," Marcello has been quoted as saying by Ed Reid, the investigative writer who specializes in Mafia sources. Marcello, however, knew that "to rid himself of Robert Kennedy he would first have to remove the President," Reid wrote in his book, *The Grim Reapers.* "Any killer of the attorney general would be hunted down by his brother; the death of the President would seal the fate of his attorney general."

Or as Jimmy Hoffa put it, in terms The Private Government could understand, without John F. Kennedy around, Robert F. Kennedy would be "just another lawyer."

The Warren Commission found no significance in Jack Ruby's dealings with Jimmy Hoffa's associates, such as Irwin S. Weiner and Barney Baker, in the weeks leading up to President Kennedy's assassination, when Ruby's movements were supposed to be reconstructed in that daily chronicle which snapped a series of unfocused box-camera-like pictures of a killer on his way to work.[23]

The Commission chronicle, that thumbnail calendar of Ruby's activities,[24] shows us for instance that on October 4, October 5, November 6 and

November 20, 1963, Ruby had appointments for scalp treatments with a trichologist, Bruce McLean. But the chronicle entirely fails to list Ruby's appointments in September and on October 15, 1963, in the office of a dermatologist, Dr. Coleman Jacobson, for penicillin treatments to cure his gonorrhea. Medical records show[25] that Ruby was a recurrent victim of venereal disease but the Commission's chronicle only portrayed his baldness.

Another entry in the chronicle shows that Ruby visited the "Edw. Fein tailor shop for suit," on November 9. But nowhere is there an entry to show that while Ruby frequently walked out of his apartment in the Oak Cliff section of Dallas dressed like some kind of George Raft, the apartment he left behind usually was strewn with his discarded newspapers, soiled clothing and unwashed dishes, according to the testimony of several Commission witnesses. The Warren Commission submitted an external view of what appeared to be an external man. After all, Ruby was absorbed in his outer appearance. He pampered himself with skin oils, shaved twice a day and often bathed three times a day. He maintained a strong interest in the way he looked to others, but otherwise treated himself like a caveman. The Warren Commission's Burt Griffin asked Mrs. Eileen Kaminsky, Ruby's sister who lived in Chicago, "Did you notice whether he had any books or magazines or anything like that in the apartment?" regarding her visit to Ruby in the last week of August, 1963. "Oh, nothing outstanding, maybe pictures of strippers, something like that," Mrs. Kaminsky replied about the reading tastes of her 52-year-old brother.

But the Warren Commission's chronicled distortions of who Jack Ruby really was assumes greater proportions than simply failing to show that behind his apartment door Ruby was a slob. The chronicle is filled with the trivia of an average man's daily comings and goings, and omits the very things that did set Ruby apart from the average man. It would be like publishing a road map that leaves out some of the essential connecting routes.

For instance, on October 12, 1963, "Amos C. Flint saw and talked to Ruby," according to the chronicle. Flint was a conventional insurance salesman who hadn't seen Ruby in at least two years. On this occasion they encountered each other in passing on the street. Previously Flint had been a patron in a private drinking club Ruby had operated, at a time when the only places in Texas that could sell mixed drinks across the bar were private clubs. Flint and Ruby exchanged a few moments of small talk and continued on their separate paths. But exactly two weeks later, October 26, at 12:07 p.m., Ruby telephoned a most unconventional insurance agent, Irwin S. Weiner, in Chicago, and talked to Weiner for 12 minutes. The FBI provided the Warren Commission with the information about Ruby's telephone call to Weiner from the Carousel Club, but the

Commission decided not to include the call in the chronicle of Ruby's activities.

At the time he got the call from Ruby, Weiner was a business associate of Lewis Barbe, an insurance man who, three months later, January 27, 1964, was blown up by the mob for talking out of turn. At the time of Barbe's gangland murder, *The Chicago Daily News* identified Weiner as "the mob's favored front-man."

Front-men normally have no police records and certainly no convictions. Weiner operated a hoodlum-tainted food service business in Chicago and was a professional bondsman who got mob members sprung from jail. He also headed the Illinois branch of the Summit Fidelity & Insurance Co. of Akron, Ohio, the company that underwrote 50 percent of the bonds covering Teamsters Union pension funds, according to information obtained by Senator McClellan's rackets subcommittee. Weiner became entrenched as an investments adviser to Hoffa before Hoffa went to prison in 1967. By 1975, Weiner was a defendant in a case brought by the Justice Department, charging that he helped defraud the Teamsters Central States Pension Fund of $1.4 million. But Weiner was found not guilty after the government's chief witness was shot to death in front of his family by masked men on the eve of the trial.

If Weiner was Hoffa's money counselor, then Barney Baker at times was Hoffa's chief thug. And Ruby telephoned Baker two weeks after he had contacted Weiner.

A 370-pound gorilla of a man, Baker was especially despised by Robert F. Kennedy, who had been chief counsel to McClellan's Senate subcommittee before he became head of the Justice Department.

During one Senate hearing in which Baker was accompanied to the witness table by George S. Fitzgerald, one of Hoffa's attorneys, Robert Kennedy scowled at the witness and said the record showed Baker was closely tied in with "underworld lice . . . the scum of the United States. Everywhere you go, there has been violence." An FBI rap sheet on Baker says he was Hoffa's bagman and muscleman, having slugged his way out of the tough New York City waterfront docks as a union organizer. Baker fled New York after an honest pier boss, Anthony Hintz, was murdered. Baker was closely linked to Eddie (Cockeyed) Dunn, who got the electric chair in the Hintz case. Baker survived charges of dealing in stolen jewelry in Miami, handling kidnap money from Kansas City and being responsible for the mysterious disappearance of a lawyer in Indianapolis who had lost money invested by the Teamsters in a taxi cab company. But at last Baker, a bully who repeatedly beat up people, was convicted in Pittsburgh for having extorted three bribes from a trucking firm official who was told to make the payments to avoid a strike. Baker had been out of prison four months when Jack Ruby reached him in Chicago 11 days before the murder of John F. Kennedy.

Unlike Ruby's October 26 call to Weiner, the Warren Commission's chronicle did list Ruby's telephone call to Baker's Chicago apartment. But the chronicle failed to show that Ruby's visit to a Dallas physician that same day, November 11, caused the doctor to prescribe a drug to calm Ruby's nerves. Ruby refilled that prescription on November 15, according to the records of a downtown Dallas drug store, confirmed by Dallas police.[26] Normally Ruby wouldn't take anything that would calm him down. In fact, during the autumn of 1963, he regularly took Preludin, a stimulant which Ruby described as something that "makes you a positive thinker, you don't have any inferiority, your reflexes are great."[27] But it is easily possible that whatever Baker told him, Ruby's nerves went bad.

The Warren Commission chronicle also omitted a listing of phone calls by Baker that might have related to Ruby. The night before President Kennedy's murder, for example, telephone records obtained by the FBI show Baker placed a person-to-person call from his Chicago apartment to David Yaras in Miami. Yaras was a feared Chicago hoodlum, who told the FBI he had known Ruby. Yaras had a string of arrests for robbery, burglary and murder charges.

Robert Kennedy, in his role as counsel on the Senate rackets subcommittee, charged Yaras with helping set up a corrupt Teamsters local in Miami and with muscling in on gambling activities in Cuba in the late 1950s, the same time period when Ruby showed up in Havana as a guest of syndicate gambler McWillie. Yaras also appears to have had a direct and sinister role in Ruby's entry into the Dallas crime market shortly after World War II—a time when Yaras was charged in Chicago with participating in the murder of James M. (Jack) Ragen.

Ragen controlled Continental Press, a horse-race wire hooked into back-room bookie shops across much of the nation. Continental made annual net profits of more than $2 million and was the bedrock of extortion rackets, political graft and police payoffs in a large slice of America. Ragen's power was enormous because whoever controlled the syndicate wire in town could then control that town's gambling operations. But Ragen felt threatened because Tony (Joe Batters) Accardo and Jake (Greasy Thumb) Guzik, Chicago operators of a rival gangland wire, Trans-America Press, were determined to seize control of Continental and dispose of Ragen in the traditional Chicago way. In an effort to save his life Ragen made an arrangement through U.S. Attorney General Tom Clark in 1946 to meet with the FBI and, in exchange for federal protection, explain intricacies of the wire-empire profits that reached into the executive suites of some of the nation's most respected "front-men" in business circles. But FBI Director Hoover refused to provide bodyguard protection for Ragen in exchange for the information, and Ragen became an immediate gangland murder victim. Yaras was part of a triumvirate—which included that other old Chicago friend of Ruby's, Lenny Patrick—indicted for the murder of Ragen. But the suspects went free when the prosecution's key witness was murdered. Two other witnesses quickly changed their stories and the fourth witness vanished.

That was Ruby's background. He emerged from a place and time when men like Irwin Weiner, Yaras and Patrick didn't face trials because key witnesses were eliminated. And when it came time for Giancana and Rosselli to become key witnesses, they also were eliminated. In the same pattern, Jack Ruby showed up with a gun—before Lee Harvey Oswald could be sworn in to talk.

The Accardo-Guzik takeover of Ragen's race wire brought their Chicago mob into negotiations with Dallas law officers late in 1946 for control of the gambling action there and a system of payoffs for police protection. The negotiations were undertaken by Paul Rowland Jones (the same negotiator who would turn up suddenly in Dallas 17 years later to meet with Ruby the day after Ruby talked with Baker), who offered substantial bribes to Steve Guthrie, the newly elected Dallas county sheriff. But Guthrie helped make the bribes a public issue—and subsequently identified Ruby as a part of the Chicago syndicate's takeover plan in Dallas. Ruby, who did move from Chicago to Dallas in 1947, would have been a front for mob activities had the deal gone through, according to what Guthrie later told the FBI.

The FBI interviewed both Barney Baker and Yaras about Ruby but never asked why Baker had called Yaras in Miami on November 21, 1963, on the eve of President Kennedy's assassination in Dallas. Was it because the mountainous Baker wanted to brag that he knew what was about to happen to Kennedy? After all, Kennedy himself, two years before he was elected President and while a member of the McClellan Senate rackets subcommittee as the junior senator from Massachusetts, had labeled Baker as "a braggard and a ham."

The Warren Commission's chronicle also ignored an earlier phone call by Baker, made October 9, 1963, a month before Baker's known conversation with Ruby: a call to California, to the business headquarters of Victor Emanuel Pereira. Pereira was in business principally with two people.

One was Earl Scheib, head of a national chain of auto-paint shops and father of Philip Earl Scheib, a machine-gun toting leader in the hate-oriented, extreme-rightwing secret military movement, the Minutemen. Pereira's other partner was Eugene Hale Brading, whose arrests and convictions had been only for small-time stuff—burglary, bookmaking, black-marketeering—until Brading hooked up with Pereira in El Paso, Texas, in 1950. The two men, handsome and slick, became widely known swindlers and confidence men as a team. Dallas Sheriff Bill Decker ran them out of

Dallas County in 1952 because of their links to organized crime.

By then Pereira and Brading were making bigtime connections with the Mafia. They moved into plush headquarters in Beverly Hills until both were sent to federal prison in 1954 for having embezzled $50,000 from a rich New Mexico widow in an interstate swindle. Five years later, when both were paroled, they picked up where they had left off. Pereira was handsomely financed by the savings of his fifth wife. Or was she his sixth? And Brading was to become one of the 100 charter members of La Costa Country Club, built with Teamster Central States pension funds and frequented by such finely manicured gangsters as Rosselli and Giancana. Brading cemented his position in the Irwin Weiner-Barney Baker axis by marrying Mildred Bollman and moving into a Palm Springs mansion once owned by Bing Crosby. Mildred's late husband had been indicted for labor racketeering and subsequently died of a gunshot wound, after using his position as a Teamster official in Illinois to amass a personal fortune. According to Peter Noyes, a skilled investigative reporter who has pursued the mysteries of Brading more relentlessly than anyone else, word began to circulate among the Palm Springs, California, country club set that Brading's wooing and winning of Mrs. Bollman had been financed by the mob. After all, her late husband had left her an estimated $4 million and the mob felt entitled to it.

Pereira and Brading parlayed some of their growing holdings into Texas oil investments, and Brading sought permission, September 11, 1963, from Los Angeles federal parole officer Sam Barrett, to make a trip to Houston "in connection with Tidewater Oil Co. litigation." Barrett didn't know it at the time but one day earlier, September 10, the California Department of Motor Vehicles had changed the name on Eugene Hale Brading's driver's license to Jim Braden for "business reasons," at Brading's request.

Another thing Barrett didn't know: the White House already had decided the fixed dates and places for President Kennedy's November 21-22 trip to Texas. The decision had been reached shortly before September 11, the day Brading told Barrett he needed "to discuss business with a Mr. D. D. Ford, land man with Tidewater Oil Co." in Texas.

No public announcement of the President's trip had been made. But Brading easily could have known the President's plans before there was a public announcement. After all, Brading reportedly had become both courier and bagman for the highest echelons of organized crime, and there was an easy flow of communication from Giancana and Rosselli to Brading. Giancana had at least a pair of potential sources of information open to him in the early 1960s—the CIA and President Kennedy himself.

In his role as a legally illegal double-agent for The Private Government and the federal government, Giancana had been supplied by the CIA with electronic equipment. In turn, Giancana's friend, Judith Katherine Campbell, had been supplied to President Kennedy.[28] Mrs. Campbell's intimate visits to the residential quarters of the White House were known to a handful of people, including Giancana. With lookouts such as the CIA and Judith Campbell, Sam Giancana didn't need to wait for the newspapers to come out.

A Dallas newspaper printed the first unofficial report on September 13—a foreboding Friday the 13th—that President Kennedy would include Dallas in his November Texas itinerary. That same day federal parole officer Sam Barrett approved Eugene Brading's request to go to Texas.

Brading's parole allowed him to leave Los Angeles by plane on September 15 and spend the next 10 days in Houston. But Brading's contacts and movements during those 10 days remain unexplained, except it is known he did not go to see D. D. Ford, the land man at Tidewater Oil, which was the supposed purpose of his trip.

September 25, Brading's last scheduled day in Houston, was also the day that Lee Harvey Oswald reached Houston from New Orleans for a brief stopover, according to the Warren Commission's own accounts, in the course of Oswald's mystery-shrouded journey to Mexico City.

Two weeks later, when Barney Baker placed that October 9 phone call to Pereira's offices, the Chicago mob had good reason to be jittery about any investment it might have had in Brading's marriage. Brading had been caught siphoning off $40,000 of his wife's personal funds to Pereira, and she was outraged enough to be heard back in Illinois. She ordered Brading out of the Palm Springs mansion they shared and her lawyer found a quick, easy reason to get her marriage to Brading annulled in Indio, California, on October 24: Brading had not divorced two earlier wives.

Next, Brading secured permission from Barrett, his Los Angeles parole officer, to return to Texas on oil business—starting in Dallas on November 21, the same day President Kennedy and his entourage arrived in Texas. Brading showed up in Dallas with Morgan H. Brown, whose California oil company had been shut down for repeated failures to pay state taxes and who later went to prison for selling shares of stock in oil wells that didn't exist.

Brown registered at the Cabana Motel in Dallas for himself and Brading, advising the registration clerk they would be staying until November 24. They moved into suite 301, with windows overlooking Stemmons Freeway—the known route President Kennedy was to take the next day. But Kennedy never made it that far. He was shot to death moments before the presidential car turned onto Stemmons—not two minutes from the Cabana Motel.

Brading's traveling companion, Brown, looked out at Stemmons as a man with a hair-trigger mind. In 1964, for instance, when a young Los Angeles police officer tried to arrest Brown on a felony warrant growing out of Brown's phony oil stock swindles, Brown grabbed the policeman's gun and shot up the area with it. Brown escaped, leaving the frightened but uninjured officer tied up, and it took 12 more policemen to capture him.

Earl Golz, the *Dallas Morning News* investigative reporter who has devoted a great deal of energy to mining veins of information never explored by the Warren Commission, found that Brading kept his trip to Texas with Brown a secret from Barrett, the parole officer, because to travel with Brown was in itself enough of a parole violation to have put Brading back in prison.

Golz also met with Roger Carroll, chief U.S. probation officer in Dallas. Brading checked in with Carroll on November 21, 1963, as required. Carroll then filed a report which said Brading "advised that he planned to see Lamar Hunt and other oil speculators while here." Hunt was a scion of the Hunt Oil Company dynasty, captained by his father, the puritanical H. L. Hunt, who regularly would eat a sparse lunch from a brown paper bag at his unadorned desk, while in command of a personal fortune worth hundreds of millions of dollars. Much of that fortune was pumped into ultra-conservative political causes.

Jack Ruby appeared to admire H. L. Hunt's causes. Found in the trunk of Ruby's car the day he shot Oswald were two scripts of already-aired "Life Line" broadcasts, the politically conservative series of radio commentaries paid for by Hunt.

Ruby also was at least in the vicinity of Lamar Hunt's office on November 21, the day Brading said he planned to see Hunt. Ruby later told authorities he merely had escorted Connie Trammell, a young woman who had a job interview with Lamar Hunt. Ruby said he didn't go to the seventh floor of the Mercantile Bank Building where the Hunt men, including Lamar's brother, Bunker, operated out of a joint suite of offices.

It actually was Bunker Hunt who Brading and Brown came to see on November 21, according to a former Hunt Oil official, who said he saw them in the reception room that day.

Bunker Hunt had pulled more than $200 in loose bills from his pocket to pay for his share of a full-page advertisement that appeared in *The Dallas Morning News* on November 22, the day President Kennedy reached Dallas. The hateful ad questioned the President's Americanism, and its sponsors disguised themselves behind the name of a nonexistent organization, which designated itself as "The American Fact-Finding Committee" for that day.[29]

November 22, Brading was at Dealey Plaza and was arrested minutes after the President was shot there. According to the arrest report filed by sheriff's deputy C. L. (Lummie) Lewis, who took Brading into custody, Brading "was in building when Pres. assassinated." The building Lewis referred to was the Dal-Tex Building on Dealey Plaza, directly across the street from the Texas School Book Depository Building, where Lee Harvey Oswald was employed.

When he was arrested, Brading gave his name only as Jim Braden—the name he'd had put on his driver's license in September—and then made the following statement to Dallas Chief Deputy Sheriff Allan Sweatt:

> I am here on business [oil business] and was walking down Elm Street trying to get a cab and there wasn't any. I heard people talking, saying—"My God, the President has been shot." Police cars were passing me, coming down the triple underpass, and I walked up among other people and this building was surrounded by police officers with guns and we all were watching them. I moved on up to the building across the street from the building which was surrounded and I ask one of the girls if there was a telephone that I could use and she said, "Yes, there is one on the third floor of the building, where I work." I walked through a passage to the elevator where they were all getting on [the freight elevator] and I got off on the third floor of the building with all of the other people, and there was a lady using the pay phone and I ask her if I could use it when she hung up and she said it was out of order, and I tried to use it but without success. I ask her how I can get out of this building and she said, "There is an exit right there," and then she said, "Wait a minute, here is an elevator now." I got on the elevator and returned to the ground floor and the colored man who ran the elevator said, "You are a stranger in this building and I was not supposed to let you up," and he ran outside to an officer and said to the officer that he had just taken me up and down the elevator and the officer said for me to identify myself and I presented him with a credit card and he said, "Well we have to check out everything" and took me to his superior and said for me to wait and "we will check it out." I was then taken to the sheriff's office and interrogated.

While Brading was waiting to be interrogated, his traveling companion Brown abruptly checked out of their suite in the Cabana Motel at about 2 p.m.—only a half hour after President Kennedy officially was reported dead.

There is no explanation for where Brown went or why he checked out so quickly, when originally Brown had told the desk clerk he and Brading would want the room two more days, until November 24.

Brading, meanwhile, got away with his alias. No one there took his fingerprints or knew in any way that he was Eugene Hale Brading, a man they had on file as a criminal, and the same man Sheriff Decker had run out of Dallas 11 years earlier. Unlike Brading, "Braden" claimed to be unfamiliar with Dallas.

Since Brading never had used the name Jim Braden with federal authorities, there was no cross-check made of him in Los Angeles parole files. He signed the statement he had made, handed it to Decker's chief deputy Sweatt and walked out of the sheriff's office in one of his all-time shining moments as a confidence man.

To compound the police blunder, the FBI interviewed "Braden" two months later in Beverly Hills, concerning his arrest in Dallas as a suspicious person on November 22.[30] The FBI never realized it was talking to Brading. The interview was strictly routine. As a result, federal authorities never questioned what Brading's connection might have been with Jack Ruby.

The paths of Ruby and Brading could have passed at least twice in the 24 hours before the President's murder: once at the Mercantile Bank Building, where the Hunt offices were; another time—12 hours before the President was shot—at the Cabana Motel, where Brading and Brown were lodged on the presidential motorcade route.

According to the Warren Commission's Ruby chronicle, Ruby arrived at the Cabana late on the night of November 21 for a midnight rendezvous with a Chicago friend in the Cabana's dimly lighted private club, the Bon Vivant Room. Ruby frequented the Cabana, which had been built with Teamsters money.

The Chicago friend, Lawrence V. Meyers, appeared to be a legitimate businessman but had some contacts he was not anxious to have known.

One such contact was with him. She was Jean Aase of Chicago, also known as Jean West, who wasn't known to Meyers' family or business associates and who Meyers described to the FBI as "a rather dumb but accommodating broad." Meyers and Miss West had checked into a Ramada Inn in Dallas on November 20. Then they checked out and shifted to the Cabana on November 21.

Ruby spent only a short time in the Bon Vivant Room with Meyers, drinking a cup of coffee (he rarely drank anything alcoholic, having grown up traumatized by his drunken, despotic father), and his movements for the next two hours are unknown. But at 2:30 a.m., according to the Commission's chronicle, Ruby telephoned an employee at his own club,[31] the Carousel, and said he was still at the Cabana.

Was Ruby meeting with the slick and slippery ex-convict Eugene Hale Brading, and with Brading's trigger-happy companion, Morgan Brown, during those early morning hours of the day the President was slain? The Warren Commission never asked Ruby. The Commission never asked anything of Brading; didn't question Brown; ignored Pereira; overlooked Alex Gruber; never talked to Barney Baker; stayed away from Irwin Weiner; failed to meet with H. L., Lamar and Bunker Hunt or to examine their office visitor logs; never went near gunman Yaras; and avoided gunman Patrick.

The Warren Commission clearly didn't want to distort its image of Jack Ruby with too much detail.

CHAPTER 3

The Weekend

Part I—Friday
"I Saw a Man Who Wasn't There"

Camelot for Jack Ruby was not an Anglo-Saxon enclave on Cape Cod, nor a late-night brandy in Georgetown. Jack Ruby had never seen these places and could imagine them only vaguely. *Bang.* What he knew about Jacqueline Kennedy was that she had two sweetheart-looking little children and the mannerisms of a broad who probably wouldn't walk up the flight of narrow stairs to see the strip show at his Carousel. *Bang.* Ruby didn't quite understand how grand the entertainment had become at White House state dinners since the Eisenhower administration, any more than he grasped the nuances of Kennedy's worsening relationship with Congress. Ruby had grown up in a neighborhood where the quality of life was measured in terms of was it good for the Jews, which apparently it was under Kennedy. *Bang.* But whatever the hell Camelot was, it was all over.

Ruby was five blocks away from the shooting at Dealey Plaza when it happened at 12:30 p.m., Friday, November 22. He was at the desk of John Newnam, an advertising salesman for *The Dallas Morning News,* in a large room with many desks and phones on the second floor of the *Morn-*

ing News building. The *Morning News* had found him to be a bad credit risk and careless about getting his advertisements in on time to meet the paper's deadlines. But this day he had arrived on time with weekend copy to run in Saturday and Sunday editions for both of his nightclubs, the Carousel and the Vegas, and had brought Newnam some cash to make an overdue payment on an ad that already had run. Ruby, however, was in an unpleasant mood. He had the day's *Morning News* opened to page 14, section one, on Newnam's desk.

Covering the whole page was a black-bordered advertisement, headed in large letters, "Welcome Mr. Kennedy," and signed at the bottom by the nonexistent organization named The American Fact-Finding Committee, Bernard Weissman, Chairman. The ad accused the President of capitulating to the communists internationally, with a series of questions that asked, for instance: "Why have you ordered or permitted your brother Bobby, the Attorney General, to go soft on Communists, fellow-travelers, and the ultraleftists in America, while permitting him to persecute loyal Americans who criticize you, your administration, and your leadership?" (Who were these loyal Americans persecuted by Bobby Kennedy and not named in the ad? Were they the members of the underworld who had been under contract to the CIA, or the Teamster racketeers who were bitterly opposed to the Kennedy administration?) The ad—paid for in part by the oil-rich conservative Bunker Hunt, who had reached in his pocket and pulled out more than $200 in cash to pay his share—demanded answers from the President on behalf of the "America-thinking citizens of Dallas" and "a Constitution largely ignored by you."

It was the name of Bernard Weissman on that ad which bothered Ruby a lot. A Jewish name. "Who is this Weissman?" Ruby began to complain about the "lousy taste" of the ad to Newnam (who'd had nothing to do with its getting into the paper) when news of the gunshots burst upon the large room. There was a great deal of confusion, anguished sounds, phones ringing, and at about 12:40 p.m., some 10 minutes after the shooting, advertising salesman Richard L. Saunders encountered Ruby standing numbly amid the confusion, uncharacteristically subdued and pale. It was Ruby's quietness that startled Saunders. He had known Ruby several years and always had found him to be an excessive talker, but Ruby was no more than barely responding to comments everyone else seemed to be making about how terrible the situation was.

Intermittently, Ruby and others crowded into the corner office of Dick Jeffrey, promotion manager, where there was a television set announcing bulletins and carrying interviews from Dealey Plaza. But then Ruby retreated back to Newnam's desk, to the telephone there, and called his sister, Eva Grant, at her apartment in a different part of Dallas from where he lived. She was crying. Ruby reasoned that "you want other people to feel that you feel emotionally disturbed the same way as other people, so I let John listen to the phone that my sister was crying hysterically."[1] Ruby had been in Dallas 16 years but he had all the moves of a man who would always be an outsider.

Newnam heard Eva Grant cry out, "My God, what do they want?" and silently handed the phone back to Ruby. Newnam was both embarrassed by her grief, and busy, because people spontaneously were beginning to phone in ad cancellations for the weekend editions. They were merchants who intended to mourn the shooting of the President in their city by closing down. Many of them expressed bitterness about the anti-Kennedy ad on page 14. Before Ruby left, he said he would shut the Carousel and the Vegas for that night, and Newnam believed Ruby had reached the decision because he was aware of the growing numbers of calls from merchants closing their doors.

Saunders estimated that Ruby left the advertising and promotion departments at about 1:10 p.m., and seemed certain that Ruby was gone by the time Dick Jeffrey's TV set broadcast a bulletin at 1:30 that a police officer had been shot down in the street in the Oak Cliff section of Dallas.[2]

Ruby said he was crying when he left the *Morning News*. At the time he got in his car there was no definite word yet from Parkland Hospital on the exact condition of the President. At the same time that he got in his car, I was in the central corridor of Parkland's emergency room area, dictating a harried account of what was going on in the area, from hospital extension phone no. 430. I was there as White House correspondent for the Washington bureau of the Scripps-Howard Newspaper Alliance, on the trip with the President. I watched a priest go through a guarded doorway across the hall from me, to where the President had been placed in Trauma Room No. 1. I described Lady Bird Johnson, her face almost colorless, being escorted from that doorway by two men. She looked as if she would be ill in another moment. I struggled to reconstruct the choked words of Senator Ralph W. Yarborough, who had been two cars behind the presidential limousine. He told me how the shots had sounded like "three explosions from our right rear" and as if "from a deer rifle." Earlier in the day, Senator Yarborough and Vice-President Lyndon B. Johnson had not been on speaking terms because of their constant political and personal differences. Suddenly, they were huddled together on the floor of the car they shared as Lyndon Johnson drew the short, frightened breath of a man who no longer would ride two cars back. On the other end of the telephone line, in the Washington office of Scripps-Howard, I had a first-rate rewrite man—Jim Lucas, the Pulitzer-winning war correspondent who kept pulling my faltering narrative back together again, especially as I described the blood and crushed flowers I had seen in the open limousine parked outside.

Earlier in the day I had heard Texas Congressman Henry B. Gonzalez[3] joke about "the luck of the Irish," because it had stopped raining and

President Kennedy would be able to ride through Dallas in an open limousine, for all to see. Leaving the phone, I walked down the corridor and encountered Congressman Gonzalez standing numbly against a wall. He seemed unable to talk as he clutched a small paper bag that contained Governor Connally's possessions. Next to him was Congressman Albert Thomas of Houston, who told me of the President's head wounds. Just then, Malcolm Kilduff, the acting White House press secretary, passed quickly behind me and told me to follow him.

Only a handful of reporters had been able to get into the hospital emergency area. There were four of us who accompanied Kilduff out of the building. He refused to answer any questions. He led us around the outside of the hospital to another entrance. Just inside, there was a stairway. As Kilduff started up, I felt a tug behind me on my suit coat. It was Jack Ruby.

I had been in Washington a year and a half as correspondent for Scripps-Howard's Texas newspapers, and before that had been a reporter in Dallas on the afternoon paper, the *Times Herald,* where I had known Ruby.

Ruby called me by my first name and I grasped his extended hand. He looked miserable. Grim. Pale. There were tears brimming in his eyes. He commented on the obvious—how terrible the moment was—and did I have any word on the President's condition? There was nothing I knew to tell him and I only wanted to get away. Kilduff was disappearing up the steps. Certainly there was nothing unusual about seeing Jack Ruby there. He regularly turned up at spectacles in Dallas.[4] In a subdued voice he asked me if I thought it was a good idea for him to close his places for three nights because of the tragedy. Instead of shrugging, I told him I thought it was a good idea and then took off on the run, up the steps.

A minute later, a faint Kilduff stood behind a desk at the front of a medical teaching room hastily converted into a press conference room. It was jammed with reporters. Kilduff leaned forward on the desk, his fingers spread to support him, his knuckles white. His voice almost broke as he said it. The President was dead.

A month later, the first time authorities asked him about it, Ruby denied having rushed to Parkland Hospital that Friday, just as he denied other overt and suspicious actions that weekend.

What would make Jack Ruby seek out a news reporter he knew at the hospital on Friday and then deny, after Sunday, having been there?

It's because Ruby was not involved in a plot to kill anyone on Friday. But by Sunday he was.

About 10 minutes after Kilduff's announcement, Ruby appeared at the Carousel, his downtown club that normally didn't open until evening. Andrew Armstrong Jr., who Ruby referred to as "the colored boy," was there. So was Curtis LaVerne Crafard, known as Larry, a drifter who slept at the club. Andy Armstrong was 27 and had put up with Ruby's hot temper and swift mood swings since the spring of 1962, which was considerably more longevity than most employees ever had with him. Armstrong was a reliable assistant who fed Ruby's dogs, took care of purchase orders, handled cash transactions for the club and weathered what he estimated to be the 50 to 100 times that Ruby actually fired him, in addition to the threats of being fired by Ruby that came nearly every day.

Ruby appeared very distressed when he walked in. He told Armstrong right off to call Little Lynn, a Carousel stripper who lived 35 miles away in Fort Worth, and tell her not to come into Dallas that night. The Carousel would be closed. The call, placed at 1:45 p.m., according to Southwestern Bell Telephone Co. records, took a minute and was the first of six long-distance calls undertaken by Ruby in the next hour.

During these and a series of local calls, Ruby's emotions welled up into tears several times, especially when he talked at least twice more with Eva Grant, his sister in Dallas, and then with Eileen Kaminsky, his sister in Chicago, "I felt like a nothing person," he stated a month later in a jailhouse interview with Dr. Walter Bromberg, psychiatrist. "My first thought was to close the club. I was afraid I would crack up. Such a great person, and then to be snuffed out," he said of Kennedy. Ruby telephoned Dr. Coleman Jacobson, who had been ministering to Ruby's venereal disease. Ruby anticipated there would be a special memorial service for Kennedy that night at the synagogue and asked Dr. Jacobson what time Friday night services would begin. Ruby "sounded ill on the telephone," Dr. Bromberg was told by Dr. Jacobson. Mrs. Kaminsky said Ruby appeared so upset that he suggested that he might fly to Chicago, his home town, to be with her. Several years earlier when life had looked bleak to him, Ruby had fled Dallas in dishevelment and had hibernated for weeks in Chicago until he could face reality again. But Mrs. Kaminsky urged him to stay this time and take care of Eva Grant, convalescing from major surgery.

Another of Ruby's earliest calls that afternoon was to Alex Gruber in Los Angeles, the ex-convict and associate of hoodlums who had shown up in Dallas for no apparent reason earlier in the month and had spent several days seeing Ruby. Gruber subsequently told the FBI he didn't really know why Ruby called.

Before leaving the Carousel, Ruby told Armstrong he was thinking of keeping the club shut for three nights. The two discussed the damage the assassination would cause to convention business in Dallas. Ruby said he considered the shooting to have been "a black mark for the city."

At about 3:15 p.m., Ruby drove out to Eva Grant's place, to help calm her down. Normally they were at each other's throats and sometimes were so angry they wouldn't speak to each other for prolonged periods, even though Mrs. Grant, a divorcee, managed the Vegas Club for Ruby. One of their most bitter arguments had occurred nearly three months earlier, on the evening of August 29, while they were driving to a restaurant for dinner. With them in the car was their sister, Mrs. Kaminsky, who was visiting from Chicago with her two young daughters. First the two began to rage at each other, then the car swerved dangerously in traffic as Ruby slapped his sister. He stopped the car just long enough to shove her out, then he roared on. Ruby was no great shakes as a driver anyway. Between 1950 and 1963, Texas state motor vehicle records show, Ruby had been ticketed for 20 major traffic violations—most of them for running red lights and speeding. In 1959 he had been convicted as a habitual motor vehicle violator and his license was suspended for 12 months. But even though Ruby's relations with his sister also had been suspended for more than two months, the two had been drawn closely together again when Mrs. Grant underwent abdominal surgery in early November. Now, on the afternoon of November 22, the two of them decided that what they needed was a delicatessen snack to comfort them.

Ruby was trying to lose some weight and was taking Preludin, the drug that he said made him "a positive thinker." It was an appetite depressant but also an "upper," which kept the high-strung Ruby higher strung. For Ruby, who wasn't a drinker, food was the real balm his system craved to ward off depression. "I wanted to get drunk on kosher food," Ruby told Dr. Bromberg. So the "snack" the dieter brought from the Ritz Delicatessen to the patient recovering from abdominal surgery included three bottles of celery tonic for each of them, a pound of smoked salmon, a pound of roast beef, a pound of smoked white fish, a pound of tongue, bread, onions, oranges, and six cakes. Mrs. Grant was shocked by her brother's compulsiveness. He had spent $22 for the food, which in 1963 would have fed an average family of four in Dallas comfortably for a week.

But the bags of food went untouched as Ruby and his sister soon lost their appetites. "He kept thinking of what a sacrifice the young President had made in taking the presidency," wrote another psychiatrist, Dr. Manfred S. Guttmacher, who interviewed Ruby a month later as part of Ruby's trial defense team. (But Guttmacher was jarred by what Ruby said next about the slain John Kennedy: "He needed the job like he needed a hole in the head.") Television news reports that the prime suspect in custody, Oswald, had been a defector to Russia and was reportedly an avowed Marxist, created new waves of emotion for Ruby and his sister. "That lousy commie. Don't worry. The commie. We'll get him," Mrs. Grant told her brother. "I would never conceive of anybody in his right mind that would want this President hurt."

The Warren Commission asked Mrs. Grant what Ruby replied to that. "He didn't say nothing," Eva Grant responded. " . . . he went in the bathroom and threw up."

The question Ruby had raised with me and then with Armstrong of whether to close down the Vegas and Carousel for three nights was resolved at Mrs. Grant's apartment. The two of them decided to close for the weekend and change their newspaper ads to that effect. Sunday would be slow anyway. But they would give up the Saturday as well as the Friday trade. Ruby only hoped his competitors in the striptease business, the Weinsteins, whom he considered to be unpatriotic, insensitive and greedy, would stay open for all to see and shun.

Eva Grant said her brother looked "broken, a broken man already. He did make the remark, he said, 'I never felt so bad in my life, even when Ma or Pa died.'" The thought of President Kennedy's tragedy as a death in the family caused an overwhelming need in Ruby to go to the Friday night religious service at Congregation Shearith Israel, where he went only very occasionally. There he could grieve—or be seen grieving, just as he had put Mrs. Grant on the phone to be heard crying hysterically. At about 7 p.m. the man concerned with outer appearances took the total opposite route from his sister's place to Shearith Israel, in order to drive across town first to his apartment to change clothes. Ruby looked so bad that his sister worried about him getting killed in traffic en route to the synagogue.

With him in his car was the pocket-sized revolver he had bought nearly four years earlier, January 19, 1960, at Ray's Hardware Store in Dallas. A police officer had accompanied him when the buy was made, and now Ruby aimed the car toward the police station, where this Oswald was, instead of going straight home.

The first time I was aware of Oswald had been four years earlier. He had defected to Russia and his mother, Marguerite Oswald of Fort Worth, was trying to get him to come home. I was on Scripps-Howard's *Fort Worth Press* then and Kent Biffle, another reporter on the *Press*, spent hours one day setting up a three-way telephone call involving Mrs. Oswald, her son at the Hotel Metropole in Moscow, and our city desk. When Oswald at last got on the line and Kent shouted, "Lee, your mother is on the line, too, and wants to talk with you," Oswald hung up. Now he was just as unresponsive, being led at intervals to and from the jail elevator and Room 317, the Homicide Bureau office, through a gauntlet of angry, taunting reporters, shouting questions at him. More than 200 news people clogged the narrow, seven-foot-wide corridor. Each time Captain J. Will Fritz, the homicide chief, moved from doorway to doorway in the third floor corridor and did not have the prisoner with him, we gathered thickly around him, straining to hear what might be said. But Fritz spoke in his low, somewhat gravelly voice and could not be heard beyond the front ranks pressed practically against his face. Almost immediately the reporters up close began the custom of radiating Fritz's words out to others in the pack. With television cables, bright lights and large cameras set up, and radio newsmen with tape recorders, reporters were being interviewed by other reporters with microphones on latest developments.

By early evening, Friday, the intensity of the anger and confusion among reporters had grown on the third floor, as more reporters were arriving from all directions, as many as a planeload at a time. *The New York Times*, for instance, immediately dispatched six reporters to Dallas to concentrate on the police work of the assassination story. Correspondents for several foreign newspapers dropped United Nations and Washington assignments to rush to the story. Shortly after 7 p.m., John Rutledge, a veteran police reporter for *The Dallas Morning News*, saw Jack Ruby, whom he easily recognized by sight, step from a public elevator onto the third floor.

Ruby was between two men who wore lapel credentials identifying them as out-of-town reporters. The three walked rapidly past a police officer stationed at the elevators to keep out anyone not on official business. Ruby was hunched over, writing something on a piece of paper and then showing it to one of the reporters as they walked toward Room 317, where Oswald was being interrogated by captain Fritz and others.

Across the hall from 317 was the Burglary and Theft Bureau, where Ruby exchanged greetings with at least three detectives he knew. Ruby had been an informant on a check forgery and narcotics trafficking case for one of the three, August M. (Mike) Eberhardt. A guard was posted at the bureau door to keep reporters from getting in to use the phones, but Ruby had no trouble easing in. He knew the guard. Ruby walked in and shook hands with Eberhardt, who asked him what he was doing. Ruby had note paper in his hand and said he was acting as translator for the foreign press. Eberhardt figured Ruby was talking about the Israeli press or the Yiddish-speaking reporters Eberhardt guessed he heard in the bedlam of the corridor. Soon after, Victor F. Robertson Jr., city hall reporter for WFAA radio and TV in Dallas, who had patronized the Carousel and had seen Ruby frequently there and elsewhere, saw him again. This time, Ruby was in the corridor, attempting to enter 317, while Oswald was in there. The guard on the door turned him away.

Ruby vigorously denied that whole appearance at the police station and complained about those who said they saw and talked with him, because "it looked like I was trying to find out who this Oswald was and [as] if I went down there more than once [that night]." As a result, the Warren Commission did not dispute Ruby's word.

The Commission concluded that the detectives who said they talked with Ruby early Friday night, and the two reporters who said they saw him then on the third floor, "may well have been mistaken as to time," even though Rutledge further reported watching Ruby loiter on the third floor, pointing out police authorities and spelling their names for the benefit of out-of-town reporters.

To bolster its conclusion, the Commission produced Clyde F. Goodson, the officer assigned to guard the Homicide Bureau door in the early evening, Friday, but who may already have been replaced by another guard at the time Robertson reported seeing Ruby turned away. Goodson recalled leaving the post at "about 7:30 or so; around 7:30," and couldn't recall who replaced him. He did recall turning away a man about 6 p.m. and said "possibly someone would mistake him for Jack Ruby . . . [but] I don't think he fit the description of him close enough that anyone who knew him or had seen him before—I don't believe he fit the description close enough to assume that that was him." But could Goodson even identify Ruby if he saw him? The FBI showed officer Goodson six crowd-scene pictures taken that Friday night at police headquarters, which included front and back views of Ruby. Goodson said he "does not feel that he knew Ruby well enough to make an unqualified identification of Ruby in any of these six photographs," the FBI reported.

Robertson was shown the same pictures on the same day Goodson looked at them. Robertson "identified, without any qualifications," the frontal views of Ruby, according to the FBI.

Those pictures showed Ruby dressed as he was later that night, after attending services at Shearith Israel. The services began at 8 p.m. but Ruby didn't get there until close to 10, almost at the end. As he drove from the synagogue, "in my mind suddenly it mulled over me that the police department was working overtime," he later told the Warren Commission. "I have always been very close to the police department, I don't know why." So Ruby figured the best way to the department's heart, and maybe to its Room 317, had to be through its stomach. He stopped at Phil's Delicatessen this time and ordered a dozen corned beef sandwiches and some celery tonic to be sacked up for the Homicide Bureau. He telephoned homicide detective Richard M. Sims and offered to deliver the free food right to the office. Sims thanked him but said the day's work was about over and they wouldn't need anything to eat. Ruby found another reason to go anyway and, at about 11:30 p.m., he stepped off the elevator on the third floor again. This time he looked like a detective in his dark suit and snap-brim fedora. The hard steel bulge in his trouser pocket was not noticeable.

This time a uniformed patrolman was stationed at the elevator and asked the intruder to state his business. Ruby said he was looking for radio station KLIF newsman Joe Long. He said he had sandwiches down in the car to be delivered to the KLIF staff. Before he could be told to leave, Ruby began smiling and waving at other officers he knew, and one of them volunteered to undertake a search for Joe Long in the mass of reporters. Ruby took careful notice that "no one has tears in their eyes" on the third floor, just as he had closely observed which saloons and clubs out there on the street were not darkened out of respect to the slain President.

But then "suddenly I'm in a world of history"[5] as Police Chief Jesse E. Curry and District Attorney Henry M. Wade appeared in the corridor with an announcement that Oswald would be put on display in the basement police assembly room for all to see. Ruby easily got caught up with the movement of people going to the basement.

Chief Curry specifically warned us that if there were any unusual movements toward Oswald or any continuing of the cannon-volley of questions that Captain Fritz had been enduring (reporters shouting, yelling, drowning out answers, drowning out questions), then the prisoner would be withdrawn.

At that point Oswald had been formally charged with the murder of officer Tippit and was to be charged in little more than an hour with the murder of the President. Chief Curry was displaying Oswald so the nation could see he was not being beaten by police in search of a confession. Oswald's face had been bruised earlier, during the course of his arrest, and he had shouted at reporters in the third-floor corridor that the police were abusing his civil rights to take a shower. Scores of newly arrived photographers and reporters had been clamoring through the evening to get a good look at the world's most essential prisoner, and all jammed into the assembly room so tightly that Captain Fritz, who arrived late, could not get in. He was forced to stay outside, straining to hear.

Ruby stood on a table in the rear of the room. He observed that Oswald seemed to smirk at the police around him. Dr. Bromberg, the psychiatrist, talked to Ruby about his feelings at the time: "He thought, 'I am above everybody. They cannot move me.' He felt like a 'big guy.' He also had a strong feeling he was in with the police; he was a 'right guy,'" Dr. Bromberg reported. The Warren Commission portrayed Ruby simply as a casual bystander at Oswald's midnight press conference. Nowhere in its 888-page report to the public did the Commission include Ruby's admission to the FBI, a month after the crime, that he was carrying a loaded, snub-nosed revolver in his right-hand pocket during the Oswald press session in the assembly room. If Ruby had considered using his gun to execute Oswald then and there, he could not have gotten off a clean shot. Reporters stood on tables in front of him and a barrier of photographers stood before Oswald. The photographers began to push, shove and close in on Oswald. Questions began to rage at him. Oswald's answers were barely audible and the pasty-faced prisoner, his hands manacled behind him, was abruptly removed from the medieval-like pit.

District Attorney Wade remained to outline to reporters what was known about Oswald, and when he got to Oswald's activities in the pro-Castro, Fair Play for Cuba Committee, Wade misstated the organization's name. He called it the Free Cuba Committee. Ruby shouted out the correct name.

Had Ruby simply heard of Oswald's connection with Fair Play for

Cuba on a news broadcast that evening, or perhaps from one of his police friends? It seems strange that a man such as Ruby, considered politically naive by those who knew him best, would come up with the correction in a room full of reporters. The explanation might simply have been in one of several newspaper odds and ends Ruby had in his car: that partial copy of *The New York Sunday Mirror* dated September 8, 1963, in which columnist Walter Winchell discussed what should be done with 58 Americans who had defied a State Department ban against visiting communist Cuba.[6] "They should be treated like any citizens who violate the law," wrote Winchell in his lead item. "It is important to note that their excursion was partly paid for by Castro and was organized by members of the Fair Play for Cuba Committee. This committee derives its financial support from Castro."

Perhaps it was because he spoke out at the press conference or maybe it was because of the electricity of the moment, and all the camera flashguns, but Ruby no longer was the grim, crying, beaten man he had appeared to be earlier on Friday. Ruby became animated. Ludicrously he began shaking hands with out-of-town reporters, handing them "Jack Ruby Your Host at the Carousel" calling cards and urging them to come by for drinks and a show when the club reopened. Now effervescent, Ruby felt himself becoming "like a reporter." When New York radio newsman Ike Pappas had trouble getting Wade to his open telephone line to New York for an interview, Ruby went over and got the district attorney to go to Pappas. When KLIF sent Russ Knight (real name: Russell Lee Moore), a disc jockey known on the air as the Weird Beard, over to the police station to interview Wade, Weird Beard didn't know whom to look for. But he knew Ruby and Ruby not only set him up with Wade but supplied a question to ask: Is Oswald insane? Wade responded, no, the murder of the President had been a premeditated act by a sane man.

Ruby then went to KLIF headquarters with the sandwiches and celery tonic, and excitedly heard himself get a vague but free plug when Weird Beard went on the 2 a.m. news: "Through a tip from a local nightclub owner I asked Mr. Wade the question of Oswald's insanity."

Despite the hour, Ruby had no intention of going home yet. He got in his car and headed for *The Dallas Times Herald*, but he saw police officer Harry Olsen and Kay Helen Coleman together at a downtown parking garage, and stopped. The three of them talked for more than an hour in Olsen's car.

Mrs. Coleman, a divorcee, was 27, a blonde and curvy stripper, born in London, and worked for Ruby as Kathy Kay at the Carousel. Ruby heard her say that if Oswald had committed the crime in England, he would have been dragged through the streets and hanged. She and officer Olsen heard Ruby curse Oswald, calling him a son of a bitch, and Ruby heard the policeman agree with Kathy Kay that a trial was too good for the cop killer, advocating that Oswald should be cut to ribbons.

Joe Tonahill, one of Ruby's lawyers, is convinced that "Ruby could have been used" by others to kill Oswald. "It wouldn't have been any problem to reach in and get Ruby to do something like this, through the power of suggestion, through innuendo, without Ruby even realizing it. The conversation with Olsen and Kay could have been the beginning of it. It could have been a lot stronger. We don't know who all he talked with."[7]

Tonahill expresses the strong possibility that Ruby's conversation with the police officer was much more explicit. "Ruby didn't want to talk about that conversation because he had enough sense to know that was premeditation," Tonahill says of Ruby's skill in keeping the fact that there even had been a dark encounter with Olsen secret until after Ruby's trial was over.

Ruby was a man of secrets in the same paradoxical way that he was a man of great disorder. On the outside he appeared well groomed, while the trunk of his white Oldsmobile and his apartment contained the strewn contents of an undisciplined life. Similarly, he appeared on the outside to run off at the mouth about anything that came to mind; not sticking too well to the theme of any conversation. But in reality he was "a very complex person," as John C. Jackson of Lafayette, Louisiana, who lived with Ruby from 1956 to 1958, described him. Jack Ruby was—as he was described by both his business partner and his tax lawyer—a secretive person.

Ruby kept his appearances at Parkland Hospital and at the Dallas police station on Friday and Saturday secret. He concealed the relationships he had with a wide range of people—such as Tom Davis, the gunrunner, and such as a mystery telephone voice he dealt with in the days leading up to the shooting of President Kennedy. Ruby was getting a series of phone calls at the Carousel from an unidentified man who never would leave a message when Ruby was out. Larry Crafard, the young handyman at the club, asked Ruby about these strange telephone calls but Ruby told him to mind his own business. And there was Mrs. Doris [Curtis L.] Warner. She was 19 and a beauty. She and her husband managed the apartment house on Ewing where Ruby lived. But when the rent was due it was strictly Doris whom Ruby would pay. Ruby certainly kept her a secret, as they corresponded privately.

"You have been the only person that I have constantly thought of, outside of my immediate family," Ruby wrote in a four-page letter to Doris on June 8, 1966, one of several letters he had smuggled out of jail to her. "I surely realize what a wonderful and blissful life we had both been cheated out of. Had I known how much you really cared for me, perhaps I too would have been more serious in our future for us." He signed the letter: "All my love, Jack."[8]

Sometime after 3:30 a.m., Ruby left police officer Olsen and the exotic dancer at the garage and continued on to the *Times Herald*, where he checked his advertisement in the composing room for the next afternoon's paper, making sure a black border was on the ad that said his clubs would be closed. Ruby complained to printers at the *Times Herald* about that *other* black-bordered ad—the ugly Welcome Mr. Kennedy ad the *Morning News* had accepted over the name of Bernard Weissman. By now Ruby had decided rightwing extremists had used the name "to make the Jews look bad."

Another reason for his visit to the composing room was that Ruby had promised something called the Twist Waist Exerciser to one of the employees there. Here was one of Ruby's get-rich-quick schemes. A $3.95 exercise gimmick based on the dance, the "Twist," it was a platform to stand on, the size and height of a bathroom platform scale. Set on 70 ball bearings, it rotated and swiveled and Ruby was excited over the possibilities of handling its national distribution. After 4 a.m. Ruby was giving a demonstration on the twist board, with the printers gathered around and everybody laughing. Then he encouraged a woman proofreader to get on the board, a performance that Ruby and everybody seemed to enjoy. Off again into the cold, black morning.

Driving home toward the Oak Cliff section of Dallas, Ruby began to brood about a signboard he had seen hours earlier. It demanded in red, white and blue, and in large letters, "Impeach Earl Warren." He wondered if there had been any connection between the Weissman advertisement and the impeach-Warren billboard. He would find out, he promised himself.

George Senator and Larry Crafard had nothing much in common except that both were aimless men who at the moment needed Jack Ruby.

Crafard was a high school dropout who had grown up in small Michigan and California towns. At 22 he had been employed at a lot of places, from Georgia to Oregon, frequently with carnivals and often quitting or getting fired from them after a few days. Crafard, whose eyes blinked constantly from a nervous tic, had no idea where his wife was. She had left him twice, the second time after he had taken her and their two infants hitchhiking at random on the interstate highways in search of work. Crafard had landed in Dallas in the fall of 1963 and had gotten a job at $5 a day as caretaker for an event at the State Fair of Texas called "How Hollywood Makes Movies," another of Ruby's get-rich schemes. Ruby was a financial partner in the crude show but it quickly went broke and closed several days before the two-week state fair itself had concluded in October. Even the $5 daily pay hadn't fully materialized. Some days Crafard was paid off in meals and cigarettes, and then Ruby offered Crafard a similar arrangement at the Carousel, where he could sleep at the club and draw money for food and smokes, in exchange for working the spotlight during striptease acts, and for odd jobs.

Senator, on the other hand, was 50 years old, a New Yorker whose marriage had fallen apart years earlier and who much preferred the company of men. He had failed as a traveling salesman of cheap dresses and novelties and now was drawing $61.45 a week as a picture postcard salesman. A bloated man who drank frequently and had been arrested in Dallas for drunkenness, Senator changed apartments and slept on other people's couches often when he was out of work. He had roomed with Ruby in 1962 but had left him because basically Ruby got on his nerves. They were a lowlife version of Neil Simon's *The Odd Couple.*

"Jack don't live too clean," Senator complained to the Warren Commission. I mean he is a type—in other words, he comes home, he is reading a newspaper, on the floor, if he is in the bathroom the newspaper goes on the floor and things of that nature. Though he was very clean about himself, he wasn't clean around the apartment . . . I couldn't cook right for him. He is a funny guy in cooking. If I don't broil right for him, if I make him eggs, it has got to be so much of this in the butter because he was watching his diet, and I got so tired of it I says, 'make your own eggs.' You just couldn't make anything right for him. . . . He would buy what [food] would suit himself, and if I don't like it that is too bad."

But in the fall of 1963 George Senator was foundering and Ruby took him in again, to sleep in Ruby's spare bedroom. Senator referred to Ruby as "my boyfriend." Senator would pay no rent, in exchange for occasional evening duties at the club, such as receiving admission fees at the door.

There was one other thing that Senator and Crafard had in common, though. Ruby treated them as though he owned them.

It was approximately 4:30 a.m. when Ruby reached No. 207, his place at 223 S. Ewing, a cheaply built two-story apartment house. Senator had been to a couple of bars Friday night. He was sleeping pretty well, he recalled to Leon Hubert and Burt Griffin, the two Warren Commission lawyers in charge of the Ruby detail:

> SENATOR: The next thing I know somebody was hollering at me and shaking me up.
> QUESTION: That was who?
> S: Jack Ruby.
> Q: Now describe him to us at that time. What was his condition?
> S: He was excited. He was moody; and the first thing come out of his mouth is the incident. Of course, the incident what happened to President Kennedy, and he said, "Gee, his poor children and Mrs. Kennedy, what a terrible thing to happen."

Q: Had he been drinking?

S: Jack don't drink.

Q: He wasn't drinking on this occasion?

S: No; he don't drink, no.

Q: And his remarks were concerning the children?

S: The children and Mrs. Kennedy and how sorry he felt for them.

Q: What other comments did he make?

S: Then he brought up the situation where he saw this poster of Justice of the Peace [*sic*] Earl Warren; impeach him, Earl Warren.

Q: He said he had seen that poster?

S: Yes, he had saw the poster . . . and he made me get dressed.

Q: What did he tell you when he made you get dressed?

S: He was telling me about this sign here.

Q: Why did he want you to get dressed?

S: He wanted me to go down to see the sign, and meanwhile he had called . . . He had a kid sleeping in the club who helps around, and he has got a Polaroid camera. So he calls the kid up, wakes him up . . . he calls him up and says, "Larry, get up, get dressed," something of that nature, "and get that Polaroid with the flashbulbs and meet me downstairs. I'll be right downtown."

The camera was a gimmick of Ruby's, used for taking good-natured pictures of volunteer customers dancing the twist with the strippers, as part of the show. Then the pictures would be made available to the customers as free souvenirs. When Crafard got in the car with the camera, about 5 a.m., Ruby didn't bother to tell him where they were going or what he was supposed to shoot.

Ruby drove to the location of the impeachment sign posted on the side of a building in a prominent location at the edge of downtown Dallas. Three pictures were taken of it. Ruby was excited because the sign encouraged people who wanted Earl Warren ousted to write to post office box no. 1754—a number vaguely similar to post office box no. 1792 in the Weissman ad. Ruby thought he was on to Something Big.

"He is trying to combine these two together," Senator recalled, "which I did hear him say, 'This is the work of the John Birch Society or the Communist Party or maybe a combination of both.'"

Later in the day, Saturday, Ruby would telephone his friend Weird Beard, the disc jockey, and ask who is this Earl Warren.

From the signboard the three drove to the main post office, where Ruby tried to get the night clerk to tell him who paid for box 1792. The clerk said he wasn't permitted to give out such information and said it would have to come from the postmaster. Ruby looked through a slot in no. 1792 and grew angry when he saw it was filled with responses. His anger seemed to build as the three then went to the coffee shop in the Southland Hotel. Senator recalled that Ruby's "voice of speech . . . was different [and] . . . he had sort of a stare look in his eye." Ruby was miserable. The killing of President Kennedy in Dallas ... the Weissman ad ... the Earl Warren sign ... it was all going to reflect badly on the city. He couldn't get to Bernard Weissman. There was no such person in the Dallas phone book. He had checked. Ruby didn't know who was behind the movement to impeach Warren yet, and for all he knew it was the same people who may have concocted a Jewish name to sign to the hateful advertisement aimed at President Kennedy. But the whereabouts of Oswald the killer was known. Oswald was right there in Dallas, where Ruby already had found him.

When Crafard was being dropped off again at the Carousel in the first traces of daylight, he commented to Ruby and Senator that it probably wasn't worth their while even to go to bed at that point. Ruby agreed. After all, it was after 6 a.m.

But when Crafard telephoned the apartment at 8:30 to tell Ruby there was no more processed food to feed the pet dogs that Ruby kept in a back room at the club, Ruby was outraged. He berated Crafard for not having brains enough to let a man sleep.

That did it for Crafard. He punched out $5 from the cash register late that morning, added it to the $2 he already had in his pocket and took off for Michigan, hitching rides. The last thing he heard at the Carousel when he left was the barking of hungry dogs.

Part II—Saturday
"He Wasn't There Again Today"

There was exhaustion in the faces of the reporters by Saturday as the physical impact of the assassination coverage had set in. The atmosphere in the third-floor corridor was one of despair, despite the crackle of the biggest police story anyone there had ever covered. The corridor seemed totally isolated from the outside world. Nothing else seemed to matter.

Shortly after noon that day, Saturday, November 23, Captain Fritz received a phone call from Chief Curry, who wanted to know when Oswald could be transferred to the sheriff's custody at county jail. The transfer was the legal procedure for a prisoner arraigned on a felony charge. Curry was most anxious to shift the focus of emotion from the 170-foot-long corridor outside his third-floor office, into Sheriff Bill Decker's building about a mile away at Dealey Plaza. But Fritz, a relentless old detective with a first-rate local reputation for cracking murder cases, and with the immobile face and understated characteristics of a Charlie Chan, was in no way done with Oswald.

Fritz planned to resume his interrogation of the prisoner after the lunch hour and Chief Curry wondered if in that case a 4 p.m. transfer of Oswald could be arranged. Fritz was skeptical. He would see. Meanwhile the police chief went ahead with quietly laid plans to move Oswald the mile at 4 p.m., without public notice. A few trusted people around the police station knew about it. And so did Jack Ruby.

At close to 3 p.m., Sergeant D. V. Harkness of the police traffic division asked a small group of people to move from the vehicular entrance of the county jail, the transfer point. Among the loiterers he saw Jack Ruby. Ruby then walked behind the Texas School Book Depository, the building Oswald was charged with having used as a sniper's nest to fire on the presidential motorcade. There Ruby encountered Wesley A. Wise, who was inside the KRLD station wagon mobile news unit. Wise was sports director for the KRLD radio and television stations[9] but had been pressed into frontline news duties during the extraordinary weekend in Dallas. Like I had, Wes Wise had seen Ruby numerous times at events and knew him to be an especially emotional fan at professional boxing matches. Wise also knew Ruby was always on the make around news people, in search of publicity.

Ruby proudly told Wise he had been the tipster identified as the "local nightclub owner" prominently mentioned on KLIF in an early-morning newscast that Wise had heard, and said he would be glad to get Wise a "scoop," too. Wise tried not to sound abrupt but indicated he was busy. Ruby walked on. But in a few minutes he was back at Wes Wise's station wagon, this time in his own car and with information that Chief Curry and Captain Fritz were at that moment examining the assassination scene. Then Ruby drove to the Nichols Garage, next to the Carousel, told garage manager Garnett Claud Hallmark he was "acting like a reporter," and asked to use the phone. One of the calls he made was to KLIF, where he talked to disc jockey Ken Dowe on the hot line—a private phone line that only station personnel were supposed to know, but Ruby had it now.

"I understand they are moving Oswald over to the county jail," Dowe heard Ruby say. "Would you like me to cover it, because I am a pretty good friend of Henry Wade's and I believe I can get some news stories." Hallmark was standing less than two feet from Ruby and heard the conversation from that end. Dowe checked with the news department and was told to let Ruby go ahead and help out. So Dowe told Ruby if he happened to be there at the time of the transfer, a phone tip would be appreciated.

"You know I'll be there," Hallmark heard Ruby reply meaningfully.

But on their inspection trip, Chief Curry and Captain Fritz found traffic was impossible in the Dealey Plaza area. Mourners were driving at a funereal pace past the shooting scene by the hundreds, many of them placing flowers and heart-sick notes on the bordering grass. Captain Fritz feared that Oswald's transfer would become mired in the sepulchral flow of traffic, word would get out that Oswald had been taken from city jail, and he would be killed in the street by a mob. The transfer was postponed.

Frederic Rheinstein, an NBC producer-director from California, was coordinating his network's national television coverage of the third floor at Dallas police headquarters that Saturday. He was working late in the morning inside a WBAP-Fort Worth remote TV van that was parked adjacent to the municipal building, when an intruder poked his face inside a window of the van, brushed aside a curtain and began to watch activities up in the third-floor corridor on a closed-circuit monitor. Rheinstein was annoyed at the intrusion and got a good look at the pushy man's face. The man became a familiar figure to Rheinstein and members of his crew that day, and they always referred to him as The Creep.

Later in the day they watched The Creep appear on their monitor, as he walked into a third-floor office being used by District Attorney Wade—an office barred to reporters by police. At that point a WBAP engineer identified The Creep as the person he had seen at the WBAP van, taking one of 14 fried chicken lunches brought in for the NBC crew.

Still later, a cameraman and stage manager reported to Rheinstein that "The Creep from down at the van" had told them he knew Wade personally and could furnish NBC information or could get the district attorney himself to come out and talk. He was observed on the sidewalk outside police headquarters and on the third floor, at intervals ranging from late morning and early afternoon, to late afternoon. When Ruby shot Oswald the next day, the NBC crew knew The Creep had a name.

Here was a man identified in Dallas police files as having underworld connections, roaming the police station halls unhampered and without credentials, possibly stalking Oswald and certainly able to overhear or participate in some police conversations. Many of Ruby's movements on Saturday, contacts he made, and his whereabouts in large time-chunks, remained blank, so far as the Warren Commission was concerned. The Commission did not pin down where Ruby was during much of the day—in the late morning, early afternoon, late afternoon and in parts of the evening—when "in fact, it was pretty well established that Ruby arrived at the police station apparently by late afternoon or early evening, Friday, and he spent a lot of time there from Friday, after the assassination, until Sunday, when he finally shot Oswald," according to one Dallas police authority in a position to know: Chief Jesse Curry.[10]

Ruby was reported to have brought sandwiches to reporters in the police press room on Saturday. Other reliable outside witnesses reported seeing Ruby or talking with him at intervals during Saturday afternoon—witnesses such as Jeremiah A. O'Leary Jr. of *The Washington Star* and Thayer Waldo, a reporter for *The Fort Worth Star-Telegram*. Waldo met Ruby in the third-floor corridor, talked with him and was handed a Carousel card by Ruby after 4 p.m. Yet the Warren Commission said it could reach "no firm conclusion as to whether or not Ruby visited the Dallas police department on Saturday" because "no police officer has reported Ruby's presence on that day" and because "Ruby has not mentioned such a visit."

In other words, the Warren Commission decided there had been no conspiracy between Dallas police officers and Jack Ruby because none of them reported it at the time.

First the Commission chose to disbelieve those police who said they saw and talked with Ruby in the early evening of Friday, and then elected to believe that Ruby wasn't there again on Saturday because none of the police brought it up.

Perhaps the Commission should have dedicated the Ruby portion of its Warren Report to Hughes Mearns, the author of the quatrain that went:

> As I was going up the stair
> I met a man who wasn't there
> He wasn't there again today—
> I wish, I *wish*, he'd stay away

Meanwhile, the Commission failed to ask a large number of police who were in the station and who knew Ruby if they had seen him at all on Saturday. In fact the Commission primarily relied on an investigation by Dallas police officials to clear the police of any collusion with Ruby.

In a report filed December 16, 1963, the panel of eight police officials said it had talked with 90 (20 patrolmen, 21 reserves, 30 detectives and 19 supervisors) of the nearly 1,200 police force members. Chief Curry was led to believe, or at least told the Commission he believed, Ruby had between 25 and 50 acquaintances on the force, when actually Ruby knew several times that number. Only a few of those were examined by the special police investigatory panel.

The Warren Commission itself never checked the records of two major Dallas banks, the Republic and First National, after Dallas Peace Justice David L. Johnston told the FBI he had heard that Ruby's signature was on cosigned loans made to Dallas policemen at those two banks. The Commission also failed to question several of the police who were known associates of Ruby and who were in the police station at critical times during the weekend.

Instead, the Commission supported findings made by the police department's own inspectors who, by their own admission, were too limited both in time and money to be thorough. Their final report exonerating any and all members of the department from collusion with Ruby was filed with Chief Curry three weeks after the shooting of Oswald.

It would have been like asking the Chicago White Sox baseball team of 1919 to examine charges that some of its players had conspired with gamblers to throw the World Series. The resulting "Black Sox" scandal that got eight Chicago players indicted and shook the good name of the national pastime to its foundations would not have come to light. The mob's Arnold (The Brain) Rothstein was the outside force behind the baseball scandal, although it was Abe Attel, the flashy dresser and former world's featherweight boxing champion, who got caught in the act of handling the "fix."

The conspiracy of the police and Ruby in Dallas was much the same as what had happened with the Chicago team and Abe Attel, with Ruby caught in the act. The question is, who was The Brain in Dallas? In Dallas, as with the Black Sox, the key players were involved; not necessarily the manager and coach, such as Curry and Fritz. The plot appeared to take place further down in the ranks, where there were sergeants and lieutenants, and it seemed to take shape after 4 p.m., Saturday.

After 4 p.m. Chief Curry suggested to Captain Fritz that Oswald be moved under cover of dark to the county jail that night. But Fritz felt the darkness would work against a safe transfer instead of for it. There would be limited protection for Oswald against lurking figures in the shadows or a sudden assault from behind bright blinding lights, Fritz reasoned. At that point Fritz was certain in his own mind that Oswald would never, under any circumstances, admit killing John F. Kennedy or officer Tippit. But he wanted at least to question the prisoner again at 6 p.m. Chief Curry then asked if 10 a.m. the next day seemed like a logical transfer time and the chief of detectives reckoned it probably was.

Word got out among police in the building that there would be no transfer of Oswald that night. Word also circulated among police that proof existed to show Oswald had been the hired gun of a foreign power, a communist agent sent in as part of an international conspiracy to destroy the leadership of the United States. That view was spread as fact in angry asides by William F. Alexander, who had been in and out of Room 317, where Oswald was being questioned, and who had participated in the police search of Oswald's living quarters. Alexander was the squint-eyed, severe assistant district attorney in charge of Henry Wade's criminal cases. Alexander also knew Ruby, who had issued him permanent free pass no. 235 to the Carousel.

So there was Ruby, an armed outsider in the police station at a time when police knew of the changed transfer plan for a prisoner believed to be communist saboteur and cop killer, and known to be close-mouthed and surly.

At 8:15 p.m. Chief Curry made the transfer plan official. He stepped from his administrative offices into the 170-foot-long corridor. He stood still a moment and was instantly surrounded by reporters. It was difficult to breathe in the swarm of people as the chief inched into position in front of the network cameras. As he began to make his statement, the crowd was bunched so tightly I saw one reporter writing notes on paper pressed against the chief's right shoulderblade. The chief said Oswald would not be transferred during the night but, if we were to return by 10 a.m. the next day, there would be ample time "to observe anything you care to observe."

Discussing this a little later with other reporters I found general agreement that Curry's statement probably was a planned deception and the police would slip Oswald out during the night to avoid mob action. We expected it.

But Curry kept his word. As a result, the FBI and sheriff's department received anonymous telephone threats during the early hours of Sunday, warning there would be a fully armed, organized street attack on the transfer vehicle and advising the police not to risk their own safety to protect the prisoner. But Ruby's friends on the police force didn't intend to risk their own safety.

Part III—Sunday
That Man upon the Stair

George Senator told the Warren Commission he awoke Sunday morning, November 24, at "maybe around 8 or 9," while Ruby still slept, and remained right there in the apartment they shared clad only in his underwear, until Ruby's departure after 10:30 a.m. Senator was insistent on that point. Yet the Commission Report states without hesitation that "Senator said that when he arose, before 9 a.m., he began to do his laundry in the basement of the apartment building while Ruby slept." Senator never mentioned doing his laundry that morning in sessions with the Commission, the FBI and the district attorney's office. However, in one interview conducted December 3, 1963, by Secret Service agent Elmer W. Moore, Senator said he spent some time doing laundry before Ruby got up. Commission lawyers decided to overlook what Senator told them on April 21, 1964, five months after the weekend of the shootings, partly because Senator's memory should have been a lot fresher when he met with agent Moore only nine days after Ruby shot Oswald, and largely because a witness described having seen someone resembling Ruby, in undershirt and slacks, carrying finished laundry up from the basement to Ruby's apartment No. 207 that morning. Another witness said he saw the same individual entering No. 207, minutes later, not carrying anything. Both witnesses, a pair of truck drivers who shared a nearby apartment, were short-term, transient residents of the building and didn't know either Ruby or Senator by sight. They made the identification only after Ruby's picture appeared all over the news, and even then neither witness seemed aware of Senator's existence. Under those circumstances it might have been possible to confuse Ruby with his roommate. Senator virtually was Ruby's age and, at 5'7", 190 pounds, he was roughly Ruby's size. The two had dark hair, both wore horn-rimmed glasses and had generally similar features. Besides, the Commission was advised that Ruby never did his laundry in the apartment building's basement washers and driers, but had it done for him by attendants at a professionally run washeteria elsewhere. Meanwhile, Senator took his laundry to the basement faithfully each weekend. So the Commission probably was right: The two truck drivers probably did see Senator that morning at two different times; a vital point, because Senator could remember Ruby getting only one phone call all morning, and it is known that he got more than one.

Senator said the only phone call Ruby received that morning was one from Little Lynn, the Carousel stripper who lived in Fort Worth. That toll call was placed at 10:19 a.m., according to telephone company records. Senator said he had no knowledge of other calls to Ruby, including one from Elnora Pitts, a cleaning lady who was able to tell authorities in detail about an unusual conversation she'd had with Ruby that morning, at a time she established as between 8:30 and 9.

Senator could not have been in the apartment at intervals when he cared for his laundry. During those intervals he had no way of knowing about any local calls received by Ruby—whether from Mrs. Pitts or from Ruby's police contacts.

Ruby had reason to expect the police to call. He also knew he would hear from Karen Bennett Carlin, the performer known as Little Lynn. She was pestering him for money.

Payday at the Carousel normally was Sunday, but, since the club would not be open, Little Lynn had begun asking for her pay on Saturday. To mollify her, Ruby had arranged to provide $5 for her on Saturday night so she and her husband could get home from a bar. Little Lynn always seemed to have hard-luck stories and already had drawn an advance on her week's salary. She told Ruby she would need more money on Sunday to pay house rent and buy groceries but he was angry with her and told her not to bother him again about the money until Sunday.

Shortly before 9, Sunday morning, Senator was downstairs with the laundry when the phone rang. Ruby sounded "uptight" when he answered.

"What do you want?" Ruby asked angrily, according to Elnora Pitts, the woman who cleaned his apartment each Sunday, as she reconstructed the conversation for the Warren Commission.

"I says, 'This is Elnora.' He says, 'Yes, well what—you need some money?' And I says, 'No; I was coming to clean today.'"

Ruby obviously was surprised. He was irritated because he expected Little Lynn to be calling to hit him up for more money. He was on edge as a man would be who expected a call from one of his police sources, telling him what time to be at the police station for an appointment with Oswald.

But the widow Pitts always telephoned him on Sunday mornings to make sure when it would be all right for her to be there, and she was baffled because he sounded so strange and didn't seem to recognize her.

Elnora Pitts identified herself again and Ruby asked if she would be coming to his apartment. She asked in return if it would be all right for her to be there at about 2 p.m., but since Ruby could have known full well he was going to the police station to shoot somebody he told her not to set out for his place without checking first by telephone.

"That's what I'm doing now, calling you so I won't have to call you again," said a thoroughly puzzled 60-year-old cleaning woman. But Ruby insisted she phone him again before making the trip to his place ("he sounded terrible strange to me," she told the Warren Commission).

The Warren Report mentioned the conversation between Ruby and Mrs. Pitts only in passing and stressed a statement by her that "there was something wrong with him, the way he was talking to me." A clear inference brought out by the Report was that Ruby had awakened that morning as a man going crackers . . . a man losing touch with reality. But the opposite was true. He knew what lay ahead. It was the Warren Commission that had lost touch.

As Elnora Pitts and Ruby were on the phone, Chief Curry and Sheriff Decker were reaching an agreement as to who would escort Oswald the mile from one jail to another. The normal procedure in such a transfer was for the constable's office to accompany the prisoner. But this was an extraordinary situation and the city police had both the manpower and firepower to handle it better, the chief and the sheriff agreed. What was shameful, though, was that there had been no earlier planning. The two men didn't discuss this basic point until more than 12 hours after Curry's public announcement at 8:15 the night before that Oswald would not be moved until at least 10 in the morning. Once the issue of which department would handle the transfer officially was settled, Assistant Police Chief Charles Batchelor suggested to Curry that an armored van be obtained as the transfer vehicle, because of the anonymous threats to murder the prisoner in the streets. Batchelor's plan was to borrow a large "money wagon," the kind used by armed guards to transfer negotiable securities, and back it into the jail basement to pick up Oswald. Deputy Chief M. W. Stevenson was in on some of that discussion in which Chief Curry told Batchelor to go ahead and get the van.

At 9 a.m., Stevenson walked into the Juvenile Bureau on the third floor of the police station and said he wanted all those on duty to remain in the office. They would be needed to form security for Oswald in the basement at the time of the transfer. One of those in the basement at the time of the transfer, W. J. (Jay) Cutchshaw, told the desk officer to contact two of the bureau's investigators who were on a coffee break and get them back into the bureau.

The two investigators, detective L. D. Miller and officer W. J. (Blackie) Harrison,[11] were reached by phone at the Delux Diner, down the block on Commerce, at a time when the police knew this set of facts: 1.

There would be no more delays, as in the previous day's transfer plans for Oswald. He was going. 2. He would be taken out through the basement, protected there by detectives and placed in an armored vehicle to safeguard his ride through the streets. 3. Escort cars would not be driven by the sheriff's deputies, which meant the city police would have their lives on the line against whatever mob action developed in the streets. To avoid that kind of bloodshed, Oswald would have to be hit before getting into the van.

Moments after the call to the Delux Diner, it is consistent with the facts to believe, the unlisted phone, WHitehall 1-5601, rang at Ruby's apartment and he had the information.

Detective L. D. Miller acted more like a hoodlum than a policeman on March 24, 1964, when Burt Griffin attempted to question him on behalf of the Warren Commission about Miller's activities at the Delux Diner and in the next two hours. Miller refused to be sworn in as a witness and had to be brought back the next day, whereupon he displayed a great "lack of memory," Griffin said in an April 2, 1964, memorandum to Commission Chief Counsel Rankin. Officer Blackie Harrison even showed up with a lawyer on March 24, 1964, to help him fend off questions by Griffin.

Harrison already was under intensive scrutiny by the Dallas police department because of his activities on the morning Ruby shot Oswald. Harrison had known Ruby for 12 years. He was one of two officers singled out by the police department to take a lie-detector test concerning his movements as they could have involved Ruby on that morning.

The day of the lie-detector test, December 13, 1963, word spread through the department that Harrison had taken strong tranquilizers to muffle his reactions to all questions. The Secret Service then informed the Warren Commission of what the police were saying Harrison had done, but the Commission failed to look into the tip and didn't check out any of Harrison's personal contacts with Ruby over the years. Results of Harrison's lie-detector test, administered by Dallas police department detective Paul L. Bentley, were *not conclusive.* Bentley was hardly an impartial tester. He was emotionally involved as one of the Dallas police who had arrested Oswald inside the Texas Theatre. Bentley had been injured in the scuffle with the suspected cop-killer.

At 9 a.m., as Stevenson reached the bureau where Harrison and Miller worked, Police Lieutenant Rio Sam Pierce was instructing Sergeant Patrick T. Dean to assemble a group of men and search the basement garage area thoroughly—vehicles, overhanging pipes, air-conditioning ducts, entrances and exits. Dean got 13 reserve officers from the detail room, two regular patrolmen and Sergeant J. A. Putnam to conduct a systematic search for weapons and to make sure all doors were locked.

Five months later, Warren Commission attorney Griffin was questioning Sergeant Dean about those doors: "Who checked the stairway door in the garage that leads up into the Municipal Building?"

"Sergeant Putnam checked it once and I checked it once, and it was locked," Dean replied.

"Did you know at the time you checked it that even though the door was locked from the outside, it could be opened from the inside?"

Dean did not respond. He sat there and stared at Griffin, and said nothing.

"Let me state this again," said the attorney. "Even though the door would be locked from the garage side, that from the stairway side it would be unlocked. Were you aware of that?"

"I believe we asked the maintenance man about this, and I believe he locked it so as it couldn't be unlocked from either side unless they had a key. I believe Sergeant Putnam called this to the maintenance man's attention, and I recall being there at the time they were discussing it, and I think at the time the maintenance man locked the door so it couldn't be unlocked from either side, other than with a key." Dean's words betrayed a great deal of uncertainty.

The Warren Commission talked with Sergeant Putnam[12] that same day, and again a few days later, but never asked him about the door. The Commission also failed to find the maintenance man and interview him.

By 9:15 a.m., having put one load of wash in the drier, Senator was back in the apartment and noticed Ruby was up. Ruby remained in his underwear while eating scrambled eggs, looking at a Sunday newspaper and watching some television with Senator. Mournful activities at the Capitol Building in Washington, where the President's body was borne by caisson to rest on the same catafalque that had held the remains of Abraham Lincoln, were on the TV screen. It was then that Ruby blurted out what he was about to do.

"Did you tell anyone that you intended to shoot Oswald?" Warren Commission attorney Allen Specter asked Ruby on July 18, 1964, in formulating a question for the lie-detector test Ruby insisted on taking.

> RUBY: Yes; Sunday morning.
> SPECTER: And whom did you tell?
> R: George Senator.
> S: And where were you at the time you discussed it with him?

R: In my apartment.

S: And state in as precise words as you can remember, just what you said to him and he said to you at that time.

R: Well, he didn't say anything—the funny part—he was reading the paper and I doubt if he even recalled me saying it. I have to elaborate on it, but I was so carried away emotionally that I said—I don't know how I said it—I didn't say it in any vulgar manner—I said, "If something happened to this person, that then Mrs. Kennedy won't have to come back for the trial."

Perhaps that was the way Ruby remembered phrasing it, on the day of his polygraph test in July, 1964. But much earlier in 1964 Ruby wrote a note to one of his trial lawyers, Joe Tonahill, that said his first lawyer, Tom Howard, had supplied him with the line about sparing Mrs. Kennedy the return trip to Dallas for Oswald's trial, as a patriotic alibi for the shooting.

At 9:30 a.m., Oswald was removed from his fifth-floor cell and taken down the jail elevator to the third floor, where Captain Fritz would question him again.

Between 9:30 and 9:40, Harold J. Fleming, the general operations manager of Armored Motor Service, Inc., was at home, shaving, preparing to go to 10 o'clock church services with his wife, when Assistant Chief Batchelor telephoned to ask for the use of an armored van with an experienced driver. Fleming said he was ready to help but it might take some time to locate a company driver and to ready the equipment on a Sunday morning.

Shortly before 10, Sidney Evans Jr., a driver for Red Ball Motor Freight and a second-floor neighbor of Ruby and Senator, saw Senator carrying up some folded laundry to Apartment 207. Then, at 10:05, Malcolm Slaughter also saw Senator. Slaughter was another Red Ball trucker. He and Evans were transients in Apartment 204, which was rented by Red Ball as a "bunk house" for its freight drivers from out of town. This time, Senator was again heading to No. 207 but was empty-handed, presumably having just put his second load into the drier.

Once the clock passed 10, the reporters and most of the police expected the transfer might occur at any moment. One reporter, Jerry O'Leary of *The Washington Star*, wanted to see Oswald taken from Room 317 and placed on the elevator. Then O'Leary wanted to be in the basement to see Oswald taken from the elevator. The only way he could do that, O'Leary figured, was to race down the stairway from the third floor to the basement, once the elevator door closed with Oswald inside, and the reporter set up a test race to see if the idea would work. O'Leary took off down the steps in a matched race with a colleague who took the elevator. When O'Leary reached bottom, he bounded from the basement stairwell into the jail office vestibule where Oswald would arrive, and did beat the elevator.

At 10:19, Ruby got the call from Little Lynn in Fort Worth. He was abrupt with her but said he would send her $25 by Western Union money order since he was going downtown anyway. He told her he was taking Sheba, his dachshund, from the apartment to the Carousel. The other dogs stayed at the club but Ruby was fond of Sheba's company. He took her home most nights.

Ruby was anxious to get Little Lynn off the phone since he likely was impatient for a second call from his police contact—the call that would tell him everything was in motion. When he bathed, shaved and dressed, Ruby seemed to Senator to be obsessed, mumbling to himself. Now Ruby began to pace nervously from room to room, his lips moving. Senator felt uneasy about Ruby's actions and went downstairs to pick up the second load from the drier.

At about 10:35, Fleming was on the phone from the Armored Motor Service Terminal to Assistant Chief Batchelor. The company's large van, capable of carrying several police inside with Oswald, had a dead battery. A new battery could be installed quickly and Fleming said he would be on the way to police headquarters by 10:50 with two vans. One would be small and not the most ideal carrier for a cargo requiring several guards, but it could be used as a backup in case the big van malfunctioned.

Over at the county jail there were several hundred soberly quiet bystanders in the streets. Many had portable radios, to follow the movements of Oswald. It was a grim crowd, numbering as many as 600 near the county jail entrance, according to police estimates. Others congregated outside the city jail—most of them on the Commerce Street side, where the exit ramp was, leading out of the basement.

At this point, Ruby investigators had reason to believe, a call was placed to the unlisted phone in Ruby's apartment; Ruby was told where to enter the station and that the transfer van was en route. Ruby made sure the snub-nosed gun with its two-inch barrel was loaded. He put it in his trouser pocket. Never in his jacket. It got the jacket out of shape.

Ruby's chief concern now would be in making the shooting look like a spur-of-the-moment matter so he could be back out in the street as soon as possible to reap the rewards of being a popular hero. He already had the perfect reason for being in the same block as the police station by going on a legitimate errand to the Western Union office there. Next he would need a reason for the gun. He stuffed nine $100 bills, 30 $10 bills, 40 $20 bills and a number of smaller bills into a pocket. It was supposed to be the federal excise tax money Ruby owed. By carrying it with him, he created an understandable reason under Texas law to pack the gun, too, even though he had no license to carry any hidden weapon. But the excise tax payment story was a phony. Only five days earlier he had signed the power-of-attorney in the office of his tax lawyer, Graham Koch, granting Koch the right to negotiate with the IRS for an extended time period to make those federal tax payments. There was no logical reason for Ruby to be carrying all that money, except to establish an alibi.

Getting the money was no problem since he always had bills scattered around the apartment. It was one of the things that made Elnora Pitts nervous about Ruby. He expected her to dust *around* the money, which bothered her because of the risk of being accused if some of it were missing. Even taking $2,040, including the $25 he would send to Little Lynn in Fort Worth, Ruby still had cash left over. There was a paper sack with $131.41, and an additional $125.39 in a closet and a dresser drawer. By the time Senator returned to the apartment, Ruby had his alibi money tucked away.

"George, I am taking the dog down to the club," Ruby said, and that's all he said. He had on his snap-brim gray fedora, a white shirt, an all-silk black tie, charcoal brown suit and black shoes. It was hardly the kind of attire one would normally wear in Dallas on a Sunday, to take a dog down to a place of business that was closed. Instead, Ruby was dressed to blend in with the scenery of where he actually was going. He was dressed precisely like a detective and he never did take Sheba to the club.

By 10:45 the basement garage area was jammed with more than 70 police, many of them detectives in plain clothes, about 50 reporters and some cameramen with still photo and television equipment. I took an elevator to the basement from the third floor and was immediately challenged by a uniformed officer to show identification. I produced my White House press credentials, issued by the Secret Service, as well as my White House accreditation for the trip of the President to Texas. The officer refused to let me pass with just that *out-of-town* identification. Meanwhile, Jimmy Turner, a director for WBAP-TV in Fort Worth, entered the basement by showing nothing more than an admission card that had been issued to him by the Sheraton Hotel in Dallas for a press drinking party to help celebrate the opening of that hotel. The reporter for The London *Daily Telegraph* filed an account from the scene that he had "walked down the stairs to the basement of the police station, unchecked. If anyone had wanted to silence Oswald the police could not have helped them more." Meanwhile, Ike Pappas, the New York City radio reporter, also entered the basement without any police officer asking to see his identification by using those same stairs—which were the ones reporter O'Leary had tried out earlier. A detective came over to the elevator's edge, where I was raising a fuss with the officer and, after examining my credentials, said they were all right.

Aside from the public elevator I had used, there were other entrances with guards posted. The building was bordered on the north by Main

Street, where there was a ramp leading down onto the basement for in-
coming vehicles, and on the south by Commerce Street, where there was a
ramp leading out of the basement for departing vehicles. A guard was
posted at the top of each ramp to keep unauthorized people from walking
in. A lone guard had been assigned to a locked engine room entrance, and
another at the "locked" door leading to the Municipal Building, adjoining
the Police and Courts Building. The open stairway used by Pappas,
O'Leary and the *London Daily Telegraph* man had no special guard assigned to it—no one designated to stop strangers from using it. The
stairway led directly to the first-floor public lobby, which had an entrance
leading out to Main Street.

At about 11 a.m., Fleming and his drivers reached the Commerce
Street side. The smaller van was parked outside and the bigger one was
backed onto the Commerce ramp. But the top of the armored truck was
too high to clear the overhead pipes and it was feared the back-heavy
truck would stall if it were backed partway down the ramp and parked
there. So it was left at rest at the top of the ramp, its front wheels on the
sidewalk, facing Commerce. Soon after that, police lieutenant George E.
Butler stood by the van and seemed inexplicably upset.

Thayer Waldo of *The Star-Telegram*, a veteran reporter, had been
talking with Butler through the weekend, using him as an information
source. Waldo had found Butler to be a man of "almost stolid poise," as
Waldo described it to the Warren Commission. But in the moments before
Oswald's appearance in the police station basement, Waldo found Butler
to be "an extremely nervous man," whose lips were trembling, and Waldo
said, "I had by then spent enough hours talking to this man so that it
struck me as something totally out of character."

Butler was a tough veteran of the Dallas police department. His
knowledge of organized crime was so intimate that he had been the key
man in the department contacted by the Chicago mob when the mob
chose to move into Dallas in 1946 and make police payoffs. Butler then
had been loaned by the Dallas police department to aid three different
U.S. Senate investigatory groups as an expert on gangster operations.

I found Butler living with his wife in seclusion in Rockwall County,
Texas, in 1976—a vigorous and tough 69-year-old man, retired from the
police force. His phone was unlisted; his rural mail box unmarked. The
yard was fenced, the gate was locked and a cadre of angry dogs within the
fence lived up to the sign out front, warning visitors to beware. The only
way I had found Butler was through records in the Rockwall County tax
assessor's office, which showed him as owner of an acre out on Route 2,
Box 79-C, a remote location pinpointed for me by a post office clerk. Once
past the dogs, I found out why Butler's nickname in the department had
been "Mr. Hard Fists." The handshake he proffered was like one of Jack
Dempsey's brine-toughened hands.

Butler didn't deny Waldo's account of his total loss of poise in the time period approaching Oswald's execution. But Butler told me it was because he was "tense and angry on account of the poor transfer plans for Oswald—the lack of preparation." But there was a great deal more to George Butler than just his concern for Oswald. He had known Ruby for years and told me he had considered Ruby to be a "sleeper"—a member of organized crime who maintained the image of a law-abiding citizen. Butler also worked in the same detail, the Juvenile Bureau, with Blackie Harrison, the officer most likely to have contacted Ruby by telephone on that fatal Sunday morning. One of the most obvious mistakes made by the Warren Commission in its skin-deep dealings with the Dallas police department was its failure even to interview Butler, who had an expert's view of both Ruby and Harrison and whose unusual case of nerves developed just before Ruby appeared in the basement.

Butler and all other on-duty members of the Juvenile Bureau—with the single exception of Blackie Harrison—left their third-floor bureau together at about 11:10 a.m. and proceeded to the jail basement. En route they encountered Harrison emerging from the sub-basement where, he later said, he had gone *before 11 a.m.*, to use a cigar-vending machine. He had also had access to any of four different public telephones on the path between his desk in the bureau and the officers' lockers in the sub-basement. There were no witnesses to any of Harrison's movements for a significant amount of time that morning.

Between 11:10 and 11:15, Chief Curry advised Captain Fritz that the armored van was in place on the basement's Commerce-side ramp, so that Oswald could be escorted up the ramp to its rear door. It was the first Will Fritz had heard of any plan to use such a vehicle to transfer the prisoner. Fritz was as angry as he was surprised and he put the problem quickly into focus for the chief. First, the background of the driver of the van was not even known to the police; secondly, the van would be clumsy and awkward to handle in an attack by a mob. The homicide detective quickly got Curry to agree to using the van as a decoy. Next, he outlined a substitute plan. The detectives in the basement would form a human corridor for Oswald to walk through, to a waiting unmarked police car that would be backed into place, close to the jail elevator. All the news people were to be moved behind a railing so that the unmarked car could maneuver into position. With Oswald inside, the car then would follow the decoy van out onto Commerce, and would soon cut away from the police convoy to take a separate route to the county jail, accompanied only by an unmarked escort car of its own. Fritz would send down two homicide detectives, Charles W. Brown and Charles N. Dhority, who could be trusted to handle the two unmarked cars to be used in the actual movement of the prisoner.

As Curry and Fritz talked, Ruby walked into the Western Union office close to the Main Street side of the police station. Ruby already had seen the nose of the armored truck jutting out from the Commerce Street ramp. He waited while Western Union clerk Doyle Lane took care of another customer, then Ruby arranged to send $25 to Little Lynn. The completed transaction with Ruby was validated by Lane at 11:17 with a stamping device that recorded the date and time.

Lane noted that Ruby promptly stepped out the door and turned left. Ruby then walked purposefully toward the Main Street ramp, which was guarded by patrolman Roy E. Vaughn (repeated time measurements on November 29, 1963, by the Dallas police, showed it would have taken one minute and 13 seconds for Ruby to have covered the distance from Doyle Lane's counter to the center of the Main Street ramp). But there is strong evidence to show that Ruby did not go down the ramp—continuing instead another 55 feet to the double-doored Main Street entrance to the police station's first floor. Then he could have eased down the same stairway that reporters O'Leary, Pappas and the *London Daily Telegraph* man were using without being questioned by any authority. Ruby, who kept himself facile with workouts at the YMCA, covered the distance comfortably in less than two minutes, at a steady gait.

Undisputed evidence does show that Ruby sent a Western Union money order at 11:17 that morning and then reached the police station within the next 90 to 100 seconds.

At that point the Warren Commission was willing to buy Ruby's contention that he scurried down the ramp unnoticed by more than 70 police in the basement and without a prior plan for killing Oswald. Ten years after the killing, David Belin, who had served as an importantly placed lawyer for the Commission, argued:

"It took only a minute-and-a-half to get from the Western Union office to the basement of the Dallas police station where Ruby killed Oswald. The time of the murder of Oswald was 11:21 a.m. Suppose there had been another customer or two waiting in line at the Western Union office. This in itself could have caused sufficient delay so that Ruby could not have descended the ramp into the basement of the Dallas police station in time to kill Oswald. Circumstances of this nature are strong proof of the fact that there was no conspiracy."[13] Belin comes off in that statement like a wise counselor to the court in the year 1491, who looked to the horizons and found the earth to be flat. For the Warren Commission never could establish that Ruby actually did go down the ramp, and let itself be conned into thinking that the arrival first of Ruby, then of Oswald, simply were unsynchronized parallels.

Instead, Ruby could have reached his destination by using the public stairway to the basement jail office area. His arrival could have triggered the go-ahead signal for Oswald to be brought down. The most logical person to have forwarded the word that everything was ready was Lieutenant Woodrow Wiggins, in charge of the basement jail office. Wiggins, who had been acquainted with Ruby for some years, acknowledged to the Warren Commission that he had received a phone call from the third floor when Oswald was being brought down the jail elevator to his death. But the Commission's Ruby probers, Leon Hubert and Burt Griffin, failed to ask Wiggins if he had telephoned a come-ahead signal upstairs, either on his own or at the request of a superior. Hubert and Griffin also neglected to ask the four ranking officials in the basement at the time—Batchelor, Stevenson, and captains O. A. Jones and Cecil E. Talbert—if any of them had sent word upstairs that the arena was ready.

"We might not have grasped the connection as we should have," Griffin told me. Their concern with how Ruby got into the basement did not tie closely with Oswald's movements into the basement.

"Hubert and I never carried on an inquiry into the whole system for protecting Oswald," Griffin said. Failing to do that, they ignored the final mechanics of a conspiracy in action.

Could such a conspiracy to kill Oswald, using Ruby, develop during the weekend after President Kennedy's murder—a conspiracy that could have involved some of the police with Ruby?

"Why sure," said Tonahill, the Ruby lawyer. "I don't say that it did, but it could have happened. My position, and my whole argument, is that if there was a conspiracy for Ruby to kill Oswald then the police had to be in on it—because of the time lag of less than two minutes in walking from that Western Union office on the corner, down into the basement where Ruby killed Oswald. If there was a conspiracy to kill Oswald, then the police had to be in on it because of the strange coincidence in the timing of their arrivals—first Ruby; then Oswald soon after."[14]

Jesse Curry, meanwhile, remains convinced that "it just seemed like an act of God that Ruby got in there." Curry said, "I've thought about it a thousand times. We backtracked and walked the distance. We investigated from every possible angle." The retired police chief remains convinced that Ruby walked down the ramp past officer Vaughn on the spur of the moment. Curry discussed the episode, July 27, 1976, in the small living room of his modest house in the White Rock Lake area of East Dallas. Curry was reminded that after Ruby was arrested, Ruby at first said he had entered the station from the Main Street side. Ruby didn't say the Main Street ramp; just simply that he came off Main Street. I asked Curry if the large double-doored entrance to the station, near the ramp, was locked.

"No, the doors were not locked," he said. "In fact at that time I don't believe you could even lock them." As a reporter, my relationship with Curry goes back a number of years and we talked comfortably with each other. He is an honest cop. But when I asked him where the double-doored street-level entrance would have led Ruby, there were several uncharacteristic hesitations in Curry's answer for the only time in our two-hour, tape-recorded conversation.

"To the first floor of the building," Curry answered. "Now, there was one stairway from the street level of city hall that went down to the basement. Had he taken that, he would have come out in the—well, you know, the main aisle that runs north and south in the basement there [Curry pauses to draw a sketch of the stairway entering a vestibule area of the police station basement]. Well, we just had men strung everywhere down there. If he had attempted that stairway he would have had to [pause] get somebody [pause] to okay him—and that was the—nobody ever (uh) established—I mean admitted that anybody ever came here [pointing to stairway] to try and get in here [pointing to basement]. But there were just so many men here and all over here—had he come in the first floor, we had men up there, too. . . ."

But Curry looked unhappy at the thought, because he already had recalled in his conversation with me that Ruby had come and gone at will in the heavily guarded police station all through the weekend.

Coming off the public elevator in the basement vestibule area at about 11:18 a.m. were Dave Timmons and John Tankersly, a pair of WBAP cameramen for Channel 5 TV in Fort Worth. They were struggling with a large camera on tripod legs, set on a dolly. Timmons was wearing a green shirt; Tankersly a dark raincoat. They were quickly trying to get the camera out into the garage area before Oswald was brought down.

Jay Cutchshaw of the Juvenile Bureau's Criminal Investigation Division was standing next to the door leading to the basement jail booking office, when he saw three men pushing the large Channel 5 camera. He saw a man in a green shirt on the right, a man wearing a dark raincoat on the left and, in the middle, a man in a dark suit.

The man in the middle seemed to Cutchshaw to be especially well dressed, but was bent so low, pushing the dolly, Cutchshaw couldn't see his face.

A moment later, detective Roy Lee Lowery saw the camera wobble as it passed through the doorway that led from the jail office hallway into the garage area. He saw three men pushing the dolly and he went over to help steady the camera by clutching one of the tripod legs.

Jimmy Turner of WBAP quickly left the position he had taken up with another Channel 5 camera in order to help Timmons and Tankersly. When he got to them, there no longer was a third man helping them push. Jack Ruby kept his head down until he got just to the left rear of where his friend Blackie Harrison was standing.

Shielded by Harrison's larger frame, Ruby was facing the direction Oswald would come from. It was 11:19 a.m.

(Eight months later Warren Commission lawyers saw Ruby standing just behind Harrison when they viewed a television tape of events in the police station basement, leading to the shooting of Oswald. They looked at reel 13 of KRLD-TV, the CBS station in Dallas. Reel 13 also showed the Channel 5 camera "being pushed past the detectives by only two men," said the Warren Report.

(On March 31, 1977, I went to Dallas to examine reel 13 at KDFW-TV, the successor station to KRLD-TV. Reel 13 and all the other films and tapes shot during the weekend of the Kennedy assassination were being kept at the station under lock and key, and several weeks of negotiations were required before the important reel could be viewed for this book. From the angle of the KRLD pedestal camera which photographed the Channel 5 camera being pushed into the police garage, it was impossible for me and others with me to see who or even how many people were pushing that camera, because a number of detectives were blocking the view, swirling around in front of it.

(That either means the Warren Commission never could see whether Ruby was helping to push the camera, or it means reel 13 was tampered with at some point. At any rate, as of now, reel 13 doesn't show the camera being pushed "by only two men," as the Warren Report said.)

Lieutenant Jack Revill, supervisor of criminal intelligence for the Dallas police department, was one of the eight department officers appointed by Curry to investigate what had gone wrong in the attempted transfer of Oswald. Revill proposed that Harrison be given the lie-detector test and was the only one of the eight-member team who insisted on it. The other seven were reluctant. Eight days after the shooting, Revill interviewed Ruby in front of the other law-enforcement officers and Ruby's lawyer. When Revill told Ruby the television tapes showed him standing at Harrison's shoulder, Ruby lost his temper. He cursed Revill and accused the police investigator of being "a hatchet man," out to destroy Harrison. Ruby also refused to discuss with Revill how he actually had gotten into the basement—and this was eight days after his entry. Then Revill interviewed Harrison, who maintained he'd had no contact with Ruby on the morning of the shooting. But Revill later told the Warren Commission that he never was satisfied with Harrison's statement. Revill told the Commission he didn't choose to comment on the record on Harrison's truthfulness.

Captain Fritz had given up on further questioning of his tight-lipped prisoner, and had asked if any of the federal officers sitting in on the session in Room 317 had any questions for Oswald. Forrest V. Sorrels, in charge of the Dallas district of the Secret Service, said he had one.

Sorrels wanted Oswald to admit to the use of the alias "A. Hidell," since that was the name Oswald was supposed to have used in purchasing the weapon that apparently had killed the President. Sorrels held a post office change-of-address card that Oswald had filed in New Orleans, which showed the name "A. Hidell" listed as someone also to receive mail at a new address for Oswald shown on the card. But Oswald would admit nothing and the questioning was interrupted.

"I might have attempted to ask him more questions," Sorrels said later. But word had been sent in that everything was ready downstairs.

At 11:20, Lieutenant Rio Sam Pierce, accompanied by two sergeants, drove a black car up the Main Street ramp as part of the decoy plan. He would swing around onto Commerce, to lead the way for the armored truck. Detective Brown drove a plain green car from the garage area onto the Commerce ramp, behind the armored truck. Detective Dhority drove un unmarked white car to a point just behind Brown. Dhority then attempted to move his car, to draw even with the jail office hall, so Oswald could be put into his car. But there were too many people in the way.

When the dour Captain Fritz emerged from 317 with Oswald, a mob of reporters began to shout questions charged with taunts and emotion at the prisoner. A cordon of police separated the reporters in the third-floor corridor from Oswald as he was hurried to the waiting jail elevator. Reporter O'Leary bolted down the stairs. No officer was guarding the stairway of the entrance to the basement. O'Leary passed unchallenged into the basement jail hallway through the same doorway that Ruby had come through two minutes earlier.

As the jail elevator door opened, Fritz was one of the first to step out. He asked Lieutenant Wiggins: "Are you ready?" Wiggins stepped out of the prisoner booking office, into the hallway, and indicated everything was all set.

Lieutenant Richard E. Swain of the Burglary and Theft Bureau, who had known Ruby for several years, then went ahead first into the garage area. Someone in the crowd shouted, "Here he comes!" Swain, who was never questioned by the Warren Commission, surveyed the confused scene quickly and then looked back to the inside corridor where Fritz waited. Everything was in good shape, he indicated. Come ahead.

Nothing was in good shape. Dhority was frantically trying to move the car, gunning the motor, honking the horn, but blocked by detectives and reporters who weren't where they were supposed to be. There was no protective corridor of detectives through which Oswald was to walk to the car that wasn't there. Reporters mixed among the police instead of being held behind the railing. Homicide detective James R. Leavelle, handcuffed to Oswald's right wrist, asked Cutchshaw inside the jail hallway if everything was all right. Cutchshaw, like almost all of the cops down there at 11:21 a.m., had no idea what the plan was supposed to be. But Leavelle was assured by Cutchshaw that there were no problems. Chief Curry, ludicrously, was upstairs in his office, responding to a phone call from Dallas mayor Earle Cabell, and had not checked for himself to see if orders were being carried out properly in the basement. Curry told me he had detailed Assistant Chief Batchelor and Deputy Chief Stevenson to set up the corridor of detectives so that Oswald would be shielded, and to move the news people behind the railing so Oswald's transfer car could move. "There were several higher, supervisory officers in the basement," Curry said, "and 70 detectives, which should have been enough, you know, to guard against any kind of assault that might be attempted to come into the basement. I was trying to let them [reporters and cameramen] have all the freedom they could. I knew this was something the American people were interested in. They were watching it by the millions. But I had told Batchelor and Stevenson to keep them behind the iron railing."

Fritz followed Swain and was promptly blinded by the bright television lights that came from behind Ruby to illuminate the target. Oswald came out next, flanked by Leavelle and Detective L. C. Graves. Billy H. Combest, a detective from the vice section, saw Ruby lunge past Blackie Harrison. Combest shouted, "Jack, you son of a bitch!" as the shot went off pointblank at Oswald's stomach.

In the melee that followed, Ruby seemed surprised that he was dragged to the hard basement pavement and pounced on by six detectives. "You all know me," he said. "I'm Jack Ruby." But while he had his pockets stuffed with enough reason for being in the vicinity with a gun (the Western Union receipt and the large amount of cash), there were police who needed a reason of their own to establish Ruby as a loner who got into their station strictly by himself.

"It no longer was important that Ruby had gotten in, but how he'd gotten in was vital," Jay Cutchshaw said. Cutchshaw was one of two detectives who seemed certain that Ruby was the well-dressed man bent over, helping to push the TV dolly into the police garage. Just after Ruby fired the shot and the turmoil that followed, Cutchshaw excitedly reported to Deputy Chief Stevenson what he had seen. "Stevenson just pulled away from me. He wouldn't listen," Cutchshaw recalls.

Cutchshaw has left the police force and sounds bitter when he talks about the Ruby episode. He lives not far from the town of Prosper, Texas, and operates a sizable wholesale cactus nursery on state highway 380.[15] He was particularly upset that the Dallas police department, when it conducted its own probe of how Ruby got into the basement that morning, refused to explore the eyewitness accounts by him and Roy Lee Lowery that Ruby had been the third man on the camera dolly.

One of the preserved NBC television tapes of events in the Dallas police station, from that weekend of November 22-24, shows announcer Tom Pettit thrusting his microphone into an animated conversation among police shortly after the shooting of Oswald, in which Lowery is describing to Lieutenant Swain how the man who shot Oswald had come into the garage with the TV camera. Lowery is upset and his voice is highly agitated.

After that, Lowery detained Tankersly and Timmons, the two TV cameramen, for more than an hour. But then he was instructed just to take their names and addresses and let them go. The Dallas police department had decided Jack Ruby had slipped past the vigil of officer Vaughn at the top of the eight-foot-wide ramp. Vaughn, it was thought, had been distracted by the movement of Rio Sam Pierce's car as it came past him, and so Vaughn became the departmental scapegoat.

Curry said he never criticized Vaughn, or called the patrolman into his office, or put any reprimand into the record. "Well, for years I didn't even mention it to anybody," said Curry. "I just didn't want them to think I was trying to shift the blame onto him. But actually when it comes down to it, that's what happened. He let Ruby get by him there. All he had was eight feet to look after, and he didn't look after it."

Until the moment Ruby's gun barked in the basement, Vaughn's record on the force was exemplary. Vaughn stoutly maintained that the movement of Lieutenant Pierce's car up the ramp and into the street had not distracted his vigil over the ramp entrance, and he had not let Ruby in, intentionally or otherwise.

Vaughn was not alone in his insistence. Lieutenant Pierce told his superiors that he had been in position to see what was happening. Pierce put it strongly, using salty language, when he told his superiors that Ruby positively had not gone down that ramp.

Vaughn was the other Dallas police officer who was told by the department to take a lie-detector test. Unlike Blackie Harrison, Vaughn had to be asked each question only once by Detective Bentley of the Identification Bureau, who administered the test. "It is the opinion of this examiner this person answered each of the questions with the truth," Bentley wrote at the bottom of Vaughn's test. Bently wrote nothing like that after Harrison's test.

Soon after the moribund Oswald was loaded into an ambulance and taken away, police sergeant Patrick T. Dean wound up where Ruby would be undergoing questions concerning the shooting. Dean had been the officer in charge of securing the basement entrances, including the stairway used by Ruby. The sergeant went up to the third floor shortly after noon that Sunday, perhaps expecting to find Ruby as the new man in Room 317 (the interrogation room).

Instead, Dean encountered Chief Curry standing with Forrest Sorrels, the Secret Service district chief. Ruby had not yet been questioned and was in a holding cell on the fifth floor. Curry's face reflected the horror he was going through, having been presiding officer at the biggest police blunder in Dallas history. His words clanked like a slow, empty train as he asked Dean to escort Sorrels upstairs.

The fifth-floor jailer had searched all of Ruby's clothing and the prisoner was in his underdrawers; in the custody of three detectives from the Auto Theft Bureau—Barnard S. Clardy, T. D. McMillon and Don Ray Archer—when Sorrels and Dean arrived. Sorrels was in a hurry to get basic background information from Ruby for Secret Service headquarters in Washington. Name. Origins. Motives. In 10 minutes Sorrels was gone.

Two days later, Dean filed a departmental report which said, "After Mr. Sorrels interrogated the subject I questioned Ruby as to how he had entered the basement and the length of time he had been there. Ruby then stated to me in the presence of Mr. Sorrels that he had entered the basement through the ramp entering on Main Street."

Sorrels was astonished. He knew Ruby had said nothing of the kind in front of him during that interview. Sorrels was 62 years old, a Secret Service employee for 40 years and a veteran supervisor of other federal agents. He had been sure to make written notes as Ruby talked and the notes said nothing of how Ruby had penetrated police security that morning—an essential point that Sorrels would have reported to Washington.

Even though Dean had kept no notes, the Warren Commission supported him and did not include Sorrel's clear denial in its report.

The Warren Commission did that because Dean's story was backed, but only as an afterthought, by the three detectives who had been on the fifth floor at the time. Archer, Clardy and McMillon subsequently told the police department's own investigatory team that they had heard Ruby say he walked down the Main Street ramp after Lieutenant Pierce's car came up the ramp, distracting Vaughn's attention.

But none of the three detectives filed that information in reports they submitted on events of the day. Their typed-up reports were not even sent to Curry's office until November 27, *three days after the shooting.*

McMillon, who had worked under Dean as a downtown patrolman before becoming a detective, said he didn't put the information in his initial report to the chief because he didn't think it was important—at a time when any facts on how Ruby had entered the basement were considered vital. McMillon said he did include the information in a second report, which somehow "disappeared" and was never found.

Archer and Clardy waited until six days after the shooting to report they had heard Ruby fully confess how he got into the police station.

What is astounding about the performance of these detectives is that a few minutes after Sorrels left to telephone Washington, FBI agent C. Ray Hall arrived in the fifth-floor cell block to interview Ruby. Present with Hall and the prisoner, from 12:40 to 3:15 that Sunday afternoon, were Clardy and McMillon. Hall had been a special agent with the FBI for 21 years. He took notes both in shorthand and longhand. He told the Warren Commission that Ruby "did not wish to say how he got into the basement or at what time he entered."

We are expected to believe that Ruby is supposed to have already told three detectives and Sergeant Dean how and when he entered, but then unaccountably refused to tell agent Hall.

If that is true then why wouldn't Clardy and McMillon as responsible detectives have volunteered the information to Hall? Why would they withhold vital information on the committing of a crime, itself a punishable offense?

The reason was that the story had not been worked out yet for Ruby. After Sorrels left, Dean remained briefly with Ruby. Then Hall arrived after Dean left. The only information on that point that Ruby was willing to share with Hall was that he had entered the Police and Courts Building from Main Street. Ruby would not go further than that. Just Main Street.

The rest of the entrance fable appears to have been slipped to Ruby between 1:56 and 2:02 that afternoon, when Hall's interview with the prisoner was interrupted so that Ruby could meet privately with Tom Howard, the first of the procession of attorneys who would guide and misguide Ruby's affairs as a murderer.

Howard, a flashy criminal lawyer with a large letter H stickpin in his tie, had been lurking in the police station basement not long before Ruby shot Oswald. Howard had numerous police contacts. He was a brawling, emotional man who had been fined and jailed in Dallas for shouting, bickering and fist-fighting in court. When he had failed to pay federal income taxes he tried to alibi his way out of it in a tax court hearing by telling the judge he would have paid but his drinking problem required a lot of money. In the six minutes he had with Ruby that Sunday afternoon, he was able to round out details of when and where his client was to have entered the building. He also told Ruby to tell authorities that he had shot Oswald in order to keep the widow Kennedy and her daughter Caroline from having to come to Dallas for Oswald's murder trial.[16]

At 3:15, Ruby was taken down to the third floor to be questioned by Captain Fritz. By now Ruby was more sure of himself. When certain questions were asked, he was quick to say, "That's something I won't answer now," or, "I'm not going to comment on that." He told the veteran homicide detective about having entered the basement by the Main Street ramp just as Rio Sam Pierce drove out, but at one point said, "Don't you think I would make a good actor?"

Ruby told Fritz he thought the police department was wonderful. He said his heart always was with the department. He said he always had hoped that if ever there were an opportunity for him to participate in a battle involving the police, he could take up the cause of the police.

By 5:40 p.m., Ruby was taken to the Identification Bureau to be fingerprinted and photographed by Ed Carlson, the ID officer. He kidded around with Carlson, whom he knew, and with other officers there, calling them by their first names.

Ruby's sister emphasized that point when she telephoned Will Fritz that afternoon and said, "You know that no one else could have gotten in that building—but all the boys knew Jack."

She told the homicide chief that Ruby had been upset because the President could be shot down, while "no one could get to Joe Valachi to kill him" (a revelation of Ruby's preoccupation with Valachi, the gangland stoolpigeon).

Ruby was talking to Eva Grant over a visitors' room communications system, shortly after 6 p.m., seeming full of self-assurance. "I got lots of friends here," he said. Ruby told his sister that Fred Bruner, another of his attorneys, would be down in the morning to post bond so that he could leave jail.

But Ruby was mistaken. He would be held without bond and never be free again. Some of those friends of his on the police force would see to that.

CHAPTER 4

A Stillness On The Fifth Floor

Monday, November 25, the day after Ruby shot Oswald, there was a telephone conversation between Texas Attorney General Waggoner Carr in Austin and Walter Jenkins in Washington. Jenkins had been the principal aide to Lyndon Johnson as Vice-President, and now was the sleepless, special assistant to Johnson as President. After their conversation Carr issued a public statement that he would head a Texas court of inquiry "to develop fully and disclose openly" the hows and whys of the grisly shooting of John F. Kennedy and the permissive killing of Oswald.

But by November 26 there were outcries on Capitol Hill for an all-out congressional investigation into the murders. Senate Minority Leader Everett M. Dirksen called for a Judiciary Committee probe. Dirksen was the ranking member on the Republican side of that committee and President Johnson had visions of the oily-voiced Dirksen demagoguing his way through politically influenced public hearings, deep into the presidential election year of 1964. Meanwhile, compounding the problem for Johnson, Republican Charles E. Goodell of New York proposed formation of a 14-member joint House-Senate committee to conduct the congressional probe. The President acted quickly to move the momentum of the investigation away from the politicians on Capitol Hill. He had Abe Fortas see to that.

In a private memorandum to himself on November 26, Waggoner Carr noted that Jenkins had put him in touch with President Johnson's private counsel, Abe Fortas, and "Mr. Fortas informed me that he had been assigned to coordinate the FBI, Department of Justice and [my] efforts regarding the assassination of the President. He pledged the full cooperation of the federal government in working with the State of Texas. To illustrate this to the world, he noted he had ordered Assistant Attorney General Herbert Miller, chief of the criminal division of the Department of Justice in Washington, to call on me that night. Mr. Fortas suggested a press conference and pictures which would aptly point out the close cooperation between the two governments.[1] He stated that the report of the FBI would be made available to us in order that the State of Texas might conduct our court of inquiry. He authorized me to say upon questioning that I had, at all times, been in contact with and consulted with the White House staff."

But Carr lost control of the investigation even as he was on the phone with Fortas, because Dallas District Attorney Henry Wade was turning over the state's evidence to the FBI. Wade told Carr that the federal investigators "agreed to let us have it back any time we wanted it." Wade said, according to the Carr memorandum, "he thought it would be good to have the FBI do it and get it out of the hands of the state for the time being." If Carr realized the impact of that transaction—the evidence being taken over by J. Edgar Hoover, who could control the files—Carr made no comment.

Wade's delivery of the files to Hoover was the end of the ball game for Carr. Three days later, November 29, Lyndon B. Johnson made it official. He announced formation of a blue-ribbon commission to be headed by Chief Justice Earl Warren, "to avoid parallel investigations and to concentrate fact-finding in a body having the broadest national mandate." Johnson was very big on establishing commissions. The Warren Commission would be the first of several. There would be the commissions to study the problems of women, of poverty in Appalachia, of prisons, of Puerto Rican statehood, of narcotics abuse, of almost anything to get a given set of problems off the streets and into meditation. First the new President had eased the assassination probe—a potential national and international fire-bomb—out of the hands of Congress and into a smaller Texas arena where open hearings could be better controlled. Now Johnson was removing it from public view; getting it behind the doors of the Warren Commission. Johnson did mention in passing, as he announced formation of the Commission, that "an inquiry is also scheduled by the Texas court of inquiry, convened by the attorney general of Texas under

Texas law," but he stressed the dominance the new Warren panel would have.

Six members were named to the panel, to serve with Warren. There were two senators: Richard B. Russell, a Georgia Democrat, considered the single most influential member of the Senate; and John Sherman Cooper, a Kentucky Republican who cast sort of an elder-statesman image in the Senate, largely because of short assignments as ambassador to India and as a U.S. adviser in United Nations and North Atlantic Treaty Organization roles. There were two House members and in both cases they were the third highest-ranking members of their political parties: Hale Boggs of Louisiana, the Democratic whip; and Gerald R. Ford, chairman of the House Republican conference. The remaining two men were lawyers in private practice but who were influential in the international intelligence markets. One was Allen W. Dulles, who had headed the Central Intelligence Agency; the other was John J. McCloy, who was chairman of the general advisory committee of the U.S. Arms Control and Disarmanent Agency. President Johnson felt he had found seven men whose ultimate findings would not touch off any foreign crises or riots in the streets of America—seven men who would find no hidden conspiracies[2] nor stir the fears of mankind.[3] Only one of the Commission members, Richard Russell, showed ferocity. Russell confided to the FBI that he had tried to talk the President out of naming him to the panel because it was "a nasty job [and] very distasteful to him . . . to serve on the same commission as Chief Justice Warren, inasmuch as he had no respect for Warren."[4] Russell tended mostly to his Senate business and missed much of the testimony by major witnesses. But he had a Georgia lawyer, Alfredda Scobey, placed on the Commission staff to be his eyes and ears. Miss Scobey asked penetrating questions and paid close attention to the day-to-day detail. She was unique in that no other Commission member had that kind of aide to keep him regularly informed on what was and wasn't being investigated. As a result, Russell challenged the testimony of Oswald's widow, Marina, and put her through a sharp cross-examination that showed gaping inconsistencies in her statements. In the end, Russell was so dissatisfied with certain Commission conclusions—such as the determination that one bullet had passed through both Kennedy and Connally and was barely disfigured when found on a stretcher at Parkland Hospital—he threatened not to sign the final report. Russell didn't make a public fuss. He was too much of an establishment man for that. But he expressed strong reservations among Senate colleagues about the kind of job the Commission had done.

One trouble with the Commission was that it functioned like a misshapen hourglass—a small-headed, big-bodied hourglass that was too narrow in the neck. The seven Commission members were assembled in the head of the hourglass. The staff members worked in the part below. Operating in between the two was J. Lee Rankin, whom some considered to be a bottleneck.

"None of us ever knew what went on between Rankin and the Commission members," recalls one of Rankin's assistant lawyers. "He always kept his door closed. The rest of us kept our doors open, but communicating with Rankin, you practically needed a pass to get to him."

Another staff member recollects that "Rankin seldom came out to see us. He was a very bureaucratic, martinetish man, a very formal individual. You knew him six months and he still addressed you as mister, while of course you were forced to call him Mr. Rankin in return. The feeling you had was that he put up this kind of wall, not because he was trying to protect the Commission, but himself. It was, I guess, a personal thing with him. A matter of a lack of security. There were times when he appeared to be a weak and totally inadequate man."

"Rankin in my opinion was a very complex person," recalls still another attorney on the Commission staff. "You never quite knew what he was thinking." There were some on the staff, such as lawyer Arlen Specter, who had easy access to Rankin. But not many.

Both Rankin and Warren had come to Washington in 1953 as appointees of President Eisenhower in the first year of the Eisenhower administration. Warren, the former governor of California, was installed as Chief Justice of the Supreme Court, while Rankin, a Nebraska lawyer, was brought into the Justice Department as assistant attorney general in charge of the office of legal counsel. By 1956 President Eisenhower appointed Rankin as U.S. solicitor general, which meant Rankin would present arguments on behalf of the federal government before the Warren court. Warren told members of the Commission at their first meeting, December 5, 1963, that he wanted to name Rankin, at that point in private practice in New York City, as chief counsel for the investigation into the killings of John Kennedy and Oswald. There was unanimous agreement.

But Rankin had not been Warren's first choice. A few days earlier the Chief Justice had decided Warren Olney III should have the job. He and Olney had been close since 1930, when Earl Warren was district attorney of Alameda County and Warren Olney his deputy. Later, when Warren was California attorney general, Olney was his assistant, in charge of the criminal division. Still later when Warren was governor, Olney served as the power behind two state crime commissions that took strong action against the organized rackets in California. Then, with Warren's endorsement, Olney served as head of the U.S. Justice Department's criminal division during the Eisenhower administration. It was only natural that Warren would want Olney with him at the Commission.

"Warren did talk to me about this," Olney recalls. "He told me he had advanced my name to the Commission but they said they wanted someone with a more nationally prominent name to take over."[5]

But there was more to it than that. As assistant U.S. attorney general, Olney once had been asked as a favor by the CIA to hold back on prosecution of a New York company that was a CIA front and had been caught smuggling arms into Cuba before the Castro takeover. Instead, Olney pushed for prosecutions and convictions against the law-breakers.

Word was passed to Allen Dulles on the Warren Commission from within the CIA not to accept Olney as staff director—that it would be bad news for the CIA. Dulles "protested quite violently," and Congressmen Ford and Boggs supported the Dulles stand. Boggs even threatened to quit if Warren insisted on forcing Olney on the Commission.[6] Olney was turned down.

Rankin was accepted, not because he was "more nationally prominent," but because he was safer.

One of Rankin's most immediate duties was to set up the bottom half of the hourglass—assembling the staff and establishing six areas of investigation. Each area would be handled by a senior lawyer, to be paid $100 a day, and a junior lawyer at $75 a day. The investigation would concentrate on Oswald, while one-sixth of the Commission's effort would go into Ruby. Because of that preconceived lack of emphasis on Ruby detail, it generally was supposed by Commission staff members that Rankin concentrated the best talent he could muster on establishing Oswald's guilt or innocence, and his least talent on Ruby. Indeed, Rankin's selection of Leon D. Hubert Jr. as chief of the Ruby area, and Burt W. Griffin as assistant counsel, seemed to several on the Commission staff to illustrate the point. Griffin was aggressive and sharp but, at 31, he was the youngest of the six team assistants and looked even younger. Hubert was considered by some to be the least effectual of the staff lawyers.

It was the beginning of January, 1964, when Hubert got an unexpected telephone call in his New Orleans home from J. Lee Rankin in Washington, asking him to join the assassination investigation. Hubert got off to a shaky start right there. He mistook the former solicitor general for John E. Rankin, a rabble-rousing, race-baiting Mississippi congressman who actually had been dead for three years. "Frankly I thought it was a joke at first," Hubert would remember with a pleasant laugh. But once he got his Rankins straightened out, Hubert was on a plane that same day, bound for Washington where he instantly rented an apartment. To the day he died in 1977, Hubert didn't know who recommended him to Rankin, but suspected it was either Commission member Hale Boggs or Washington Federal Appellate Court Judge James Skelly Wright, since both were old friends of his. Hubert never asked Rankin about it because the two never established more than an arms-length relationship. But even from the beginning Rankin noted that Hubert, at 52, was both courtly and obliging, a deep-voiced man who spoke in cultured ways. Leon Hubert was in every sense a gentleman and a scholar.

Hubert had been a law professor at Tulane, an expert in the tedious business of procedural law, who had written needed revisions in the statutes and codes of criminal and civil law for the state of Louisiana. He had served four years in the 1950s as district attorney in New Orleans. But he and Carlos Marcello, the Mafia *capo*, couldn't understand each other well enough to do business and one of them had to go. Before that, during most of President Franklin Roosevelt's administration, Hubert had served as an assistant U.S. attorney for the eastern district of Louisiana and was well-backgrounded for the Warren Commission assignment. Like others joining the Commission staff in early January, Hubert didn't know anybody there and had never heard of the young man who would be assigned to be his partner, Burt Griffin.

Griffin got his phone call from Washington by default. It came from Phil Filvaroff, an attorney in the administrative area of the Justice Department, assigned to search for Commission legal talent. Among the guidelines Filvaroff kept in mind was a need for lawyers from a broad geographic distribution with backgrounds in criminal law. Filvaroff had worked for a Cleveland law firm and telephoned a former associate there with an offer to join this unprecedented presidential commission empaneled to solve a spectacular crime. What lawyer could ask for more of a challenge? Unpredictably, the guy turned it down. He was at work on a major project for his law firm and felt his career with the firm would suffer if he turned away from it to go for the glamour deal in Washington. So Griffin got the call. Griffin was working in another Cleveland law office and Filvaroff had known him to be a serious and diligent young lawyer.

A native of Cleveland, Griffin was educated in the East, at Amherst and Yale. Like Hubert, he had been an assistant U.S. attorney, serving in the northern district of Ohio before entering private practice. Griffin was familiar with Washington because he had clerked there four years earlier for Judge George T. Washington of the federal appeals court, not far from 200 Maryland Avenue, Northeast. That was the address of the Veterans of Foreign Wars Building on the edge of Capitol Hill, where the Warren Commission was setting up its staff headquarters on the entire fifth floor, the top floor. The six teams of lawyers were assigned office space there by the categories they would investigate:

1. *Basic Facts of the Assassination* . . . such as, how many shots had been fired at the President and from where? Francis W. H. Adams, 59, was assigned as senior counsel. He was former New York City police commissioner and member of a prominent New York-Washington law firm. His name lent prestige to the caliber of talent on the Commission staff but

Adams was typical of some of the high-powered attorneys named to the Commission. He barely showed up and contributed little at all. His assistant, Arlen Specter, 33, a Philadelphia lawyer, was the workhorse.[7]

2. *The Assassin* . . . an evaluation of all the evidence that led to naming Oswald as the killer of both the President and officer Tippit. The senior lawyer was Joseph A. Ball, 61, ranking partner in a noted California law firm. Ball was teamed with David W. Belin, 35, a well-established Des Moines attorney.[8]

3. *Oswald's Background and Motives* . . . his Soviet years and other influences. Albert E. Jenner Jr.,[9] Chicago attorney and former Northwestern University law professor, was the senior man. Wesley J. Liebeler, 32, a New York City lawyer, born in North Dakota, was the junior.

4. *Was There a Conspiracy?* . . . What was the impact of others on Oswald and had he concealed conspiratorial relationships? William T. Coleman Jr., 43,[10] member of a leading Philadelphia law firm and onetime clerk to Supreme Court Associate Justice Felix Frankfurter, headed the conspiracy detail. Coleman was another who was on hand for Commission business infrequently. Assisting him was W. David Slawson, 32, a Denver attorney, originally from Michigan.

5. *Oswald's Death* . . . the Ruby detail. Had Ruby acted alone? Did Ruby have any connections leading to Oswald? Originally there were to be five areas of investigation, in descending importance. The Ruby detail was considered the fifth and least significant. Hubert and Griffin were introduced to each other and deposited there.

6. *Presidential Protection* . . . involving sensitive precautions taken and not taken by the Secret Service, FBI and Dallas police in advance of the President's trip to Dallas. The Commission decided this category was essential and added it on. Rankin was placed in charge of it. Samuel A. Stern, 35, a Washington lawyer who had clerked for Chief Justice Warren eight years earlier, was the day-to-day counsel on the job.

The management would have had to reinforce the fifth-floor walls of the building at 200 Maryland Avenue if these attorneys had elected to hang all their framed credentials as learned men on the walls. Yet despite that cumulation of certified intelligence, they often isolated themselves from each other. Some were pompous and didn't feel the need to hear what others on the staff were thinking. Some were too caught up with their own investigative projects to communicate with others. There were conflicts and overlaps and jealousies and grievances and most of it was because there was no simple line of contact among the men on the fifth floor.

One of the contributing factors to the Commission's overall failures was its lack of communication from top to bottom and from side to side. Rankin kept the up and down flow of information in the hourglass—between Commission members and staff—tightly controlled and limited through his office. It was all very formal and private. As a result the fifth floor took on an antiseptic atmosphere, with no system for a free exchange of facts among the working-level lawyers.

For instance, "We never had any significant dialogue, any structured dialogue among the staff members on the question of conspiracy," says one of those lawyers who still is distraught because of that critical failure. "There never were any series of hypotheses set up that we were all supposed to check into. In fact, we never really had a structured system of meeting and exchanging information so that various theories could be checked out. These two points were problems caused by Rankin—either because he was incompetent and way over his head, or because he knew something the rest of us didn't know."

Another of the lawyers, Hubert, was never, in all the months that the Commission took testimony, asked to examine any witness appearing before the Commission members. That was true not only in the Commission's badly handled questioning of Jack Ruby, but Hubert was excluded even after he and Griffin already had questioned those same witnesses in preliminary sessions when depositions were taken.

"It is not that we were overtly kept out," Hubert recalled. "We were not advised to be there." He says it was more than just a lack of simple communication. "We were all on the same floor, you know. All it would have taken was for someone to holler out."

In an attempt to change the atmosphere, Hubert and Griffin established what they hoped would be a series of informal Saturday morning meetings with the lawyers from the five other investigatory details of the Commission. The idea was to promote an exchange of professional information, so that Hubert and Griffin could find out what the others were accomplishing and to explain what they were into. There was one such meeting. After that the other lawyers didn't show enough interest to discuss evidence with each other again.

Warren himself sensed the problems of arrogance and self-importance that could come about in a 100 percent mix of independently successful lawyers. Warren specifically asked that a skilled historian, a non-lawyer, be brought in so that a perspective on the facts could be maintained. Alfred Goldberg was selected.[11] At the first staff meeting he attended, Goldberg was asked to comment on perspective. The historian told the assembled lawyers that their ultimate report to the people of America should not be some kind of oversized legal brief. It had to be written clearly for a broad audience throughout the land. The group he was speaking to received the advice coldly.

Much of the chill factor on the Commission staff was evident at the top, between Rankin's two principal aides, Howard P. Willens and Norman Redlich.

On the weekend of President Kennedy's assassination the 32-year-old Willens was second assistant in the Justice Department's criminal division,

which had been pulsating with Attorney General Kennedy's war on organized crime. A month later, when the FBI began shipping thousands of its
assassination investigative reports to the Commission, Willens was designated by Deputy Attorney General Nicholas deB. Katzenbach to serve as
liaison between the Commission and Justice in the handling of FBI information. Willens immediately became Rankin's chief administrator. He
laid out the work divisions, made staff assignments, dealt with the FBI
and CIA and became a decision-maker. "We communicated with Rankin
through Willens," Hubert recalls.

But three weeks after Willens was installed, Rankin named Norman
Redlich, a 38-year-old brusque, highly opinionated professor of law at
New York University as his special assistant.[12] Redlich was a "work-
aholic," who wrote his opinions and reworked the labors of the other lawyers on the staff seven days and nights a week. The creative, demanding
Redlich and the far more pragmatic Willens had personalities that
clashed, and each considered himself to be Rankin's true deputy. Because
their interests were not the same, though, they operated on separate but
equal plateaus on the fifth floor.

December 9, 1963, just four days after the Commission held its first
meeting, and before there even was a Commission staff, J. Edgar Hoover
turned over to Chief Justice Warren a four-volume summary report of the
FBI's probe of the Kennedy and Oswald assassinations. That instant report was the basis of the final conclusions the Warren Commission officially would reach nine months later.

Willens was upset by the superficiality of the FBI report and Rankin
agreed. Rankin assembled the staff lawyers and told them not to accept the
FBI report as gospel and to request more facts. (A few days later, at the next
staff meeting, the lawyers began to quarrel loudly among themselves. One
threatened to quit, Rankin lost control of the proceedings and from that point
on there were no more regular staff meetings.) The Commission itself didn't
have anyone on its staff designated as an investigator—and would be vulner-
able because it had to depend on such agencies as the FBI, Secret Service, CIA
and Dallas police to investigate themselves.

"It was a mistake that we never had any investigative staff of our own,"
Griffin believes. "Rankin himself indicated to us that the FBI couldn't be
trusted, yet his feeling was, from his own bureaucratic experience, that we
could make more progress by enlisting their help than we could as an agency
that would be seen as an investigative threat to them. Rankin was fearful that
our own investigation of the assassination could be interpreted by the FBI or
CIA as an attempt to investigate them. That was a tough problem for Rankin
to resolve." The way Rankin did it was to encourage the Commission lawyers
to seek additional, explicit facts from the FBI.

Hoover was outraged, especially because on the surface Rankin and Warren were highly complimentary about the FBI investigation. "Their so-called compliments of the Bureau's work are empty and have no sincerity," Hoover noted in longhand on an internal FBI memorandum.[13]

The memorandum complained that the Warren Commission was dunning the FBI with 52 questions on a subject "to which they request a reasoned response in reasonable detail and with such substantiating materials as seem appropriate. The questions are those of a cross-examination of the FBI or a part of it in the case of the assassination of President Kennedy."

When there were penetrating questions from the Warren Commission, the FBI had two primary ways of concealing vital answers from the American public.

The first was by holding out facts from the Commission, as in the Oswald-James Hosty affair. Hosty was a special FBI agent in the Dallas office, where a bitter Oswald had come to see him only a few days before the murder of President Kennedy. The purpose of Oswald's visit was to threaten Hosty and possibly other federal authorities because Hosty had been bothering Oswald's wife. Hosty wasn't there but Oswald put his threat in writing, leaving it in a note for the agent.[14] About four hours after Ruby shot Oswald, Hosty was ordered to destroy the note by Dallas FBI Bureau Chief, J. Gordon Shanklin, according to Hosty. Shanklin later discussed the Oswald-Hosty affair on a high level with the FBI, according to an affidavit by one of Hoover's key administrators, William C. Sullivan. But at no time was the angry written threat by Oswald disclosed to the public or to the Warren Commission—until 1975, which was 11 years after the Commission had concluded its business, and after Hoover's death. Acting on information it had obtained, *The Dallas Times Herald* began asking FBI officials in Dallas and Washington in July, 1975, about the hushed-up threat from Oswald and the story came out at last. Of course Oswald's November, 1963, written threat would have become a major FBI embarrassment if the Commission had been able to report it and raise an obvious question: Why hadn't the FBI taken threats from Oswald more seriously? Some of Willens' associates in a prominent Washington law firm report he became furious when he learned the FBI had held out such vital information from the public, and had destroyed the evidence immediately after the bullet from Ruby's gun kept Oswald from ever talking about the note.

The other way the FBI had of maintaining a coverup was to confide a potentially explosive fact to the Warren Commission, and ask that it be kept private, such as the use of Jack Ruby in 1959 by the FBI as an underworld contact—a crucial fact about Ruby that wasn't made public for several years after the Warren Report was issued.

On February 27, 1964, FBI Director Hoover wrote a memorandum to Commission staff director Rankin that confided "for your information"

Ruby had been contacted nine times by the FBI in 1959, from March 11 to October 2, "to furnish information" on criminal matters. Hoover asserted Ruby never was paid any money and "did not furnish any information and further contacts with him were discontinued."

As a result, the Commission never inserted a word into the Warren Report about Ruby's flow of 1959 contacts with the FBI. The Commission also failed to question Charles W. Flynn, the FBI agent in Dallas who had set up the contacts with Ruby. Another communiqué from Hoover to Rankin, on June 9, 1964, said Ruby had "expressed a willingness to furnish information" to the FBI in 1959. But that Hoover communiqué was withheld from the public until January, 1971. What emerged for public inspection with the Warren Report was Commission Document 732 (item J), which showed only that Flynn had met with Ruby on March 11, 1959, and that Flynn had filed a general description of Ruby: weight, height, age, credit information (the Dallas Credit Bureau gave him an unsatisfactory rating), address, occupation and remarks—"Known Dallas area criminal."[15] Commission Document 732, as published, gave no hint of the subsequent meetings between Flynn and Ruby.

On reflection now, Burt Griffin says, "I am confident that Leon Hubert and I saw the Hoover letter as a part of our work for the Warren Commission . . . Hubert and I had nothing to do with, and were unaware of, any decision to withhold that letter from the public once it left our hands . . . I now believe that the FBI should be asked to disclose all information about the purpose of these 1959 contacts and the information he was asked to provide, if they have not already done so."[16]

What the FBI did provide the Warren Commission on February 18, 1964—the same month Hoover first gave the Commission information to be withheld about Ruby as a covert FBI contact—was this fearless piece of additional information out of Ruby's past:

Ruby's mother, Fanny Rubenstein, wore false teeth. The FBI obtained a dental diagram from the Elgin State Hospital in Illinois, dated January 15, 1938 . . . a diagram of 32 teeth, showing Mrs. Rubenstein had full upper and lower plates; with a notation by Dr. W. J. Hoeft, staff dentist, who apparently looked into Mrs. Rubenstein's mouth and found nothing there: "Patient states she has teeth but not wearing them."

The dental report on toothless Fanny Rubenstein, 25 years before the Kennedy assassination, was dutifully reproduced as Commission Exhibit No. 1281 on page 395, Volume 22, of the Commission's findings.

Nearly three hours after Lee Harvey Oswald was pronounced dead in Parkland hospital, presidential aide Walter Jenkins prepared a memorandum for his files, reporting a telephone conversation he'd had that afternoon with J. Edgar Hoover. The memorandum quotes Hoover as saying, "The thing I am most concerned about, and so is Mr. Katzenbach,[17] is having something issued so we can convince the public that Oswald is the real assassin." Hoover simply didn't want any other governmental body prowling into the shootings of Kennedy and Oswald. On December 3, two days *before* President Johnson's appointed Warren Commission held its first meeting, United Press International carried a story on its national wire that began:

> WASHINGTON—An exhaustive FBI report now nearly ready for the White House will indicate that Lee Harvey Oswald was the lone and unaided assassin of President Kennedy, government sources said today.

Hoover himself ordered that information leaked to UPI in his zeal to "blunt the drive for an independent investigation of the assassination," according to Sullivan, the Hoover lieutenant.

Hoover's hostility toward the Commission grew as the Commission staff members were assembled in the following weeks, and he asked that any known "dirt" in the FBI files on any of them be brought to him. At this point there is "no documentary evidence" that once derogatory information was brought to Hoover's private office it was "disseminated while the Warren Commission was in session."[18] However, once derogatory information on Norman Redlich reached Hoover's desk it found its way into the hands of a group of rightwing congressmen who tried to use it to get Redlich fired as Rankin's special assistant. That move on Capitol Hill to expose Redlich as a member of a communist-front organization was well-orchestrated to prevent Redlich from getting the security clearance required for him to continue on the Commission staff. Inside the Commission itself, Gerald R. Ford led the fight to "get" Redlich. But it failed when Chief Justice Warren interceded in Redlich's behalf, much to Hoover's displeasure.

Ford was sympathetic to Hoover inside the Commission. The two men shared a private contempt for Earl Warren, and Ford regularly furnished the FBI with pieces of information about what was happening behind Commission closed doors. Senator Russell, a Ford colleague on the Commission, disliked Warren intently, too, but Russell was an independent man and maintained his distance from the FBI. During the Christmas holidays in 1963, the FBI furnished Ford with an official agent's briefcase, which could be locked, so he could take FBI investigative material on the Kennedy assassination along on a skiing vacation.[19]

From the beginning the Warren Commission made a conscious effort to pull its punches in looking into Jack Ruby's activities before and during the weekend of President Kennedy's murder.

Rankin and Warren agreed that open hearings or the pursuit of witnesses in Dallas "might interfere with Ruby's rights to a fair and impartial trial." But while their decision sounded good—and the decision was enough to put the final blocks to Waggoner Carr's hopes for public hearings in Texas—the Commission couldn't have treated Ruby's rights with more disdain. For on the day that Ruby's trial got under way, March 4, 1964, Rankin and Warren allowed New York lawyer Mark Lane to appear in an open hearing before the Commission. Over the years Lane has argued that Oswald was far less implicated and Ruby far more implicated in a murder plot than the Commission would admit. But Lane sometimes argues without presenting supporting facts. At first Lane attempted to get the Commission to appoint him as "defense counsel" for the dead Oswald, with the right to cross-examine Commission witnesses (Oswald and Lane never had encountered each other). When that failed, Lane asked for and was given a public hearing, to appear as a witness himself. On March 4, Lane testified that Ruby had met for two hours in the Carousel with Bernard Weissman and policeman J. D. Tippit, eight nights before President Kennedy was slain. Weissman was the murky figure whose name appeared on the virulent anti-Kennedy advertisement in *The Dallas Morning News*, the morning of the day both the President and Tippit were shot. "This information came to me from a witness to the alleged meeting," Lane said. But Lane has yet to produce the name of the witness. So what he gave the Commission in a public session was hearsay evidence from an unnamed person whose record for telling the truth is unknown. The Commission let itself be used as a megaphone for an unsupported charge against Ruby on the opening day of Ruby's trial. Meanwhile, after the trial was over, the Commission held back information from its final Warren Report that would be damaging to Ruby. Explain that one.

Burt Griffin attempts to explain it. He says a major problem for the Commission was that its investigation was going on before and during the trial, and then while the guilty verdict against Ruby was on appeal. Since the trial was concerned with whether there had been premeditation by Ruby or whether he even was mentally responsible when he shot Oswald, "we were trying to be very careful not to put equivocal, argumentative things into the report," says Griffin.[20] "We spent a lot of time worrying how we could write this report and not deprive him of a fair trial."

One of those equivocal, argumentative things was the gun Ruby told two FBI agents on December 21, 1963, he had carried in his pocket into the Dallas police station on Friday night, November 22, when he first viewed Oswald in the station. Six months later Ruby told the Warren Commission that he had lied to the FBI—there had been no gun in his pocket on that Friday night. He had invented the fact, he said, to prepare for his trial defense, in order to show that he might have killed Oswald at the earliest opportunity, instead of waiting until Sunday, had murder been his plan.

What emerges without dispute from the two Ruby accounts regarding the gun is that he was a liar on one of those two occasions. Yet even that much was kept out of the Warren Report. "To have put in the gun episode," says Griffin, "would have put us in the position of dealing with premeditation and we would have had to attack his credibility."

Attack Ruby's *credibility*? Why should the Warren Commission do that to a man with a criminal record, who associates with hoodlums, and who then murders the prime suspect in what might be the American crime of the century, before that suspect talks?

Because of the Commission's enunciated policy of not interfering with Ruby's day in court, the Warren Report would present a limited look at Ruby since his case still was pending in appellate court at the time of his death, which came more than two years after the Warren Report was issued and the Commission was disbanded.

Restricted by the Commission's noninterference policy, Hubert and Griffin were not even able to question witnesses knowledgeable about Ruby for more than two months after their probe began. The two former federal prosecutors spent from early January, 1964, until March 14—the day Ruby's trial ended with a death sentence—assembling as many secondhand details about him as they could in their Washington office.

For instance, Hubert and Griffin put together a profile of Ruby based on FBI interviews and reports. Hubert described the profile that emerged: "He was a violent man. He was a peculiar man. A silly man, really. Ruthless. He beat up a lot of people, very badly. Would kick a man when he was down. But he was not a guy who was going to conspire deeply. Nor was he the type of guy who would be trusted by international conspirators."[21] Hubert used as an illustration of Ruby's "silliness" the fact that Ruby bought a volume of sandwiches at the delicatessen and took them to the police on Friday and to the reporters on Saturday. The illustration doesn't concede that it was to Ruby's advantage to use the sandwiches as a ploy to reach the third floor, the nerve center, of the police station on two successive days before he murdered Oswald.

But Hubert and Griffin were painstaking in their basic search for details on Ruby. They catalogued him first in broad categories, based on periods in his past—his Chicago days, his life on the West Coast as a hustler, World War II military service, life in Dallas, rumored underworld and Cuban connections. Each of those areas was broken down into subcategories by the two former prosecutors.

Hubert and Griffin worked well and closely together. They assembled a large mockup of the Dallas police department basement in order that each known person who was there when Ruby pulled the trigger could be pinpointed and positioned. The two investigators also put together a massive time chart—the Ruby chronicle referred to in Chapter Two—showing the current of Ruby's movements over a period of months before the assassination. They attempted to identify where Ruby was at every known minute during the assassination period. Many of Ruby's movements and associations were traced through telephone records. Hubert and Griffin developed the use of these records as a technique that other lawyers on the Commission staff soon began to use, too, in different areas of the Oswald investigation.

On February 19, 1964, for instance, Hubert and Griffin compiled a list of Ruby's relatives and certain people he knew, in order that their home and business telephone records could be checked. In the course of a lengthy memorandum to Willens that day, Hubert and Griffin said:

> ... a list of all telephone calls placed from, placed to, or charged to such telephones should be obtained for members of the Ruby family and for Ralph Paul and for George Senator as far back as records are available. During the period of August 1, 1963, to November 25, 1963, information as to the exact time and duration of such calls should be obtained together with the name of the person making or receiving the call (if available). Inasmuch as the FBI reports which we have already received concerning Jack Ruby's telephones is inaccurate or incomplete in some respects, it will be necessary to obtain the original or copies of all telephone records. However, we also would like the FBI to submit those records in report form so that it will not be necessary for us to tabulate and transcribe the information obtained by the FBI unless, in particular circumstances, we find errors in the transcribing by the FBI.

Funneling their requests through Willens, Hubert and Griffin became intense in their search for basic information on Ruby. For instance, they asked for the names of "all persons who attended schools in Dallas and New Orleans when Lee Harvey Oswald was in attendance at those schools," in their pursuit of any connections that could have existed between Ruby and Oswald. Hubert and Griffin even asked for "the names, ages, home addresses and rank of all persons in any military unit in which Ruby or Oswald served." They asked that the Library of Congress be combed for any feature-length magazine articles ever written on Barney Ross, the professional prizefighter who had grown up in Chicago with Ruby and had become a narcotics addict. Ruby had contacted Ross in New York in 1963. Hubert and Griffin wanted to know if there could be a link between Ross as an addict and Ruby as a supplier. Meanwhile, some of the other attorneys on the Warren panel were annoyed by the excitement and suspicions being stirred by the two-man Ruby team.

These requests by Hubert and Griffin kept widening until at one point they actually asked for the records of everybody who had left and arrived in the United States over a total span of 90 days before and after the Kennedy assassination. That was Griffin's idea. Hubert said he went along with it but even he thought the idea was too monumental to be productive. Some of these requests were ignored or blocked at the Rankin level, such as the one seeking records on everybody leaving the United States on trips. Other requests were pigeonholed for highly questionable reasons by government officials who considered themselves beyond the reach of the Warren Commission. For instance, Hubert and Griffin wrote a 13-page memorandum on February 24, seeking information about, among other things, mysterious links between Ruby and Cuban interests.

The memorandum was sent to Richard M. Helms, the CIA's deputy director for plans. It went unanswered.

Originally the CIA appeared to be helpful and forthcoming, especially when compared with the FBI. But by the mid-1970s it had become apparent to former Warren Commission staff members that Helms and Allen W. Dulles had held back information from the Commission.

In 1964, Helms was to be the next director of the CIA[22] and Dulles was the immediate past director. Between the two of them, with Dulles sitting on the Warren council itself, they were in a strong position to block embarrassing facts. The essential difference between them and J. Edgar Hoover was that they handled the Commission more deftly. In a transcribed discussion among Commission members, January 27, 1964,[23] Dulles told his colleagues matter-of-factly that, according to the dictates of U.S. intelligence policy, Hoover and the then-current CIA Director John A. McCone should be expected to lie to the Commission to protect the identity of their operations and undercover agents.

Hoover and McCone (McCone was accompanied by Helms) were successive witnesses before the Commission on May 14.

Even though Hoover had told Rankin on February 27 and again on April 7 that Ruby had been contacted nine times by the FBI in an eight-month span during 1959, neither Rankin nor any member of the Commission asked Hoover a single question about that in May. Obviously the decision to keep the Ruby-FBI contacts quiet already had been reached.

Ruby's name might not even have come up when Hoover testified before the Commission. The questions concerned FBI investigative techniques, presidential protection and FBI information on Oswald. But Hoover brought up Ruby's name to emphasize that "we found no associations between Oswald and Ruby."

McCone and Helms were within moments of concluding their testimony before there was any mention of Ruby, who by now was being treated as an isolated figure in the events of November 22-24, 1963.

Gerald R. Ford, considered the least significant of the seven Warren Commission members but the one who focused attention on Ruby's innocent-looking Cuban connections, brought up Ruby.

FORD: Did the Central Intelligence Agency ever make an investigation or did it ever check on Mr. Ruby's trip to Cuba or any connections he might have had with the Castro government?

McCONE: Not to my knowledge.

HELMS: We had no information.

FORD: Central Intelligence Agency has no information of any connections of Ruby to the Castro government?

McCONE: That is right.

FORD: Did you ever make a check of that?

HELMS: We checked our records to see if we had information and found we did not.

FORD: What would that indicate—the fact that you checked your records?

HELMS: That would indicate that if we had received information from our own resources that the Cubans were involved with Mr. Ruby in something that would be regarded as subversive, we would then have it in our files. But we received no such information, and I don't, by saying this, mean that he did not. I simply say we don't have any record of this.

FORD: That is all.

Both the questions by Ford and the pattern of answers by McCone and Helms are revealing. Even after getting a limp answer the first time, Ford repeated his preliminary question concerning what the CIA might know about Ruby and Cuba. Helms couldn't have made it clearer to Ford that there would be no substantive answer: "I simply say we don't have any record of this." Ford of course let it drop and Warren dismissed the witnesses in the next moment, without anyone asking more than the preliminary question Ford had asked.

No one asked, had Ruby ever been a CIA contact? Had Ruby ever been a known source of information for the CIA? Ford asked if Ruby might have been connected with the Castro government. No one asked if Ruby might have been connected with anti-Castro elements.

Hubert and Griffin weren't there that morning. Even if the two experts on Ruby had been notified of the session—and invited into it—they still would not have been welcome to ask questions of their own or generate a fresh flow of questions for such Commission members as Ford. The Commission was structured, remember, so that staff lawyers communicated to members through Rankin. It meant the questions were controlled. The only thing more controlled that morning were the answers.

Dulles was there. Dulles, as well as McCone and Helms, knew about the workings of Project ZR/RIFLE, the super-secret project that had linked U.S. underworld figures with the CIA in the abortive attempts to assassinate Castro.

CIA files showed that at least one of Ruby's reported underworld contacts in Cuba, Santo Trafficante Jr., had been involved with the CIA in the project to hit Castro.

But Dulles didn't bring that up, since other Warren Commission members still had no idea that the CIA had put a Chicago-style contract out on Castro.

CHAPTER 5

Any Friend Of Needle-Nose Labriola...

When Leon Hubert and Burt Griffin looked into Jack Ruby's background as Jacob Rubenstein they found he had come from a blizzard of noise and unhappiness; from parents whose marriage was arranged through a Jewish *shadchen,* a marriage broker in the Eastern European tradition.

Fanny Rokowsky, aged 24 at the turn of the century, was not the greatest catch in the Russo-Polish *shtetl,* the small town near Warsaw where she and her family lived. It was true that she was not a bad-looking redhead and her father was a respected man in the community, a doctor's assistant. But Fanny Rokowsky was uneducated and quite emotional. She talked too much—incessantly, really—and her moods swung from laughter to weeping without perceptible cause. Her father realized that she would suffer an old maid's lot unless he arranged for a groom through the *shadchen.* The available groom who applied for the Rokowsky dowry was short, barrel-chested and fierce. His name was Joseph Rubenstein, from a family of carpenters and that was his given profession, although he lacked both the journeyman's pride and craftsmanship to make progress. Instead, he had been taken into the Russian army where he had learned to perfect other traits he would handle more expertly—abusive language, heavy drinking and woman-beating. Joseph Rubenstein was 30 when he entered into the agreement with Fanny Rokowsy's well-meaning father. From the beginning it was a marriage which had as much warmth and love as a pillaging Cossack would give.

They reached America in 1905 and settled in Chicago, where in 1911 Jacob Rubenstein became the fifth of eight children born into the poor and desperately unhappy home. When he wasn't home, Joseph Rubenstein took up with street women, squandering his money on them and on his own drunkenness. There wasn't that much money to begin with, since he sometimes didn't get paid for his carpentry jobs. His arrogance would lead to arguments with customers or bosses and he would leave jobs before they were done. When he was at home, Joseph and Fanny rarely could stand being in the same room. She became a babbling nag and they often communicated like a pair of long-range cannons, with angry blasts from different rooms. By the time Jacob was four years old, the beatings Mr. Rubenstein gave Mrs. Rubenstein led to the first of a series of assault and battery charges brought by her against him. He also slapped the children frequently and didn't want them educated beyond grade school. Jacob was 10 when his parents separated.

From then on, Jacob, his three brothers and four sisters were placed by the Jewish Home Finding Society of Chicago in various foster homes and they lived only intermittently with their mother. But she provided them with even less intellectual security than their father had done. He at least had brought in a Hebrew teacher to tutor the three youngest sons, and had taught the children the values of sharing what little they had with others. She yelled at them, hit them and had delusions about them having sexual relations with each other. As the years went on, Fanny Rubenstein remained illiterate, would ramble and shriek in Yiddish, crochet compulsively, demand that others serve her meals, and then she would eat enormous, unhealthy quantities. If she did prepare a meal for herself, the kitchen would be left in a shambles for others to clean up. Willful and lazy, she threw tantrums when she didn't get her way. At last, in 1937, when she was 61, Fanny Rubenstein was committed to the state hospital at Elgin as a deteriorating paranoia case. She told authorities there that she did not like any of her children, and insisted they were closer to their errant father than to her because he was the one with the insurance policy. In a way she was right because the children found her to be impossibly emotional and demanding and developed a bond of tormented understanding with their father as his ferocity began to wane with old age. Jacob had become Private Jack Rubenstein in the U.S. Army Air Force when his mother died of a heart attack and pneumonia at 68 in 1944. He was Jack Ruby the Dallas nightclub operator in 1958, when his father died in Chicago at 87.

He was 11 years old and his parents had been separated for a year when he showed strong signs of defiance and depression. He became a school truant. He disobeyed at home and in the classroom. He frequently stayed in bed in the mornings to avoid the realities of school discipline, and he masturbated frequently, according to a record of Jacob Rubenstein, a problem child, compiled by the Illinois State Public Welfare Department's Institute for Juvenile Research on July 6, 1922. The record showed his IQ to be "adequate," his reactions as "quick and careless," his "attention unsustained" and his attitude "egocentric." He could have been recorded identically 40 years later.

Jacob quit school after missing an average of one out of every five days in the eighth grade, while getting near-failing marks in history and English. He was 16 then and he took to the streets, fulltime. There he was known as "Sparky," which suited the feisty, quick-tempered kid who roamed Chicago's West Side in search of a fast buck or a fight, whichever came first. He got both at once one day when he was 16, scalping tickets to a football game at Soldiers Field. Two Chicago policemen arrested him, pistol-whipped him into unconsciousness and put him in jail. But most of the time Sparky moved too fast for the police. He and Barney Rasofsky—who would become World Welterweight Boxing Champion Barney Ross in the 1930s—were among about a dozen young toughs who delivered sealed envelopes at the rate of $1 per errand for Chicago's No. 1 racketeer, Al Capone.[1] A year later, the emerging Jack Ruby made his debut in the legitimate job market. "I tried to be an errand boy for a mail-order house but I couldn't be regimented," he recalled years later.[2] "I couldn't get up in the morning." His sister Eva and a younger brother, Sam, remembered Sparky was fired from another job that same year by losing his temper when told to do something; knocking the manager of the place to the floor with his fists. From that point on, Sparky decided he would work when and where he wanted to. He sold novelties briefly from a pushcart—obtaining a street vendor's license through his older brother, Hyman, a flunkie in political boss Jake Arvey's Democratic stronghold, the 24th ward. He hustled peanuts inside sporting events; scalped tickets outside sporting events; sold race-track tip sheets, carnations in dance halls, chocolates in burlesque shows and "genuine discount jewelry." He sold newspaper subscriptions in California, "hot" music sheets (in violation of the copyright law) in Chicago and punchboard chances in New York. He worked as a nightclub bouncer, was an off-key singing waiter, worked out at athletic clubs, was a sharp dresser, fashioned himself as a ladies' man, and every corner that he turned, Sparky Rubenstein had to prove two things. He was a man. He was a Jew.

His younger brother Earl remembered him coming home on repeated occasions with excited accounts and bruised knuckles from street fights that had resulted from other people's anti-Semitic statements. Jack Rubenstein usually would strike fast and savagely with his fists or with any-thing he could pick up to use as a club. One time he came home with his suit covered with the blood of somebody who had disparaged the Jews.

The rage that Jack Rubenstein felt on a gutter level has been shared in countless ways. Composer Leonard Bernstein has expressed it in a different way with his hands. "You can't live in the world without rage—and guilt," he said.[3] "Yes, I have my share. It's not the Jew's prerogative, but it's characteristic. It's the 'I'm really no good, I'm just a fraud' thing. That's where it comes from.

"It's a remarkably lucky thing, being able to storm your way through a Beethoven symphony. Think of the amount of rage you can get out. If you exhibited that kind of rage on the street or in an interpersonal rela-tionship you'd be thrown in jail. Instead, you're applauded for it."

Jack Rubenstein searched for no symphonies. Before he was in his teens, he fought in gang brawls against Italian kids who taunted the Jews. In his mid-twenties he was part of a Jewish poolhall crowd that attacked the hate-spewing, pro-Hitler German-American bundist meetings with fists and head-cracking weapons. In his mid-thirties, as an Air Force pri-vate, he beat up a sergeant who had called him a Jew bastard. In the end, in his mid-fifties, his jailhouse delusions were that the Jews were being tor-tured because he had shot Oswald. In his mind Oswald had been an im-personal Nazi image.

In 1937, Leon R. Cooke, a 25-year-old attorney, founded the Scrap Iron and Junk Handlers' Union in Chicago. Cooke became financial secre-tary and his central goal in that depression year was to help local workers in the junk business get more than the 15 cents an hour top wage they were being paid.

Union headquarters was established upstairs over a store on Roose-velt Road, five blocks from where Jack Rubenstein had grown up. At the same time, Rubenstein returned to Chicago in search of work, from a se-ries of job failures in California. His antagonistic mother had just been put away as a mental patient when Cooke hired him at $22.50 a week to be a union organizer.

There is every indication that Cooke's motives were high. But the junk and scrap metal yards attracted hoodlums and Cooke soon lost control of his own union. The officers he installed, including himself, were replaced by men tied to the Chicago rackets, such as John Martin, who seized control as president. At the same time, Martin was on the public payroll as a sanitary district clerk and was under indictment for conspiring with a well-known Chicago hoodlum to withhold tax information from revenue agents. Martin assigned Rubenstein the role of bagman in what appeared at the time to Lieutenant Thomas Kelly of the state's attorney's office in Chicago to be a shakedown racket. According to one report, Rubenstein pulled a gun one day when he was attempting to organize a group of scrap-paper workers in a plant on North Leavitt Street.[4] Near the end of 1939, when the state's attorney's office seized the union books, the union's funds were unaccounted for at the rate of several hundred dollars a month. By then Martin had installed a notorious West Side Chicago hoodlum, Carlos Fontana, as business agent for the union. Rubenstein had been given the title of union secretary by Martin but actually was no more than a money pick-up man, according to a statement furnished by Rubenstein to Chicago police on December 8, 1939, the day Leon Cooke was shot.

Officially Cooke had remained legal adviser to the union but Martin would have little to do with him. On December 8, Cooke barged angrily into Martin's office and the two argued over Martin's handling of union business. Martin pulled his gun, fired it three times and then fled down the fire escape with the witness to the shooting, Mrs. Gladys Walsh, the office secretary. After his arrest Martin admitted having pulled the trigger. Cooke lingered about a month in the hospital before dying and then Martin went free. That seemed only reasonable to the prosecutor's office in Chicago. After all, records showed Cooke was shot in the back and Martin said he had fired in self-defense.

The shooting of Leon Cooke was front-page news in Chicago and Jack Rubenstein's picture appeared in connection with it in *The Chicago Tribune.* But all police records of the incident disappeared from police files, leading the FBI to report erroneously to the Warren Commission on June 15, 1964, that Cooke had been shot by an "unknown assailant." George Bliss, a Pulitzer prize-winning reporter for the *Tribune*, explains that "arrest records and fingerprints in years past in Chicago would disappear in wholesale lots from police files. Hoods with political clout or those who could make the right payoff could get records pulled." There was no trace of an arrest record for Jack Rubenstein, going back to his first known arrest in 1927 for ticket scalping, or the 30-day sentence he received in 1930 for selling pirated music sheets.

Long after he became Jack Ruby, he spoke with deep affection for Leon Cooke and adopted Cooke's first name as his own middle name, which he used on signed documents as a mark of lasting respect. But he was not disturbed enough by the brutalization of Cooke at the time to walk out on the hoodlum-controlled union. Jack Rubenstein remained.

Captain Daniel Gilbert of the state's attorney's office confiscated the union's charter and records, and the junk workers were reorganized under the name of the Waste Material Handlers Union, Local 20467, American Federation of Labor. The new local was at once assembled and dominated by its secretary-treasurer, Paul J. Dorfman, who had numerous labor-racketeering connections in Chicago.

In his book *The Enemy Within*, Robert Kennedy wrote about Dorfman, among those he encountered in his role as chief counsel to Senator McClellan's rackets-investigating subcommittee:

> By 1949 . . . Jimmy Hoffa had consolidated his position in the Michigan Teamsters; but outside his home state he was still largely unknown. For him, the key to the entire midwest was Chicago. He needed a powerful ally there—and he found his man in Paul Dorfman. Dorfman, our testimony showed, was a big operator—a major figure in the Chicago underworld who also knew his way around certain labor and political circles.
>
> A slight man with thinning red hair and an almost benign manner, Dorfman took over as head of the Chicago Waste Handlers Union in 1939 after its founder and secretary-treasurer was murdered. In 1957 the AFL-CIO kicked him out for corruption.
>
> He has tied some strange knots in the strings he pulls. According to our testimony, he was closely linked with such underworld figures as Tony Accardo, who became head of the Chicago syndicate after the death of Al Capone, and with Abner (Longie) Zwillman—a top gangland leader in the United States (Longie Zwillman committed suicide shortly after being subpoenaed by our committee). Red Dorfman is also considered a power in some political circles, both Democratic and Republican.

Somehow the Warren Report concluded that "there is no evidence[5] that Ruby's union activities were connected with Chicago's criminal element. Several longtime members of the union reported that it had a good reputation when Ruby was affiliated with it, and employers who negotiated with it have given no indication that it had criminal connections."

Contrast the Warren Report with a July 30, 1957, internal AFL-CIO report filed by then-AFL-CIO Vice-President Joseph A. Bierne to President George Meany, which described the Waste Handlers Union as "largely a shakedown operation" in 1939.

To arrive at its conclusion the Warren Report also had to ignore a crucial FBI interview with Paul Rowland Jones, the Chicago crime syndicate's liaison to Dallas underworld operations.[6] Jones said that when he first met Ruby in Chicago, he was given immediate assurances by mobsters Jimmy Weinberg and Paul (Needle-Nose) Labriola (both of whom eventually were found together, garroted in the trunk of a car, in a double gangland killing) that Ruby was known to them and was "all right" so far as the syndicate was concerned. The FBI report said Jones understood that Ruby "had been working in Chicago as some kind of organizer for the Scrap Iron Workers Union. Jones knew that the syndicate had an interest in this union and presumed this was Ruby's connection. He emphasized this did not mean that Ruby was in any way a top man or a dominant figure in the syndicate but merely that he was accepted and to a certain extent his business operations controlled by the syndicate, at least during the time that he was in Chicago."

Another of Jack Rubenstein's associates at the time of his union job, it was reported, was Nathan Gumbin. They both frequented the same gambling place. Like Weinberg and Labriola, Gumbin was wiped out in Chicago's mob warfare, catching a shotgun blast in his car.

Several months after Dorfman took over the new union, Rubenstein left abruptly. From there he went into the business of manufacturing and distributing punchboard gambling devices, as partner in a company with no fixed address. The company operated out of a series of cheap hotel rooms. At the age of 32, in mid-1943, he obtained a more permanent address as a draftee in the Army Air Force.

Rubenstein spent his part of World War II at southern U.S. bases. He was an aircraft mechanic who sold punchboards on the side, shot craps, played poker, seldom used his fists in anger, earned a good conduct medal, kept a low profile and got his discharge on February 21, 1946, as a private first class.

He and his three brothers went into partnership then, manufacturing and distributing punchboards, miniature cedar chests, key chains, and small kitchen items such as bottle openers. It was like old times, being back together again, which meant they quarreled loudly. Hyman Rubenstein, nine years older than Jack and as if a generation removed from his brothers, was the first to stalk off from the Earl Products Company in anger. Earl, Sam and Jack remained, changing their last name legally to Ruby. Earl, who founded the company and who would be the most successful businessman of the four, believed they could attract more business with a shorter, more "American" last name. But the Rubys didn't fight among themselves any less than the Rubensteins had done. When Jack, the sales manager, decided he was going to sell another company's line of goods on the side, Earl and Sam decided he wasn't. He threatened to ruin them in court and it became a bad family split. Jack didn't speak to those two brothers for several years. Earl and Sam remained partners until about 1954—when they stopped speaking. Jack got Sam to start speaking to him again by 1955, and promptly borrowed $5,500 from Sam to get out of one of his tax jams with the federal government. As a result Sam sued Jack for the money in 1956 and they weren't speaking again.

Jack Ruby's original partnership with his brothers had lasted about a year. They paid him off with more than $14,000 in cash to get rid of him in 1947, the year he left Chicago and appeared in Dallas.

Subsequently Ruby confided that the needs of the mob got him "exiled from Chicago." He had wanted to go to California in 1947, but instead "was directed" to go to Dallas.[7]

Was that just Ruby talking to make himself out to be a necessary soldier in the Chicago gangland's takeover strategy in Dallas? Ruby was a talker and he often overrated his own importance, even as a thug.

But whatever the specific reason for Jack Ruby's settling in Dallas, it obviously was motivated by the criminal actions of unsavory people. And the Chicago syndicate's Paul Rowland Jones played a role in it.

CHAPTER 6

Put That In Your Pipe & Smoke It

In meetings on October 9 and 26, 1946, Paul Rowland Jones talked privately with Lieutenant George Butler of the Dallas police department and the two discussed large plans. To pique the policeman's interest, Jones slipped Butler $70 in two bills and a .357-magnum pistol.

Jones said his crime syndicate connections extended from coast to coast and even to other nations. The syndicate controlled a flow of post-World War II black-market commodities that reached Europe through Spain by way of Vera Cruz, he said. In addition, Jones said his crowd's flourishing Chicago policy racket was being exported into Mexico, and now there were domestic plans for Dallas. The 37-year-old Jones was tough. He had been convicted in Kansas in the murder of a state's witness, but he spoke now as a business executive outlining a timetable for a new industrial plant. His people would be ready to move in, in another six months. There would be the horse-race wire for Dallas bookie shops, operated out of Chicago by the Tony Accardo-Greasy Thumb Guzik operation. There would be slot machines, whiskey distribution and a permanent "super-duper" crap game. A prominent and influential Dallas attorney would handle the payoffs to Dallas county authorities. The two key county authorities were the sheriff and district attorney and both these posts were being filled by new men in the November elections. Dallas elections were no different from those anywhere else in Texas, in that the political winners were decided in the Democratic party primaries held earlier in the year. So of course Butler knew the new sheriff would be Steve Guthrie and Will R. Wilson would become district attorney.

Butler and Guthrie had been on the payoff-riddled Dallas police force together, and Butler advised Jones to stay away from Wilson—because Wilson was too clean to fool with. Twenty-five years later Wilson would become one of the first figures of scandal in the Nixon administration. Will Wilson was head of the Criminal Division in the Justice Department under Nixon's Attorney General, John N. Mitchell, when Wilson's name was linked to the Sharpstown banking and securities scandal in Texas. He had to be fired by Mitchell in October, 1971, when it became known that funds from Wilson's own Sharpstown bank account had been used to pay for the electronic eavesdropping of bank examiners going through the Sharpstown books.

So Steve Guthrie was the man set up for Paul Rowland Jones to deal with, except it was Jones who was being set up. In the three meetings that followed, motion pictures from a hidden camera were taken of Jones entering Guthrie's house and conversations between the sheriff-elect and the syndicate payoff man were overheard by a hidden microphone. They were monitored and recorded by officers of the Texas State Department of Public Safety.

The first meetings took place the night of November 1, with Jones, Butler and Guthrie talking for five and a half hours, until 1:30 a.m. Jones offered Guthrie a minimum annual take of $150,000 in a 50-50 split of the principal action, with the mob to call all the shots.

After that meeting Jones flew to Chicago to convey the message to syndicate bosses Accardo, Guzik and Murray (the Camel) Humphreys that they could do business with the new sheriff. On November 3, Jones telephoned Butler from Chicago and set up the second meeting with Guthrie.

November 5, election day, Jones returned to Dallas accompanied by five mob confederates—three from Chicago and two from Las Vegas—representing various areas of syndicate interests. Two of them, Pat Manno and Jack Nappi, participated in parts of the next two meetings with Jones, Butler and Guthrie on November 6 and 7. A final meeting was held December 13.

During these sessions it was determined that the mob would bring in its own man from out of town in 1947 to operate a new, expensive restaurant at the corner of Commerce and Industrial, to serve as a front for the widespread gambling and syndicate business activities to be installed in the Dallas area.

Guthrie had been out of office for several years by the time Jack Ruby shot Oswald. The former sheriff talked to the FBI then and said Ruby specifically had been named by Jones in the recorded conversations as the outsider who would be brought in to front for the syndicate in the spring of 1947.

Ruby kept a little daily memorandum book in 1947, in which he noted social and business appointments. The book was not made available to the Warren Commission and hasn't ever been made public, but it shows that Ruby began to appear in Dallas in the spring of 1947 and moved there later in the year.

The Warren Commission never talked to Guthrie and instead used two arguments to refute him: first that Lieutenant Butler of the police department said Ruby's name never came up; and secondly that Ruby's name was not heard on any of the recordings. Those were strong arguments, except for two weaknesses: the Warren Commission never talked to Butler and never heard all the 1946 recordings. One of the records (sides no. 8 and 17) from the November 1 meeting at Guthrie's house was and still is missing, according to Butler himself.[1] The final Warren Report indicated there were 22 records and Ruby's name did not come up, yet there actually were 42 records and the Warren Report never hinted that some of the recorded evidence had disappeared.

Also, the records never were played in Jones's bribery trial, despite an attempt by his lawyers to have them heard by the jury. The lawyers contended there was ample proof on the records that Jones had been enticed by Butler and Guthrie into making a deal—instead of it being the other way around.

Jones was found guilty of attempted bribery and appealed his three-year sentence on grounds that he had been entrapped by a well-established corrupt law-enforcement system in Dallas. While the sentence was on appeal, Jones had several dealings in Dallas with Eva L. Grant, Jack Ruby's sister, who was hooked up with a con-artist named Dr. Waldon Duncan, a medical quack who practiced as a chiropractor. Eva Grant and Duncan were having an affair and were preparing to open the Singapore Supper Club together in a tough section of Dallas.

Eva Grant had come to Dallas to sell Hyman Rubenstein's line of aluminum salt and pepper shakers. She was a good-looking woman, two years older than Jack Ruby, but tough-talking and at ease with mob-connected people such as Paul Rowland Jones.

Jones became involved with the shipment of narcotics in 1945 from Mexico into the United States, and at the same time made trips to Chicago, where he saw Hyman Rubenstein and Jack Ruby.[2] On one of the trips, Jones and two confederates, Taylor Crossland and Maurice C. Melton, met with Hyman Rubenstein. The next day Rubenstein mailed a "sample" three-quarter-inch piece of metal pipe to Jones in Dallas. Soon after, Eva Grant mailed a six-inch length of one-and-three-quarter-inch pipe from Dallas to Chicago. As a result of the transaction—the exchange of pipe sections—federal narcotics agents interviewed Jack Ruby and his older brother in Chicago, at the time Jones, Crossland and Melton were arrested for transporting $1 million worth of raw and smoking opium across the border at Piedra Negras.

"For all I know they were shipping narcotics in iron pipe but I didn't know anything about it," Jack Ruby later told the Secret Service.[3]

In the week before he was arrested on the narcotics deal, Jones made arrangements with Hyman Rubenstein to ship 700 gallons of bulk four-year-old whiskey to a bootlegger in Oklahoma, which still was a dry state. The shipment was to be made in cases indicating there were salt and pepper shakers inside.

Meanwhile Waldon Duncan and Eva Grant were arrested in Dallas on a $2,700 swindle charge. Jack Ruby bailed her out and got the charge against her dropped after the indictment. That was the end of her romance with Duncan, and Ruby remained to help his sister run to Singapore. But they couldn't get along any better than the Ruby brothers could. "She was temperamental and belligerent," Ruby recalled. "I have been close to her, not that I wanted to be, and wherever I went I couldn't shake her."[4] Ruby gave his sister more than $300 to go away. She went to California and didn't return to live again in Texas for several years. As sole proprietor of the Singapore Supper Club one of the first things Ruby did was to change its name to the Silver Spur. He featured Western string music and dressed himself in a pure white dude-ranch getup. But the Chicago Cowboy, as Ruby was known as at first, didn't prosper at the Silver Spur. Not only was the neighborhood bad but Paul Rowland Jones and his sinister associates hung out at the Silver Spur until Jones went away on the narcotics rap to Leavenworth and on the bribery conviction to the state penitentiary at Huntsville, in a pair of back-to-back sentences.

The Warren Commission concluded Jack Ruby's transfer to Dallas had nothing to do with syndicate plans. But the timing of his arrival and the pattern of his actions in 1947 were like his timing and pattern would be in the police station basement 16 years later: the movements of a man who was expected.

Only a few days after Ruby got the Silver Spur under way, a man who called himself Ralph Paul showed up in Dallas and leased another drinking place, similar to Ruby's, the Sky-Vu Club. Ralph Paul was 48, unmarried, an immigrant with an Eastern European Jewish accent, who had lived his American life in New York City. Texas couldn't be more foreign to him, and he claimed he knew no one there. Ralph Paul just suddenly showed up with an "entertainer" named Joe Bonds, and a considerable amount of money. The two took over the Sky-Vu. A few months later, in 1948, they bought the Blue Bonnet Bar, a notorious downtown hangout for criminals, on the first floor of a fleabag hotel.

"Entertainer" was a word Ralph Paul used to decribe his partner, Joe Bonds, whose real name was Joseph Locurto and who had a criminal background. Bonds and Ruby began to run together, as the term is applied in Texas to describe a friendly relationship.

"Ruby and Bonds always carried concealed pistols and were in constant association with James Robert Todd, better known as Jack Todd, a well-known Dallas safe-cracker. Ruby, Bonds and Todd, together with other hoodlums and safe-crackers, usually hung around Sue's Used Car Lot, 3400 Live Oak, in Dallas," according to a report filed by FBI special agent Ralph J. Miles on August 11, 1953.[5]

When Joe Bonds was arrested for committing sodomy and conducting a white slavery racket out of the Blue Bonnet, Jack Ruby was upset. His buddy was sent down to Huntsville for eight years and Ruby "felt he was suspected of being tied into the Chicago syndicate. 'They wanted to run me out of town,' " Ruby said later.[6] But Ruby stayed and his dealings with Ralph Paul were always on another level entirely. Ruby used Paul as a money supplier.

Over the years Ruby "borrowed" more than $5,000 from the older man, who remained a mysterious, silent partner behind clubs fronted by Ruby. Ralph Paul told the Warren Commission he never got a dime back from any of his loans to Ruby over the years. Paul held 50 percent of the stock in Ruby's Carousel but rarely went there and claimed he didn't know who held other controlling interests in the Carousel.

Paul operated the Bull Pen, a drive-in restaurant in Arlington, about 20 miles west of the Carousel. On the night before Ruby shot Oswald, Ralph Paul got a telephone call from Ruby at the Bull Pen, and Paul's end of the conversation was overheard by one of Paul's car-hop waitresses, Wanda Sweatt Helmick. She reported hearing Ralph Paul blurt out to Ruby at one point, "Are you crazy? A gun?" The telephone call itself was not disputed but Paul stoutly denied to the Warren Commission that there had been any mention of a gun. The Commission never explored the whole subject of Ralph Paul adequately—his background, what he knew and what he wasn't saying.

From 1947 to 1963 Jack Ruby operated a series of nightclubs, most of them failures. They were the Silver Spur, the Bob Wills Ranch House, the Vegas (in partnership with Joe Bonds at first), Hernando's Hideaway, the Sovereign and the Carousel. The failures stacked up and in 1953 Ruby was so deeply in debt that he plunged into a deep depression. Alternately he talked angrily of killing one of his partners and despondently of doing away with himself. Instead Ruby took a room in a cheap hotel, the Cotton Bowl, pulled down the shade and stayed there for weeks, barely eating. His face grew pale and he looked as shabby as he felt. Ruby hadn't felt this way since he was a kid, when his parents broke up and he had no desire to get out of bed any more to go to school. Ruby was 42 now but he felt like that kid again. Hurting. He dragged himself home to Chicago, checked into the YMCA and found he couldn't even face his family. It was the worst depression that overtook Ruby at any time before the death sentence was handed down for his murder of Oswald, but he overcame it without medical help and returned to the Dallas he knew.

He considered Dallas to be a place of honky tonks, strippers and stale, beer-stained air. "You had to know this place to know what went on," he recalled. "You could get exonerated for murder easier than you could for burglary."[7] There was a great deal of truth to Ruby's observation about Texas justice. Endless court records in Texas bear that out. And that was a factor in Ruby's thinking when he decided to kill Oswald.

Ruby was fond of recalling that on the first night he put the Silver Spur into operation he found a traditional underworld warning from an anonymous Texas gangster for Ruby to watch his step—five bullets on a table—and Ruby always claimed there were local forces trying to run him out of town, or rob him. As a result, "I always carry a gun," he told the FBI.[8] "I have no permit and the Dallas police know I carry a gun to protect my business." He was arrested once in 1953 on a charge of attempted murder with a concealed weapon, after he beat a man unmercifully with his gun. When the Dallas police located him in a booth in a late-night restaurant, Ruby had the gun in his right-hand pants pocket. But the wording on the arrest sheet showed that he had been apprehended only for possessing a concealed weapon and he was released when no charge was filed. Despite the frequency and severity of Ruby's brawls (the end of Ruby's right-hand index finger was bitten off to the first joint in one of those Dallas fights), often no charges were brought against him by his terrified victims. It was widely recognized, too, that Ruby often knew he would win his fights before they began. He liked to beat up drunks and more than once he would punch some woman hard enough to knock her down the steps at his club.

There is no doubt that Ruby was protected by certain police in Dallas. His rap sheet showed he was arrested nine times in 16 years. These included charges that Ruby was operating an illegal after-hours saloon—a serious enough offense to shut him down. But no serious charges ever stuck. The greatest penalty he had to pay was $35 for having ignored a traffic summons.

One time Ruby used his gun to slug an off-duty Dallas policeman over the head in a fight inside the Carousel. No charges were brought against him. In fact an investigating police captain assured Ruby that no apology would be necessary and the proprietor of the Carousel was allowed to continue unimpeded with his policy of supplying free bottles of booze on the side to the cops and reduced rates for them inside the club.

Jack Ruby denied any first-hand knowledge of narcotics shipments flowing into the United States from Mexico and the Caribbean, when federal agents questioned him in Chicago, in 1947, as a result of Paul Rowland Jones's activities. However, Ruby's name continued to come up in Dallas as someone knowledgeable about narcotics traffic.

Early in 1956, Eileen Curry, a Los Angeles prostitute and occasional police informant, set up shop in Dallas with James Breen, a narcotics transporter. On March 18, 1956, she telephoned a contact she had in the Los Angeles FBI office, special agent Ambrose K. Law, to report worriedly that she thought Breen had met with foul play at the hands of members of a large Texas narcotics ring. "She believes James made connections with the narcotics ring through a former associate from Seagoville Prison [a federal facility east of Dallas]," agent Law wrote in a report he filed on March 20. "In some fashion James got the okay to operate through Jack Ruby of Dallas." The ring was reported to be a major conveyor of narcotics into the nation's northeast states.

In his ongoing role of police tipster, Ruby got angry at one of his female employees who had given him a forged check in 1961. Ruby tipped the vice squad that she was handling narcotics, and when they raided her apartment they found her with dangerous drugs on the premises.

The Commission failed to look into an earlier arrest of Jack Ruby by a law officer in Aztec, New Mexico, in the course of what some Dallas sources believed to be a narcotics-related trip by Ruby.

Ruby was jailed in Aztec, in a remote area on the north side of the state near the Colorado border, after he was caught driving an overdue rental car. For Ruby, a devoted city creature, this foray off the main highways of New Mexico was an unexplained aberration.

Ruby was reported to be active in other areas of Dallas crime. Police detective Morris Brumley, for instance, learned in the fall of 1961 that the Carousel owner was obtaining false identification for a 17-year-old prostitute and former reform-school inmate, so she would appear older and have a name that wouldn't be traced by the vice squad. She was working for Ruby as a stripper.

Meanwhile, the FBI was told by a prisoner in Mobile, Alabama, Jack Hardee Jr., that in 1962 Ruby was supposed to have been in control of the policy gambling wheel in Dallas County. Hardee's information came to the FBI a month after Ruby killed Oswald and is suspect, primarily because no one ever reported that kind of power by Ruby before the Oswald affair, and Hardee had been no more than a transient in the Dallas area in 1962.

But Ruby was active in the area's gambling circles. His name was on a list of elite Dallas-Fort Worth professional gamblers found in the possession of Dallas gambler Harry Siedband, when Siedband was arrested in Oklahoma City in 1959. Also on the list was Elmer Ray Soloman, an owner of Sol's Turf Bar, where illegal bets were placed and where Ruby hung out. Ruby was there the afternoon before he shot Oswald.

Ruby also frequented a liquor store at 2700 Ross Avenue, which was a front for a bookie and horse-wire operation. Ruby especially liked to bet on boxing matches and liked to be around fighters, but he maintained a lifelong interest in all sports events and bet on whatever was in season.

One of Ruby's West Coast gambling associates was Harry Hall, also known as Harry Haller, Harry Helfgott and, on his visits to Ruby in Dallas, as Harry Sinclair Jr. or Ed Pauley Jr.

Hall was younger than Ruby but they had a lot in common. Both were from the same general Chicago neighborhood and both maintained connections with Teamsters racketeers. Like Ruby, Hall frequently was an unpaid informer to law-enforcement agencies because he thought it was a good self-interest policy. But Hall was arrested more than Ruby. He was an accomplished swindler and he hung around in the Mafia big leagues in Las Vegas and California, with such people as John Rosselli, Eugene Hale Brading and the La Costa Country Club set.

Hall and Ruby had mutual gambling connections in the early 1950s. Ruby visited Hall in California and the two traveled together to Chicago, Tulsa and Shreveport where, according to what Hall told Secret Service agents in 1963, Ruby had "good connections" among the gamblers.

With Ruby's help, Hall on occasion would set up large bets with wealthy Texans on major sporting events. Ruby would take a 40 percent cut of the profits when Hall would win "because he was supposed to have influence with the police, so there would be no worry about any gambling arrest," Hall told Guy H. Spaman, the special agent in charge of the Los Angeles Secret Service bureau. When Hall lost, using one of his fictitious names, he would skip town after writing a bad check.

One time, Hall and Ruby won a large amount of money from oil-magnate H. L. Hunt on the Cotton Bowl and Rose Bowl football games, after Ruby arranged a meeting between the two.

Because of that gambling connection and because Ruby was reported to have been in or near the Hunt offices the day before the Kennedy assassination, and had two of Hunt's politically conservative "Life Line" radio scripts in his car the day he shot Oswald, old man Hunt feared that he might become an object of investigation by the Warren Commission.

Hunt quickly bankrolled his own investigation of the Kennedy murder and related events.

The Hunt probe was tightly kept secret but it was extensive and was headed by Paul M. Rothermel, a former FBI agent, in charge of security for H. L. Hunt.

About the only thing of lasting interest from the Hunt probe is the smattering of FBI reports in the file. Hunt was getting the top-secret FBI reports at a time when the American public wasn't allowed to see them.

One thing H. L. Hunt certainly learned from them was that he had lost a couple of football bets to a con-artist who wasn't really Harry Sinclair Jr. after all.

CHAPTER 7

In Search Of Class

Jack Ruby fired one shot at Lee Harvey Oswald and was thrown to the basement garage pavement in the Dallas police station. One of the arresting officers, detective Don Ray Archer, told Ruby that Oswald appeared to be dead.

Nearly three months later Archer recalled that Ruby "just looked at me straight in the eye and said, 'Well, I intended to shoot him three times.' "

Even though such a statement by Ruby would have reflected a murder plan, Archer said nothing about it in his arrest report, nor did he mention it to the police department's own team of investigators who were probing Ruby's "spur-of-the-moment" shooting of Oswald. "I just didn't recall [the alleged statement] as important information at the time," Archer said later.

When Archer did recall it, in February, 1964, three weeks before Jack Ruby's murder trial would begin, he was in a private meeting with William F. Alexander, the tight-lipped, narrow-eyed, rawboned assistant district attorney who liked to carry a gun stuffed into his belt and who would be playing a key role in the prosecution of Jack Ruby.[1]

Alexander was more the archetype East Texas prosecutor than a slick city public defender. He was a man of hatred and distrust toward those he considered to be *outsiders*. He reflected a segment of his city's establishment when he spat his tobacco juice and said, "Jack Ruby was about as handicapped as you can get in Dallas. First he was a Yankee. Second, he was a Jew. Third, he was in the nightclub business." Eventually Alexander left the district attorney's office, after stating that Chief Justice Warren didn't need impeachment—but needed hanging. Bill Alexander was an outspoken political rightwinger who maintained a network of associations within the Dallas police department.

On February 18, in the time period when Alexander was meeting with detective Archer and other police officers, a written report suddenly was filed by police sergeant Patrick Dean to Chief Jesse Curry, with bombshell information in it.

Dean had been the officer in charge of making certain no harm would come to Oswald in the police station basement on the morning of Oswald's murder. After Oswald was shot, Dean accompanied Forrest Sorrels, the Secret Service official, to question Ruby on the fifth floor of the police station.

"Sorrels asked Ruby if he thought or planned to kill Oswald," Sergeant Dean wrote to Chief Curry in his February 18 report, "and Ruby stated he first thought of killing him when he observed Oswald in the showup room two nights earlier. He stated that the thought came to him when he observed the sarcastic sneer on Oswald's face when he was on the showup stage. He stated that when he saw Oswald on that night he thought it would be ridiculous to have a trial for him when he knew the results would be the death penalty, since Oswald had killed the President and officer Tippit."

As had been the case with detective Archer, Sergeant Dean had put none of Ruby's "admission" of premeditated murder into his original departmental report on the shooting of Oswald, submitted two days after the shooting. Dean also had said nothing about it to the FBI, in an interview eight days after the shooting.

But the Dean report of February 18 set the stage for Dean and Archer to testify at the trial that Ruby had been a solitary gunman, who had contemplated the murder on his own, as much as two nights in advance of his pulling the trigger. The advantage of the police testimony, of course, would be to tighten the case against Jack Ruby as a loner.

Exactly two months after Dean's damaging public testimony, Sorrels told the Warren Commission behind closed doors that Ruby had made no such admission of premeditation in front of him.

Jack Ruby was in a hurry to start reaping publicity dividends from the moment he shot Oswald. When Sergeant Dean escorted agent Sorrels to interview Ruby, just after Ruby had been brought to the fifth floor of the jail and stripped to his underwear for a frisking, Ruby mistook Sorrels for a magazine writer or an out-of-town newspaper reporter and was ready to do business. He only hesitated about talking when he learned Sorrels was from the Secret Service. A day later, Bill Alexander brought a psychiatrist into Ruby's cell for an interview and the prisoner began seeking advice on how to hire an agent to handle the book and show-business offers he anticipated would come his way. But Ruby thought in small publicity terms, compared to his chief lawyer, Melvin M. Belli. Law professors John Kaplan and Jon R. Waltz explain:

> Belli was not only an important lawyer but, in the crudest sense, a successful one. At the traditional 30 to 40 percent contingent fee charged by plaintiffs' personal-injury lawyers, the "more adequate award" brought, at the very least, adequate compensation to those who were fortunate enough to attract the right clients. And these Belli had. In addition to all his other talents, Belli possessed a genius for publicity and, as he became better known, more and more of the seriously injured sought him out. Belli's big cases frequently gave credence to an old saying of plaintiffs' practitioners: If the injuries are bad enough, the liability will take care of itself. Melvin Belli did not often lose, and his income reflected this fact.
>
> Belli's style of living was appropriate to his income. He drove a Rolls Royce and had three residences: a $200,000 house and penthouse apartment in San Francisco, and the third, where he was to meet Earl Ruby, a retreat complete with swimming pool in the Hollywood hills.[2]

Jack Ruby's brother Earl took over his brother's business and legal arrangements immediately and it didn't take him long to decide that Tom Howard, who operated out of a store-front office across the street from the Dallas police station, didn't have enough class to manage Jack Ruby's defense. Earl, who had become established in business in Detroit, flew to California to negotiate with Belli. They agreed to a $25,000 fee, which was less than half of what Belli sought, but the lawyer figured he would make up the difference by producing a book out of the trial. Belli was a man of super-confidence and Kaplan and Waltz explain how that came naturally to him:

> Everything about his appearance was remarkable. A handsome, leonine man, grown perhaps overportly from good living, he wrapped his large frame in custom-tailored suits of Continental cut and a topcoat trimmed with Persian lamb. His suits were lined with flaming red silk and he sported a red velvet briefcase. He affected a black Homburg hat and black leather boots specially made for him in London—they were to be the subject of poorly concealed derision in Dallas, assistant prosecutor Bill Alexander christening them "fruit boots"—while a heavy gold chain and fob ran from vest pocket to vest

pocket across his paunch. His San Francisco office . . . was located in a 114-year-old beer hall which is the second oldest surviving structure in the city and a California state historical landmark. Belli renovated the structure, named it the Belli Building, and filled it with turn-of-the-century furnishings at a cost of nearly half a million dollars. A huge front window, rimmed by gaslights, gave passers-by an unobstructed view of Belli at his desk beneath a huge, idealized portrait of himself. . . . Atop the building were a cannon and flagstaff. Belli celebrated courtroom victories by firing the cannon and running a skull-and-crossbones up the staff.

Earl Ruby expected Belli to slip into Dallas quietly for a test meeting with the prisoner, to see if they could work together. But the flamboyant lawyer attracted the attention of newspapers and television. He arrived with a retinue which included a camera crew because he intended to have a movie made of his handling of the Ruby case. He was a man Jack Ruby could understand and they hit it off just fine. Ruby was not the midway impresario with rings on his pudgy fingers that Belli had expected to encounter. Ruby was making the best exterior impression he could—in trim white jail coveralls, his shoes shined, hair slicked back and his face freshly shaved. He reminded Belli of an earlier client, West Coast mobster Mickey Cohen. "If you had to pick Cohen up to drive him to court at 8:30, he would have to start getting himself ready at 5:30. Ruby was the same type."

Ruby already had checked out Belli through a contact in Chicago and had heard all-right things about the lawyer who had good underworld references. Ruby and Belli had at least one mutual Texas friend, Candy Barr, the paroled stripper with whom Ruby had been in recent contact. After Candy Barr's 1957 arrest for possession of narcotics, Mickey Cohen lined up Belli to serve as her attorney, and Belli got big Joe H. Tonahill of Jasper, Texas, as his associate in the Texas narcotics case. Again, in the Ruby case, Belli turned to Tonahill to serve as his principal Texas partner in Ruby's defense.

They were an awesome match, Belli and Tonahill—the latter looking like the former University of Texas varsity wrestler he was. Aged 50 and standing six-feet-four, Tonahill had let his size balloon to 300 pounds and every court room entrance he made was impressive, especially with a voice that dealt with judges and juries in a rich *basso-profundo*.

Belli gave the impression of an international liberal, an anathema in a Dallas court of law. But Tonahill had the cornpone in him and his office was a short piece east, through the rugged East Texas pines and swamps, from Martin Dies Jr. State Park, named after the late communist-hunting chairman of what once was the House Un-American Activities Committee on Capitol Hill.

Tonahill himself was the son-in-law of the extremely conservative

Virginia congressman, Judge Howard W. Smith, the chairman of the House Rules Committee who had blocked, or tried to block, almost every piece of progressive Kennedy administration legislation from getting to the House floor for debate. And Tonahill's town, Jasper, was nestled in the bosom of one of the most politically conservative Democratic areas of a conservative state.

The Tonahill Building on Lamar Street in Jasper is nothing like the Belli Building in San Francisco. But Tonahill works in an eclectic, cavernous office on the first floor of his building, behind a massive desk, faced by rugged cowhide-covered chairs. The office is jammed with books, oddly assorted hats, statuary and a tattered football, which had been mauled by a Baylor University mascot bear, lying snugly on a thick bearskin rug. Like Belli, Tonahill became established through personal-injury cases.

Belli, of course, called the shots on what Ruby's defense would be, and he selected two avenues. The first of these was Ruby's "insanity." Belli seemed certain from the outset that he would establish a medically sound reason for a plea that Ruby had acted uncontrollably and spontaneously in shooting Oswald.

The scientist chiefly responsible for developing the exact line of Ruby's medical defense was Dr. Roy Schafer who, after three days of extensive personal analysis of the prisoner, reported to Belli on January 7, 1964, that Ruby was a victim of psychomotor epilepsy and had killed Oswald while in a form of blackout. Dr. Schafer had impressive credentials as staff psychologist and associate clinical professor of psychiatry and psychology at Yale University. But Tonahill strongly disagreed with Belli's decision to go with a medical defense.

Tonahill says now that if he had been in charge of Ruby's defense or could run the trial over again, there are three major things he would do differently.[3]

First, he would build the case around a "state of mind defense" and appeal to the jury's strong Texas sense of anti-communism and patriotism. He explains:

"State of mind would have involved Ruby being incensed at the killing of Jack Kennedy like everybody else was: Would the jurors want to send a man to the electric chair for killing a communist? Wouldn't they consider it to be un-Texan to send an ex-soldier with a good-conduct medal [Ruby earned the medal as private-first-class draftee assigned to U.S. bases during World War II] to the electric chair for killing a communist? Would the jurors want to be the first members of a Texas jury who sent a man to the electric chair for killing a communist who had killed the President? Well, state of mind I thought was the defense. So I would go back to state of mind. Ruby's state of mind. And I would insist that he testify."

That's the second major difference between the way Tonahill would have run the defense and the way Belli ran it. Belli kept Ruby off the stand. Belli didn't trust Ruby's mouth. He didn't know what the defendant might blurt out. Perhaps Belli was not sure of Ruby's motives on the day Oswald was shot.

Thirdly, Tonahill says he would have used a radically different medical defense for Ruby than the one chosen. Tonahill would have claimed it was not Ruby's bullet but an embolysm—a clot caused by the medical treatment he was given at Parkland Hospital—which killed Oswald. Tonahill argued privately with Melvin Belli that the Oswald autopsy report should be a line of defense.

"Dr. Howard Wilcox of Beaumont was the pathologist we consulted," Tonahill recalls. "A very outstanding pathologist. One of the outstanding pathologists in America. He ascertained that Oswald died of an air embolysm instead of a gunshot wound. I wanted to develop that but Mel didn't think it would work. We could have made a good, strong issue there that he wasn't killed by the gunshot but was killed by the doctors giving him blood, new blood, that induced an air embolism that led to his death."

Dr. Tom Shires, chief of the surgery staff at Parkland, who led the skilled team that worked over Oswald, said that Oswalf was given constant transfusions, which might support Tonahill's argument. The transfusions were fed into numerous areas of the body as Oswald's blood pressure dropped drastically while the doctors worked over him. When they opened him up they found massive internal bleeding, amounting to several liters of blood. They found the aorta (the main artery from the heart) and the vena cava (which supplies blood to the right auricle of the heart) had been ruptured. The bullet also had passed through the spleen, into the pancreas, right kidney and the right lobe of the liver. With that kind of damage, even with the interior bleeding halted, heavy transfusions were required. When Belli got Dr. Earl F. Rose on the stand he just barely raised the embolysm issue. Dr. Rose was Dallas County medical examiner and had conducted the autopsy. As a witness Dr. Rose said he did discover the air embolysm but determined that it had been caused by the bullet slicing through the vena cava. With that, Belli dismissed his partner Tonahill's argument by asking Dr. Rose a leading question:

"Even from seeing the massive internal hemorrhage of spleen, kidney, stomach, aorta and other damage, to your knowledge of these cases, it would have been impossible to save this man by any surgery?

"I believe his wounds were of sufficient magnitude where it would have been impossible to save him, yes, sir," said Dr. Rose.

Instead Belli doggedly pursued the complicated psychomotor epilepsy defense. Both sides put on experts and their scientific debates were inconclusive, except that they caused the jurors noticeably to grow drowsy. Belli's argument was that Ruby's afflicted brain would at times shut out reality.

"They say Jack has brain damage," assistant prosecutor Alexander told a group of reporters with a thin-lipped smile. "Well, we'll send them his brain from Huntsville [where the state's electric chair is installed] so they can find out."

The other avenue of Belli's defense was an all-out attack on Dallas as a place to judge the actions of Jack Ruby. Belli said the Dallas area was "so self-conscious, so inflamed with shame and with the need to find a scapegoat that it was impossible to find a fair jury there." Belli raged at the city. He tried desperately to have the trial moved to some other Texas jurisdiction and, at the change-of-venue hearing, Belli produced Stanley Marcus as a witness in behalf of moving the trial.

Marcus, one of the city's most influential civic leaders, agreed to testify and said on the stand that he had "grave reservations whether the defense or the prosecution can get a fair trial in Dallas," because the city had been tied into so many psychological knots by the assassination of Kennedy and the execution of Oswald.

District Attorney Wade asked Marcus if he didn't think anti Ruby feelings would be encountered anywhere in Texas.

Marcus paused and then said, "In Dallas the feeling is more personal."

Belli of course failed to get the trial shifted and in another pre-trial hearing his resentment grew stronger. It happened when Wade's deputy, Bill Alexander, was questioning one of the defense psychiatrists, Dr. Walter Bromberg, who had been describing Ruby's upbringing in Chicago. Alexander referred to the defendant in a way Belli was certain was a racial slur.

Belli leaped up from his seat at the defense counsel table, shouting at the judge, "I didn't get that. 'Jew boy?' Is that what he referred to?" Alexander said he only had classified Ruby as a "Jewish boy" and that Wade must not have heard him clearly. There were few witnesses to the exchange and those who were there were divided over what was said but Wade brought up the issue often after that as a symptom of Dallas persecution.

During the trial, the day after the testimony of another defense psychiatrist, Dr. Manfred Guttmacher of Baltimore, Belli went into a barber shop near the courthouse to get a trim.

Belli, a Protestant of Italian-Swiss heritage, describes what happened next:

> They were talking about the Ruby case. My picture had been plastered all over the place, but they didn't recognize me. The barber had just started to adjust the towel around my neck when I heard

someone say, ". . . and they got those Jew psychiatrists out from Maryland."

"Yeah," said someone else, "those slick Jew psychiatrists with their slick Jew lawyers."

Hitler had been out of power 19 years, but that was simply Nazi stuff. I swept away the towel and, as the barber turned a startled look toward me, I stood straight up and gave the Nazi salute. *"Achtung!"* I yelled. *"Achtung! Heil Hitler!"* And I goose-stepped out of the place while the barber stood there open-mouthed, holding the towel in his outstretched hands.[4]

Belli encountered anti-Semitism and preached anti-Dallasism. He seemed to keep Dallas on the stand night and day, while he kept Jack Ruby off the stand.

"I wanted to get on the stand and tell the truth what happened that morning," Ruby said to Chief Justice Warren three months later when the Warren Commission met with Ruby in the Dallas county jail. But Belli, according to Ruby, said, " 'Jack, when they get you on the stand, you are actually speaking of a premeditated crime that you involved yourself in.' But I didn't care, because I wanted to tell the truth."

In his uninhibited, unschooled way, Ruby told Earl Warren that "Mr. Belli evidently did not go into my case thoroughly, circumstantially. If he had gone into it, he wouldn't have tried to vindicate me on an insanity plea to relieve me of all my responsibility, because circumstantially everything looks bad for me. . . . Had Mr. Belli spent more time with me, he would have realized not to try to get me out completely free; at the time we are talking, technically, how attorneys operate."

Tom Howard, the original attorney in the Ruby affair, now edged aside because he didn't have Belli's "class," would have operated differently. "I would have pleaded him guilty and use what we call the death-house defense," Howard told Allan E. Blanchard, a reporter who had been covering the trial for *The Detroit News.* "I would have put Jack at the jury's mercy, spending a lot of time in detailed description of an electrocution. No jury can be unaffected by that."

Howard told reporters that he would have put Ruby on the stand and allowed the defendant to weep and throw himself on the jury's mercy. Howard said he then would have pleaded Ruby guilty to murder without malice, which in Texas is worth five years in prison at the most. The killing, said Howard, had a pattern similar to "just another nigger murder case"—the kind of passionate thing that is expected to happen in black neighborhoods on Saturday nights and is so trivial in Texas criminal district courts that sentences are relatively minor.

But Belli had a victory cannon on top of his building in San Francisco which he wanted to fire, and a skull-and-crossbones flag he wanted to raise. So he went for all or nothing with Ruby's life.

Joe B. Brown was a good old boy. He had grown up in Dallas, quit high school and had gone to work for the railroad. With only a grade-school diploma Brown enrolled in a short-cut law school at 23 and emerged during the Depression with a law degree. Without practicing much law, Brown was elected to the bench a year after he passed the bar—becoming a peace justice in Oak Cliff, a sprawling fundamentalist and reactionary adjunct to Dallas. After some 20 years as justice of the peace, Brown was elected to the criminal district court bench, where nearly a third of his verdicts later reviewed by the state appeals court were overturned. Judge Brown was good-natured to the point of being permissive and he remained no ardent student of the law books. One of the classic stories about him in Dallas concerns the time a ruling of his was challenged by a defense lawyer during a trial, and Judge Brown suggested the best way to settle the issue was to declare a recess so that he and the attorneys could meander into another court and seek the advice of the judge there as to how the legal point should be settled. But the most notorious episode of his judicial career took place when Judge Brown was presiding at the marijuana trial of Candy Barr. He recessed the trial, rolled his eyes at the sexpot defendant and invited her into his private chambers. There she posed for pictures for him, which he snapped from various angles. Joe B. Brown was a good old boy, who liked to eat chili, drink beer, ogle the ladies and, it was reported, read comic books while on the bench.

Distraught by all the other events that had overtaken Dallas, civic leaders there—each of whom had snickered about Judge Brown before—now were torn by the prospect of his honor, Joe Brantley Brown, presiding over a trial that would draw the news media of the world to Dallas. District Attorney Wade suggested to Judge Brown that his honor might assign the trial to another district criminal court because of the, *uh,* complexities of the case. But the judge was unyielding in his insistence that he would preside.

Following the guilty verdict, when there were various motions for a new trial and a sanity hearing for the defendant, Ruby's lawyers tried to have Judge Brown removed from the case because they learned he was trying to take advantage of his duties as judge in order to make some extra money. Judge Brown subsequently wrote a private letter to an editor at Holt, Rhinehart & Winston, Inc., the New York publishing house. In part the letter he wrote on official court stationery said:

> About the book—it perhaps is a good thing that it is not finished, because they have filed a Motion to disqualify me on the grounds of having a pecuniary interest in the case. I can refute that by stating that there has been no book published or that I have not begun to write a book.
>
> We are coming along nicely. We have approximately 190 pages complete . . .

When Jack Ruby was arrested, there was an outpouring of telegrams to him, all lauding his murder of Oswald, praising him as a hero and promising him financial support. These hot-headed endorsements made Ruby feel very important. But as the weeks and months went by, Ruby's spirits sagged. Promises of aid to support his costly legal battle never materialized. His hopes even of gaining tentative freedom faded at two bail hearings. He was kept in an isolated area of the jail, in a square cell with a mattress on the floor and a toilet bowl. He had no view of the outside world from his cell window—only of a ventilator shaft. Ruby could walk from his cell into a large enclosure, where he could play dominoes or cards with a guard posted there day and night. One way he had of maintaining contacts with the outside world was through the limited use of a payphone on his floor of the jail. The sheriff's office would use the phone as a punishment device against Ruby at times when he was said to be misbehaving as a prisoner; he would be forbidden to make calls. Belli discovered the FBI was supplying Ruby with small change for use in the phone, to encourage his indiscriminate placement of carefully monitored calls. One morning during the trial Ruby desperately telephoned Belli. "Mel, I must see you before court opens," he said. Belli appeared preoccupied and told Ruby to take a cab to the hotel where Belli was staying. "Mel," the deteriorating Ruby replied, "don't you know where I am?"

Ruby's deterioration wasn't noticeable on a day-to-day basis but the prisoner steadily grew more despondent, suspicious, weary, and resentful. He poured out these feelings on paper. Ruby constantly wrote notes that harbored his secrets, particularly when he was with his lawyers who were certain their jailhouse conversations with him were under electronic surveillance.

One day he said to Tonahill, "There's something I want to get straight." So Tonahill handed Ruby his yellow legal pad and invited the prisoner to write it down. Tonahill remembers Ruby wrote: " 'It was not my idea to say that I shot Oswald to keep Jackie [Kennedy] from coming back here to testify. I did it because Tom Howard told me to.' ... What Ruby wrote down disturbed me very much. I thought about it, walking all the way back to my hotel room. I just shook my head the whole way back. It was very upsetting."[5]

At an undated time, after the trial was over and after the issuance of the Warren Report on September 27, 1964, Ruby wrote a secretive 16-page note to another prisoner, who was leaving the jail. The prisoner, whose first name was John, apparently was a trusty who may have brought Ruby his meals. Ruby told John to memorize names and facts in the note and then destroy it. Instead, once he got out, John decided to sell the unsigned document. It was pencil-written in what has been determined to be Ruby's handwriting, on the customary four-by-six-inch white note paper he used, and in Ruby's distinctive phrasing. Charles Hamilton, the New York autographs dealer, had it appraised as authentic, bought it and later resold it to a collector in Texas. The note was pitted with Ruby's growing paranoia but it warned John that "you must realize that the people here want everyone to think I am crazy . . . and then no one will believe me, because of my supposed insanity." Early in the note Ruby made this inexplicable statement:

> To start off with, don't believe the Warren Report, that was put out to make me look innocent, in that it would throw the Americans and all the European country's off guard.

Ruby went on to say he had been framed through deceptive tactics inside the county jail (explained here in Ruby's own way):

> Now this is how they did it. They had a guard with me constantly, and this one guard in particular by name of Stevenson was well versed in the bible, and he started to work on me with the Bible routine and on his person unbeknownit to me he had one of these wireless speakers, which is very small, and he kept it in his trousers pockets. Everything we talked about and everything I said was transmitted into this tiny mike and taken on a tape recorder in another room. Now everything that may be incriminating against me they would leave on the recorder and anything I said that would prove me innocent they would erase from the recorder.
> Here is what happened one nite. I was in a very delirous mood of what had transpired in the courtroom that day. That was when I had gone back to my cell and had tried to sleep without talking to the guard, and I was very low and crying, and the guard knew I at my lowest, because Phil Burleson[6] had told him so. The guard knew I was vulnerable to admit anything. He blurted out Jack aren't you talking to me tonite, and I came to where he was sitting and I fell to the floor and broke down and said that I had sent guns to Cuba. . . .

Ruby then told John in the note that in reality he had *not* sent guns to Cuba—except for four handguns sent by mail to Lewis McWillie, the syndicate gambler in Havana. But Ruby said his words, *I had sent guns to Cuba*, were recorded and were there to be used against him.

There is no doubt that Ruby and the guard, sheriff's deputy Jess W. Stevenson Jr., had grown close. One day, in a pre-trial meeting with the press, Ruby appeared radiant. He disclosed that he had been reading the Bible with the help of an unnamed "friend" and had become "a changed man." At that point the prosecution succeeded in getting Ruby's press conferences discontinued and the friend remained unidentified.

Was Ruby's "friend" acting as an information sieve for the prosecution? Belli became convinced of it. Belli later wrote:[7]

> One of the guards gave Ruby a Bible and got in the habit of talking religion with him. Ruby became more and more obsessed with his faith as the days droned on. His conversation with us often touched

on people he thought were being nice to him, and he would mention
Sheriff Decker; then, more and more, this guard who talked religion
and read the Bible to him.

I kept hearing about this religious solace without ever getting to
meet the guard who was providing it. At the same time I was getting
the impression that somehow Henry Wade and his men were hearing
a lot more about Ruby than they should have. One day it came to
me—the guard might be their source.

I asked Jack, "What have you told him?"

"I told him everything, Mel." He stared at me innocently. "I
must have told him what happened when I shot the gun, and about
Jackie and the children; and about the story we're telling for the trial.
And he [the guard] shook his head and told me, "That won't do,
Jack.' "

The guard "worked on Ruby's conscience constantly and tried to talk
him into getting rid of his lawyers and pleading guilty," Joe Tonahill recalls. "He tried to over-persuade Ruby and Ruby would tell us about it
and we told him to be careful about what he said, and so forth, and I
didn't know but what the guy was sincere. Turned out that immediately
when the trial was over, the deputy wouldn't have anything more to do
with Ruby. . . . His job had been to undermine Ruby's confidence in his
attorneys."

Tonahill describes the guard identified in Ruby's note as "some sort
of semi-preacher who was praying with Ruby; reading the Bible with
Ruby, and then the guy left him; wouldn't have anything more to do with
him after Ruby got convicted. Boy, that really turned Ruby off then.
That's when his real deterioration came about. He just never trusted anybody after that. No faith. No trust."

Jess W. Stevenson Jr., a tall, angular Texas lawman, left the sheriff's
office in 1966, and since has become a deputy constable in the Oak Cliff
section of Dallas. His desk in the County Building is right below Peace
Justice W. J. Richburg's court, where religious tracts from an Oak Cliff
church are available to spectators.

To Stevenson, religion is fundamental and he is a member of the Full
Gospel Church. He talks about the Bible discussions he had with Ruby
but says Ruby would have nothing to do with the New Testament and
"didn't seem to know an awful lot about the Old Testament." But Stevenson says he worked on Ruby in a religious sense and one night the prisoner became deeply moved because he claimed he had a vision of his
mother there with him in his cell.

Stevenson smokes nervously as he talks about it, because he never
has been publicly identified as the guard who worked his way into Ruby's
innermost feelings, and because Stevenson appears aware that Ruby felt
deceived by him.

The deputy doesn't talk about the charge in Ruby's note that he had used a hidden microphone on Ruby, but says the prisoner would go over and over his own movements on the morning that Oswald was shot, "as if he was preparing the story in his own mind."

Sergeant Dean's account of Ruby's alleged admission in front of Sorrels of premeditated murder was the single most damaging testimony against Ruby in the trial, yet Belli decided against putting the one man on the stand who could refute Dean's story—Sorrels himself, the veteran Secret Service agent.

Sorrels was questioned privately by both District Attorney Wade and Belli and each side thought Sorrels was too risky to put on the stand. Wade was against the idea because Sorrels insisted Ruby had made no such admission to him. He had taken notes of the Ruby conversation, Dean hadn't taken notes, and testimony by Sorrels obviously would weaken or destroy Dean's account.

Meanwhile, Belli chose not to put the Secret Service agent on the stand as a defense witness because, under cross-examination by Wade or Alexander, it would be brought out that Sorrels heard Ruby refer to Oswald angrily as a son of a bitch, and heard Ruby say, "I guess I just had to show the world that a Jew has guts." Both statements could indicate to the jury that Ruby had not been simply a victim of a psychomotor epilepsy variant blackout.

Instead, Belli waited until he reached his summation to the eight-man, four-woman Waspish Dallas jury before mentioning Sorrels. Then he berated Wade for having failed to bring Sorrels to the stand to corroborate Dean's testimony.

Wade, in his summation, charged that Jack Ruby had been a glory-seeker who "wanted the limelight, he wanted publicity and he wanted to go down in history as the man who killed an alleged assassin."

After the case had gone to the jury, Wade was asked by a reporter if he really thought Ruby should be electrocuted. The district attorney said that is how he would vote if he were on the jury, "but I'd regard a life term or a long sentence as a victory." What Wade was saying was that he figured the crime was worth 10 years in prison for Ruby—since Ruby could be eligible for parole in 10 years on a life sentence.

None of the out-of-town newsmen who had been covering the trial—including several nationally well-known reporters—expected the jury to acquit Ruby, who after all had shot a helpless, manacled prisoner in front of an estimated 20 million television viewers. But most seemed to expect a long-term sentence. Even *The Dallas Morning News*, generally hostile to Ruby, indicated in its Saturday, March 14, editions that nothing like a death verdict was expected.

Saturday, March 14, the day the jury brought in its verdict, was being celebrated in Dallas with an early St. Patrick's Day parade. Before the jury came in, assistant prosecutor Bill Alexander looked out a window of the criminal courts building at one of the marching units.

"Don't you think we're pushing our luck a little," Alexander said, "having another parade for an Irishman around here?"

The death verdict the jury brought in was devastating to Jack Ruby, but one of the saddest, most poignant moments in the trial for him had slipped by almost unnoticed.

It came when Alice Reaves Nichols was called to the stand to testify. Mrs. Nichols was an anomaly in Ruby's life. She was a proper lady. Quiet. Dignified. Responsible. At 49 she was secretary to the vice-president and treasurer of a major Dallas insurance firm and had been married once, many years earlier.

Mrs. Nichols and Ruby had kept company over a period of time and he had discussed marriage with her. His relationship with her was significantly different from any others. With Alice Nichols he was more subdued; more gentle. Obviously she was someone he respected enough to think of marrying out of his faith, with all his strident Jewish emphasis. But she would not marry him and gradually they broke up.

Still, the day John F. Kennedy was killed, Alice Nichols was one of the first people Jack Ruby wanted to turn to. He telephoned her early that afternoon from the Carousel Club.

Joe Tonahill recalls the heartbreak in Ruby's face as Mrs. Nichols was called to the witness stand and passed by the defense counsel table where Ruby sat, without even looking at him.

But Robert B. Denson recalls something else. Denson, a private detective in Dallas, was serving as Belli's chief investigator and was sitting at the defense table, too. He remembers that when Alice Nichols finished her testimony, and passed by again, Ruby pushed his chair back, stood and bowed gently toward her. To Ruby, Alice Nichols represented the ultimate in class.

"And what Jack Ruby wanted more than anything else," said Denson, "was class."

CHAPTER 8

Cuba

Part I—The Two Faces of Mr. Trafficante

After the Ruby trial ended, Leon Hubert and Burt Griffin, the Warren Commission's two Ruby experts, tried to convince Commission members in memorandums on March 19 and April 1, 1964, that there was "substantial evidence" showing Jack Ruby had maintained unexplained Cuban associations. But the efforts of Hubert and Griffin were blocked by the CIA and discouraged by others on the Commission staff.

Rankin, the staff director, and Willens, his chief administrator, were against putting time and energy into investigating Ruby's Cuban angles. Despite all the loose ends spotlighted by Hubert and Griffin, "these Cuban pursuits represented some kind of bottomless pit and our overall investigation had to be wrapped up," Willens said.[1] Other staff lawyers agreed with Willens.

Therefore, the Warren Commission never explored the possible links of Ruby's Cuban activities in 1959 with his FBI contacts that year and with Ruby's totally unexplained use of a safety deposit box at the time of his Cuban and FBI interests.

Ruby rented box 448 at his bank in Dallas, the Merchants State, where he maintained a small business checking account and no savings account. He'd had no known bank safety deposit box in 11 previous years as a Dallas resident—and he rented the box the day before the first of his regular meetings as an undercover FBI contact with FBI agent Charles W. Flynn. Then he used the box 12 times in 1959,[2] in exactly the same seven-month stretch in which he was meeting nine times with Flynn.

That seven-month period included much of Ruby's known Cuban related trips and meetings in 1959.

But even as they were being thwarted within the Commission from digging into Ruby's Cuban connections, Hubert and Griffin saw no special relationship between Ruby's meetings with the FBI and his activities concerning Cuba.

"I assumed in 1964," says Griffin now, "that the FBI contacts with Ruby in 1959 were rather routine requests for information about vice and organized crime . . . I don't remember if it occurred to me in 1964 that such FBI contacts in 1959 might have been in connection with Cuban matters; but I doubt that I ever had that in mind, based on other information we had from the CIA and FBI in April, 1964. I now believe the FBI should be asked to disclose all information about the purposes of those 1959 contacts with Ruby and the information he was asked to provide, if they have not already done so."[3]

The FBI so far has said the contacts were useless; that Ruby provided no worthwhile information. But what Judge Griffin is suggesting here is something different, when he asks that the FBI make public now *what kinds of information the bureau was seeking from Ruby in 1959.*

"If Hoover concealed information that the 1959 FBI contacts were about Cuban matters," Griffin says, "such a concealment would be important and serious."

By December, 1977, the FBI released some, but not all, information out of agent Flynn's file on Ruby. It shows Ruby was listed as a PCI (potential criminal informant) and was contacted on matters concerning the interstate transportation of gambling devices, lottery tickets and obscene matter—along with questions relating to the FBI's general investigative intelligence file, which ranged broadly enough to include such categories as organized crime and Cuba.

"PCI was advised of Bureau's position regarding willingness," Flynn noted in longhand, "to pay for expenses he might incur in obtaining information . . . on a COD basis. He was further advised of the fact that such money was considered as income—reported on his income tax return."

Ruby's movements at key points in 1959 indicate a proximity of his Cuban, FBI and bank box affairs as this chronology shows:

January   1 Fidel Castro takes control of Cuba.

             8 Jack Ruby is believed to have made his first contact on

this date with Robert Ray (Dick) McKeown, a Bashore, Texas, gun-runner who had been supplying Castro with arms.

February   1   Ruby tells McKeown he represents source in Las Vegas who wants to get three Castro prisoners out of jail in Cuba (at a time when Castro had several U.S. underworld figures jailed there). Ruby meets McKeown in Kemah, Texas, and offers $25,000 for personal introduction to Castro.

March   11   Ruby meets with Dallas FBI agent Charles W. Flynn and agrees to become an FBI contact.

   15   Throughout this time period, Ruby telephones and meets with Tom Davis, the gun-runner with CIA ties, in Beaumont.

April   2   The Dallas police department's Criminal Intelligence Division lists Ruby and Lewis J. McWillie among those connected with professional gambling activities in the community.

   27   Castro travels to Houston after completing a controversial trip of several days to Washington, New York and Boston.

   27   Ruby rents safety deposit box 448 at Merchants State Bank.

   28   Castro meets with McKeown and offers him a post in the Castro government, but McKeown is serving a five-year probated federal sentence as a gun-runner and would become a U.S. fugitive if he takes off in Castro's private plane as he is invited to do. McKeown turns down the offer at the airport.

   28   Ruby meets with Flynn for first time in his role as undercover contact.

May   7   Ruby uses his safety deposit box.

   15   (approx.) Elaine Mynier of Dallas carries coded message to Cuba from Ruby. She relates message to McWillie.

   22   Ruby uses safety deposit box.

June   2   Again Ruby uses the box.

   5   Meets with FBI agent Flynn.

   18   Meets again with agent Flynn.

   22   Uses safety deposit box (in May and June Ruby entered the box twice a month).

July   1   Ruby uses safety deposit box.

   3   Norman (Roughhouse) Rothman, U.S. Mafia figure and Cuban racketeer, arrested in connection with an $8.5-million Canadian bank heist of convertible bonds. Federal

authorities link the Canadian job with a large theft of arms from an Ohio national guard armory and with Rothman's $6,000 rental agreement on an airplane, as part of a massive Cuban gun-running project.

7 Ruby meets with agent Flynn.

8 The Castro cabinet decides that Florida numbers-racket boss, Santo Trafficante Jr., key figure in the Lansky gambling empire in Havana, is to be expelled from Cuba along with two others. Trafficante, meanwhile, is held in a Havana-area jail.

9 Ruby uses safety deposit box.

20 And uses box again.

21 Then meets with agent Flynn.

August 1 (approx.) The dinner Ruby shares in an airport restaurant with one of the Fox brothers and the two criminally associated Dallas attorneys, McCord and McLane, appears to have occurred in July or August.

6 Ruby meets with agent Flynn.

31 Meets again with Flynn in the week of his departure for Cuba (in June, July and August, the FBI followed a pattern of meeting every two weeks with Ruby).

September 4 Ruby uses safety deposit box and then departs for Cuba.

5 According to estimates of Ruby and others, he spends next several days, including the long Labor Day weekend, in Cuba with McWillie, the armed syndicate gambler. Ruby also visits gangster "Louis Santos" in jail more than once, according to a British witness.

12 Ruby is in the Miami area, where gangster Rothman has an interest in the Biltmore Terrace Hotel. According to airline records, Ruby flies back to Havana for one day.

13 Ruby then flies from Havana to New Orleans.

21 Ruby uses his safety deposit box again.

October 2 Meets for last time with Flynn as a contact.

28 Opens his safety deposit box for last time in 1959 (he uses it only four times more in next 17 months and, when authorities crack open box 448 late in 1963, it is empty).

Elaine Mynier was an attractive woman, and during the 1950s in Dallas she dated the big-time syndicate gambling house operator, Lewis J. McWillie.

McWillie ran illegal gambling establishments to the east and west of Dallas County, always appeared to Elaine Mynier to be in the big money and had a bodyguard living with him.[4] She also saw him frequently with Jack Ruby, whom she considered to be "a small-time character who would do anything for McWillie, who was in the habit of being surrounded by people he could use."

McWillie was approximately Ruby's size, gray-haired, expensively turned out with a flair for style. According to Ruby, McWillie was "a very high-type person" who looked like a banker and led Ruby toward "the finer things in life."[5] McWillie's FBI record, No. 4404064, showed he used the last-name aliases of Martin, Chapman and Olney, and was considered to have been a gangland killer.

Here was a man Ruby could idolize. McWillie moved to Havana in September, 1958, and returned to the United States, January 2, 1961. On the flight back, McWillie became annoyed at another man on the plane, a Chicago school teacher who was making disparaging remarks about the United States and about President Eisenhower, who was to be replaced in the White House by John Kennedy later that month. The school teacher, Laverne Kautt, was 54, the same age as McWillie. Kautt was returning with a group of pro-Castro tourists who had gone to visit Cuba in defiance of a State Department request that they stay home. As the plane landed in Miami McWillie could stand it no more. He knocked down Kautt with one punch and then reported Kautt to the FBI. McWillie's one-punch patriotism was in the mold of the Mafia's John Rosselli, who was donating his time to the CIA as a patriotic gesture, and in the mold of Jack Ruby, who never allowed the Carousel Club's stand-up comics to make an unpatriotic remark or a religious crack. Ruby often talked about how much he admired McWillie. But when he was jailed for the murder of Oswald, Ruby drew up a list of "persons who may dislike me." The list included Lewis J. McWillie.

In May, 1959, Elaine Mynier was preparing to leave Dallas for several days to visit McWillie in Havana, when Ruby went to see her at the airport. At that point Ruby already had met once with FBI agent Flynn in his role as special undercover contact, and was preparing to meet with Flynn a second time.

Ruby gave her a code of some kind—a short jumble of numbers and letters, and this message: "Tell McWillie that Sparky from Chicago is coming." Perhaps there was a special significance to Ruby's use of his boyhood nickname in the message. But when Elaine Mynier landed at Havana Airport she recited the code she had written down, and gave McWillie the message that went with it. Then she looked at McWillie kind of expectantly but the gambler only muttered, "He's nuts."

McWillie made it seem, when two FBI agents interviewed him in Las Vegas the day after Oswald's murder, that he had only happened to have seen Ruby in Havana when Ruby spent several days there in 1959. But Ruby told those close to him after his return that McWillie had picked up the tab for his trip and had looked after him while he was there: "He sent me tickets to Cuba—think of it, a man like that sending me tickets."[6]

Before Ruby departed for Cuba he told virtually no one in Dallas about the trip. He meant for it to be conducted as secretively as possible.

Ruby, McWillie and others independently told federal investigators that Ruby was in Havana for about a week, and accumulated records show the time frame as early September, 1959—the period between Ruby's final two known meetings with Flynn as an FBI contact.

There are no U.S. Immigration and Naturalization Service records to show the dates of that Ruby visit of several days to Havana—although INS records do show that Ruby did fly from Miami to Havana on Saturday, September 12, 1959, and then from Havana to New Orleans on September 13. Ruby never was asked for an explanation of that second trip—a yoyo trip in which he bounced down to Cuba and back in a 24-hour span, after having just visited Cuba for several days.

Since there were no INS records of Ruby having made the earlier visit which Ruby said was managed with tickets sent him by McWillie, it is quite possible that McWillie, who dealt in aliases, sent Ruby tickets under an assumed name, but no federal authorities ever explored that likelihood.

Ruby told the Warren Commission that he found the trip to Cuba somewhat of a bore, with little to do while McWillie was at work.[7] But a highly classified CIA message—kept from the Warren Commission staff—indicated Ruby had found someone special to talk with during the Havana trip: an American racketeer associated with McWillie, who did use an assumed name. He was known, when he wanted to be, by the name of Louis Santos.

The classified message about Santos was sent Thanksgiving Day, November 28, 1963 (four days after Ruby shot Oswald), from CIA headquarters to: McGeorge Bundy, President Johnson's special assistant for national security affairs; U. Alexis Johnson, deputy undersecretary of state; and the FBI. The message read:

> On 26 November 1963 a British journalist named John Wilson, and also known as John Wilson-Hudson, gave information to the American Embassy in London which indicated that an "American gangster-type named Ruby" visited Cuba around 1959. Wilson himself was working in Cuba at the time and was jailed by Castro before he was deported.
>
> In prison in Cuba, Wilson says he met an American gangster gambler named Santos who could not return to the USA because there were several indictments outstanding against him. Instead he preferred to live in relative luxury in a Cuban prison. While Santos was in prison, Wilson says, Santos was visited frequently by an American gangster type named Ruby. His story is being followed up. Wilson says he had once testified before the Eastland committee of the U.S. Senate, sometime in 1959 or 1960.

The next day, according to a heavily doctored memorandum in CIA files, the FBI came up with a preliminary report that the Englishman John Wilson "likely be psychopath [sic]. We gather he gave this impression when testifying before Eastland Committee in 59."

Both the CIA message on Wilson and the following day's memorandum were kept secret until mid-1976, when Washington attorney Bernard Fensterwald Jr. flushed it out through the Freedom of Information Act, along with hundreds of other CIA documents relating to the Kennedy assassination dating as far back as 1963.

A check of the files of the Senate Judiciary Subcommittee on Internal Security, headed by Senator James O. Eastland of Mississippi, shows that while the Eastland panel explored a long list of hot political areas of Latin America in 1959 and 1960, Wilson does not appear on the witness list under any of the names he used—John Wilson, John Hudson, John Wilson-Hudson, Carl (or Carlos) J. Wilson.

U.S. embassy records in London referred to Wilson only as a self-described "free-lance journalist" residing in Chile during most of the 1940s and 1950s. Wilson told American embassy officials that he actually had been working for Cuban dictator Batista in the late 1950s, and was deported by Castro after a term of imprisonment in 1959.

But a confidential November 28, 1963, memorandum from the office of Richard M. Helms, at that time CIA deputy director for plans, reveals much more about Wilson. The CIA file on him went back to 1951.

The Helms memorandum to Sam Papich at the FBI shows that Wilson, well educated at Oxford University, had been born in Liverpool, December 29, 1916, had reached Chile on January 28, 1939, from Buenos Aires, and "was a contact of one Bert Sucharov, a suspected Soviet agent in Santiago, Chile."

Wilson was outspoken as a pro-communist and foe of the United States. He posed occasionally as a British Royal Air Force captain in uniform, and two attempts by the British embassy to have him expelled from Chile failed—after Wilson apparently convinced authorities inside the embassy that he had "worked on a special mission for the British government in Germany, Egypt and Turkey at the close of World War II."

The CIA source in Chile pegged John Wilson as "very probably an intelligence agent." Wilson always seemed to have a lot of money without an apparent income. He held UN press pass no. 287, issued in Santiago, and another pass from the Chilean secret police which allowed him special access.

At the end of June, 1959, Wilson and three Americans were arrested in a suburb of Havana as they planned to carry out a sneak bomb raid on Nicaragua, using three airplanes and a small volunteer attack force. Fidel Castro had nothing to do with the attack plans and ordered Wilson and the other ringleaders arrested; thus John Wilson was in jail at the time of the Ruby visit.

Inexplicably, one of Ruby's notebooks had this entry, which Dallas police located on the day Oswald was shot: "October 29, 1963—John Wilson—bond."

The FBI checked police and sheriff's records in Dallas to see if a John Wilson had made bond. The FBI also consulted two different private attorneys in Dallas whose names were John Wilson but who had never had dealings with Ruby. The FBI said it found no reason for the notebook entry.

There are three important facts about Wilson or Wilson-Hudson which emerge: one—the FBI never offered supportive evidence that he was not a credible person; two—Wilson's prompt appearance, November 26, 1963, concerning Ruby visiting Santos in jail, came before there were public details about Ruby's 1959 Cuba visit; three—the Santos he was talking about turned out to be the assumed name used by the U.S. Mafia figure, Santo Trafficante Jr.

Santo Sorge participated in a series of vital Mafia strategy meetings from October 10 to 14, 1957. Sorge, the international exporter of illicit narcotics, was the business ally of Alfred McLane, and McLane was the moneyed Dallas lawyer who liked intrigues and maintained a shadowy association with Ruby.[8]

Sorge and other U.S.-connected Mafiosi were reported to have given their assent during the secretive strategy meetings in the Hotel des Palmes, Palermo, Sicily, for the October 25 murder of Albert Anastasia, who himself was regarded in the New York tabloids as the Lord High Executioner of Murder, Inc.

Anastasia, reaching for control of the Mafia in New York and far beyond, had decided the time had come for him to take a slice of the action in Cuba. He wanted the gambling and international narcotics riches presided over by Cuban dictator Fulgencio Batista. In order to get at them, Anastasia knew he would have to oust Meyer Lansky, developer of the crime syndicate's dynastic partnership with Batista. Anastasia reasoned that his Mafia colleague in Florida, Santo Trafficante Jr., had become close to Batista and could take over the Lansky operation as Anastasia's lieutenant without disturbing the Batista regime's bilateral gambling agreements with The Private Government.

When crime syndicate members sent word back to Anastasia to keep his nose out of Cuba, Anastasia decided to organize his own takeover force within the syndicate. He called a summit meeting of about 100 Mafia sub-leaders from throughout the United States. Some were "sleepers"—thought of as businessmen in their communities; not known for their outfit connections—and all of them were recognized by Anastasia as being greedy for more power. They were to meet October 28. Trafficante was one of those invited, but Trafficante double-crossed Anastasia in order to protect his own burgeoning interests in Cuba. He swore allegiance to the well-entrenched Lansky and became Lansky's spy.

Trafficante spent the evening of October 24 with Anastasia in New York and left hurriedly for Florida at the snap of Lansky's fingers, before two sure-shot assailants fired 10 times into Anastasia at close range the next morning as the gangster sat in a barber's chair. Anastasia's murder never was solved, but Manhattan detectives suspected Sorge and Lansky knew the killers.

Continuing in his role as Lansky's hidden agent, Trafficante then attended the Mafia summit meeting which went ahead without Anastasia, although it was postponed for two weeks out of respect for the dead man. It was the infamous meeting at Apalachin, New York—raided by the police. A number of delegates caught in the raid were major narcotics traffickers who, as Anastasia had been, seemed ready to revolt against the rising market prices of hard drugs being moved into the United States through Cuba and other Latin American points by Santo Sorge's friends. Informed underworld sources, according to Hank Messick, the Lansky biographer, indicated the Lansky-Trafficante axis played a key role in making sure the police showed up at Apalachin.

Four years later, 1961, Trafficante still was handling his Cuban affairs as expediently as possible, which, translated, means he was available to both sides at once. This time Trafficante had become involved as a principal in Project ZR/RIFLE, the bizarre CIA-Mafia operation to overthrow the Castro regime.

It was logical for mobsters Sam Giancana and John Rosselli to work through Trafficante in their CIA project. Trafficante had developed the best gangster network between Florida and Cuba and had much to gain by dumping the Castro government, since Castro had expropriated the U.S. gambling industry's enterprises in Cuba. As Meyer Lansky's operative, Trafficante could make a bundle if Castro were removed one way or another and Havana could resume its role as the Las Vegas of the Caribbean.

On the other hand, CIA chiefs began to realize that Trafficante was sabotaging the U.S. spy agency's plan to depose Castro by acting as a double-agent—furnishing Castro with advance information about the CIA-Mafia plot to get him.

What would there be in it for Trafficante to work under the table with Castro? One payoff for the Tampa numbers racketeer might have been uncovered by George Crile III, Washington editor of *Harper's*, who disclosed in 1976 that a July 21, 1961, memorandum on file in the Treasury Department's Bureau of Narcotics said there were "unconfirmed rumors in the Cuban refugee population in Miami that when Fidel Castro ran the American racketeers out of Cuba and seized the casinos, he kept Santo Trafficante Jr. in jail to make it appear that he had a personal dislike for Trafficante, when in fact Trafficante is an agent of Castro. Trafficante is alledgedly Castro's outlet for illegal contraband[9] in the country."

Another Narcotics Bureau memorandum uncovered by Crile said that "Fidel Castro has operatives in Tampa and Miami making heavy *Bo-*

lita bets with Santo Trafficante Jr.'s organization." Bolita was the name of the numbers betting racket operated by Trafficante, and Crile suggests that the numbers game "may have served as one of the paymasters to the Cuban intelligence network in the United States."

Significantly, Trafficante became "unavailable " in 1976 to congressional investigators[10] who later wanted to talk to him privately about his knowledge of Cuban-related Mafia connections with the U.S. intelligence community during the Kennedy administration. While his fellow mobsters Giancana and Rosselli were silenced in gangland-style killings before they could respond to the growing list of questions in 1975-76 from the Senate's Church committee, Trafficante ducked the questions. He camouflaged himself by disappearing into one of his aliases, such as Louis Santos.[11]

Senator Richard S. Schweiker of Pennsylvania was virtually the only member of the Church committee eager to chase clues in the Kennedy murder case that pointed to Cuban connections. By early 1977, with the Church committee defunct, Schweiker had become privately convinced that it still was essential to pursue and intently question the elusive Trafficante in the murder case.

Before he quit the House Assassinations Committee at the end of March, 1977, chief counsel Richard A. Sprague saw to it that Trafficante was found and subpoenaed to testify before the House panel. Trafficante refused to be questioned in a closed session. When he showed up before cameras and reporters on March 16, 1977, Trafficante made a point of refusing to answer any questions posed by Sprague and committee members, to demonstrate that he would not have to be otherwised silenced.

Of special significance is Trafficante's knowledge of what went on at the Churchill Farms estate of Carlos Marcello, the tough little Mafia boss of New Orleans, when Marcello called in other organized crime leaders in September, 1962.

Trafficante was invited to attend the sinister, turbulent meeting in which Marcello demanded Kennedy blood. As a result, Trafficante knew intimately what transpired at the Churchill Farms meeting.[12]

That same month, September, 1962, Trafficante confided to José Aleman, a prominent member of the Cuban exile community in Miami, that the Kennedys could not be trusted. Trafficante complained that Robert Kennedy, the attorney general and Marcello's bitter enemy, was harassing Jimmy Hoffa, portrayed by Trafficante as a friend of the working class. As a result, "Louis Santos" said menacingly, President Kennedy would get what was coming to him.

Aleman disagreed. He recalls arguing that Kennedy would be re-elected, according to Crile who talked with Aleman.

"No, José," said Trafficante. "He is going to be hit."

One of Trafficante's chief allies in Cuba and in the U.S. crime syndicate was Norman (Roughhouse) Rothman. By 1977, aged 62 and recently out of the federal penitentiary at Atlanta, Rothman was another whose interests and acquaintances in Cuba in 1959 paralleled Ruby's.

Rothman was a New York City bookmaker who made it big in Cuba. He was a Havana casino operator for The Private Government in the early 1950s;[13] then took control for the mob of the slot-machine business in the Batista regime.

Hedging his bets in the spirit of Trafficante, Rothman began running guns to Castro, the bearded revolutionary who festered in the hills that Batista ignored. Rothman, like most U.S. mobsters, figured that Castro would cut the mob in for an even bigger Cuban take, if he got guns and ammunition when he needed them.

By 1959, and at a time when Ruby was reporting to the FBI, Rothman was regarded as a major arms supplier for Castro. Rothman's arrest that summer in connection with the May 3 theft of more than $8.5 million from the Brockville Trust and Savings Co. of Brockville, Ontario, Canada (the FBI said it was the biggest burglary in history), was considered by federal investigators to be part of the underworld's arrangement to help Castro.

But the Warren Commission failed to look at that connection—or at Ruby's likely role as a courier who was being used to shuttle information between Rothman and Trafficante—while Rothman remained free on bond in the bank job, and Trafficante languished as a prisoner under comfortable conditions provided for him by Castro.

Here was Ruby in his lifelong role as an errand boy—as he had been when he ran sealed envelopes for Capone years earlier in Chicago, and as he would be some years later on a weekend in the Dallas police station, getting sandwiches to the cops and a bullet to Oswald.

Part II—Ruby's 72-Hour Passes to Havana

Both Ray McKeown and Thomas E. Davis III drew five-year probated federal sentences in 1958: McKeown for conspiring to smuggle guns to Fidel Castro from Texas; Davis for holding up a Detroit bank teller at gunpoint. By early 1959 Jack Ruby was dealing with both of them.

According to a Warren Commission staff memorandum,[14] Ruby's dealings with McKeown extended into April, 1959—the same month that Castro and McKeown conferred at Houston, and Ruby met with the FBI in his role as undercover contact.

McKeown believes Ruby "was trying to get information from me. That's all he was after."[15] Ruby told McKeown he wanted a letter of introduction to Castro and would pay $25,000 for it on behalf of an unnamed Las Vegas source seeking the release from Cuba of three Castro-held prisoners. "He led me to believe the $25,000 was easy for him to get," McKeown recalls. "He acted like a big shot, but I checked on him and found out he wasn't." McKeown says he prepared the letter but insisted on $5,000 good-faith money before even showing it to Ruby, who never came up with any money.

During their conversations, Ruby told McKeown of his dealings with another gun-runner—Tom Davis in Beaumont. Davis was 21 in June, 1958, when his wife graduated from the University of Michigan. Davis had dropped out of the university's school of business administration and needed $200 to pay a tuition debt. Perhaps he had dropped out of business administration too soon because his solution for raising money to pay the debt was to stick up a branch office of the Detroit National Bank. Federal District Judge Thomas P. Thornton of Detroit chose to put Davis on probation, partly because the young man had decided at the last moment to escape from the bank without taking the $1,000 he'd received when he'd displayed a note and a gun to a teller. It also was partly because of an outpouring of letters and telegrams from civic leaders and others in Davis's home town of Jacksboro, Texas, telling Judge Thornton what a fine family Davis came from and the good stuff he was made of. And it was partly because Davis convinced the judge he would spend his probation hard at work in Texas, probably on his daddy's land.

Davis never went near the ranch country. He got into salvage work in Beaumont and then the gun-running business in league with Cuban exiles, using a boat he helped operate on the Neches River and in the Gulf of Mexico. Davis first met Ruby when he walked into Ruby's club in Dallas with an idea to produce a porno movie with Ruby's girls in the cast. While still a convict on federal probation, Davis became involved in CIA-associated anti-Castro operations,[16] and was issued a U.S. passport at a time when the director of the State Department's passport office, Frances G. Knight, had access to a private phone line to the CIA.[17]

Whether he simply was looking for a way to make a buck, or seeking information that he could pass along to inflate his own importance, Jack Ruby frequently seemed to be dealing with a McKeown or a Davis once Castro took power in 1959.

In 1961 Ruby was involved in a plan to sell British Enfield rifles obtained in Mexico to anti-Castro Cubans, according to Warren Commission testimony from a self-described ex-prostitute, Nancy Perrin Rich, who had worked for Ruby that year. As mentioned earlier, when he was in jail in Dallas in 1964, Ruby became hysterical one evening, sobbing to his guard that he had been running guns to Cuba and was remorseful for having done it, but regained his composure later, claiming he only had been referring to four handguns he'd mailed in 1959 to gambler Lewis McWillie in Havana. (But obviously Ruby would not have lost control of himself so completely over something as trivial as ordering four registered guns from Ray's Hardware Store in Dallas to be sent by parcel to Havana several years earlier.)

As Ruby's interests in gun smuggling grew, he undertook what appears to have been a series of secretive, illegal and unexplained trips to Cuba. Even J. Lee Rankin, staff director of the Warren Commission, suspected that Ruby had slipped into Cuba as recently as the summer of 1963, less than six months before the murder of President Kennedy.

Rankin met with Richard M. Helms, the CIA's deputy director for plans, on March 12, 1964, as the Ruby trial was drawing to a close. Rankin told the intelligence official the Warren Commission had information that Ruby had managed to reach Havana in 1963—presumably using a Czechoslovakian passport with an alias and by way of Mexico City.

Helms told Rankin that the CIA "would be limited in its possibility of assisting" the Commission in establishing details about any such movements by Ruby, according to a still-censored portion of a CIA memorandum on the Helms-Rankin meeting.[18]

The CIA made no apparent effort to furnish the Warren Commission with any details of Ruby's Cuban transactions, and the Warren Commission never hinted publicly that it suspected Ruby may have made an illegal trip to Cuba in 1963. The Commission never examined any of the possible times when Ruby could have slipped out of the country in 1963.

One such time was a 72-hour period in June, when Ruby's whereabouts continue to be a mystery. According to Ruby, he was in New Orleans seeking a striptease act between June 5 and the morning of June 9. He said he was especially interested in seeing one stripper, Jada, perform, after making a 28-minute telephone call on June 5 from Dallas to Jada's agent in New Orleans.

Harold Tannenbaum, who was Jada's agent, says he had no contact with Ruby again until the night of June 8,[19] and the Warren Commission found no identifying records to show that Ruby was in a hotel or anywhere else between the nights of June 5 and June 8. That was totally out of character for Ruby.

Normally when Ruby left Dallas—for instance when he went to Houston in May, 1963, and to New York that August[20]—he made himself very visible. He talked to hotel clerks, bellboys and taxi drivers. He told them who he was and why he was there. He handed out Carousel Club cards and made long-distance telephone calls. Ruby left a trail like elephant tracks in the snow in the normal course of his out-of-town trips. But this time, on the New Orleans trip, there was not a handed-out card, not a sound, not a trace—until Saturday night, June 8, when a number of people suddenly saw and heard him. There would be every good reason to suspect he hadn't been in New Orleans any earlier that week.

Those 72 unaccounted hours in Ruby's life were not the only time he secretly could have flown to and from Cuba in 1963. There had been another 72-hour span in April as well, when there was no record of Ruby being anywhere, including Dallas. It was the second week of April—the week Bob Price of Houston claims he met Ruby while Ruby appeared to be on his way to a private plane ride to Cuba.

Price says he was in Houston's Escapade Club early one afternoon when Ruby and three other men walked in. Ruby was well known to the Escapade's day manager and was introduced to Price, who says he sat with the manager and talked with the four men for nearly four hours. One of the four was a pilot who talked knowledgeably about having flown pipeline inspections over West Texas.[21]

The pilot and other members of the Ruby party said they were on their way to a small private airfield near Alvin, Texas, south of Houston, according to Price, who says Ruby was bragging that he would bring back boxes of cigars from their trip.[22]

Whether Ruby really flew to Cuba from Mexico under an assumed name, as J. Lee Rankin had been informed, or flew there at night in a private plane from the Pearland or Clover airfields near Alvin (not far from the Gulf of Mexico), the patterns of Ruby's unexplained absences in April and June were the same. Each time there was no record of his movements for 72 hours.

Perhaps of more significance was a press-release issued on January 29, 1964, by an anti-Castro group in Miami known as the Cuban Student Directorate (DRE), which said:

> Jack Ruby, the man accused of killing President Kennedy's assassin, Lee H. Oswald, stayed in Cuba during [the end of] 1962 and the beginnings of 1963. Ruby flew to Havana from Mexico City.
> During his stay in Havana, Ruby was a habitual visitor at a Cuban souvenir store located across the street from the Sevilla Hotel, in Prado Avenue. This store belonged to a man named Salomon [sic] Pratkins.

The DRE identified none of its sources and *The Miami News* carried the story without sources prominently that day. U.S. Intelligence agents immediately began to investigate and discovered the DRE's information had come from Evido Pereira, a Cuban refugee who lived at 821 Southwest Second Street in Miami.

Pereira told the agents that he in turn had received the information from his sister-in-law in Havana, in a letter that had been postmarked December 28, 1963, and that he had made the letter available to the FBI. Pereira also told the agents that the person Ruby had visited in Havana was named Praskin; not Pratkins. Praskin, he said, owned a house on Prado Street, between Animas and Trocadero. The CIA said it could find no trace of anyone in Havana under either name, whom Ruby may have visited in late December, 1962, and early January, 1963. But the FBI developed information that Praskin was "a Czech or Pole [and] supposedly a close friend of Fidel Castro."[23]

At about the same time Pereira's sister-in-law sent him the information about Ruby, an underground anti-Castro group in Havana was distributing a mimeographed circular which gave less specific information about Ruby's reported visit than the Pereira letter had, but did say that Ruby had lodged in the Sevilla Hotel.

The underground circular, named *Acción*, referred to Jack Ruby as "El Matador," which literally means the man "appointed" to kill the bull in a bull ring.

CHAPTER 9

The Ring Of Bulls

If Jack Ruby were the matador, as *Acción* labeled him, then his bull ring that fatal Sunday would have been the basement of the Dallas police station. And the Warren Commission set out to discover on March 22, 1964, eight days after Ruby's murder trial ended, how the killer had gotten into the basement.

"I had and continue to have very great skepticism that Ruby did this on the spur of the moment," says Warren Commission Ruby expert Burt Griffin.[1] "My feeling is that at least 24 hours before Ruby shot Oswald that the thought and possibly a plan to shoot Oswald had occurred to him, and the pattern of his activities for at least 24 hours before he shot Oswald at least shows a buildup in his mind—a moving toward in his own mind a climactic event where he would shoot Oswald."

Griffin and Leon Hubert, the two Commission attorneys assigned to examine Jack Ruby's movements, spent the first two and a half months of that assignment mired in Washington, under orders not to give even the appearance of interfering with witnesses, evidence or Ruby's rights until his trial was over. Like bloodhounds straining at the leash, Griffin and

Hubert began on Sunday, March 22, to explore areas of Dallas where Ruby had lived, worked and frequented. They visited the police station and the scenes of President Kennedy's and officer Tippit's murders. The next day they held preliminary meetings with various Dallas officials, such as U.S. Attorney Barefoot Sanders, District Attorney Wade and Assistant Police Chief Batchelor. Griffin asked Batchelor about Ruby's relationship to the Dallas criminal element and Batchelor replied there "was no serious criminal problem in Dallas" to which Ruby could relate.

Over the next three days Hubert and Griffin took the depositions of 21 of the 1,175 members of the Dallas police force. One of these was detective Mike Eberhardt, who drew a different picture of Jack Ruby's Dallas. According to Griffin's notes on the interview,[2] "Eberhardt stated that, in performing his duties with the burglary and theft bureau of the police department, he found Ruby to be useful in providing information to him. He said that Ruby always knew 'who was out in the streets,' since people in Ruby's business generally were among the first to see or hear hoodlums when they were in the area. He made a practice of visiting Ruby's club almost nightly when it was open during the shift that Eberhardt was working on. And he would always try to obtain information from Ruby."

Ruby was an informer on every different police level there was. He fed tips to Eberhardt and others on the Dallas police force regularly. He met in Dallas with two Chicago detectives to provide them information, less than three months before the Kennedy assassination. He had the 1959 arrangement with the FBI, and 10 years before that, he asked a Chicago lawyer to help him get established as an informer with Senator Estes Kefauver's special Senate committee to investigate organized crime. The lawyer he approached, Luis Kutner, was accused of taking $60,000 from underworld clients to protect them from the Kefauver probe. Kutner, who had known Ruby from Ruby's days in the rackets-infested Waste Handlers Union, arranged a meeting for Ruby with Rudolph Halley, chief counsel of the Kefauver committee. Ruby said he wanted to establish himself with Halley in order to give the Senate lawyer information on certain people (Ruby was living in Dallas at the time), and find out simultaneously, if he could, what the Kefauver committee was up to. Operating as an informer was an indelible part of Ruby's pattern, as it was when he tried to get Chief Justice Warren to take him to Washington to talk, several weeks after Hubert and Griffin conducted their late-March interviews of the police in Dallas.

Hubert and Griffin attempted in those interviews to find out *how* Ruby got into the police station basement, but not *why*. And their concern with how he got in didn't relate to the movement of the prisoner Oswald from the third floor down to the basement.

"We might not have grasped the connection as we should have," Griffin says now about the movement of Oswald and the security lacks in the basement. "Hubert and I never carried on an inquiry into the whole system for protecting Oswald."[3]

Griffin soon decided that he and Hubert were not getting a complete story from the Dallas police. "I always thought all along about the Dallas police that anything that would get them into trouble or embarrass them, they would lie to us. No question about that," Griffin recalls now from his Cleveland judge's chambers. He says the problem was the same all up and down the Dallas police force. It was not always something as indelicate as a lie. Sometimes it was a matter of innuendo. Captain Fritz, the homicide chief, for instance, told federal authorities he felt that Ruby was the unidentified man who had made anonymous threatening calls to the FBI and sheriff's office in the early morning hours of Sunday, November 24, 1963, that Oswald would never make it alive in the planned transfer of the prisoner from one jail to another. For a professional lawman, Fritz's statement was surprising. He didn't hear the anonymous caller's voice on either occasion and the calls weren't recorded. There was no way for Fritz to ascertain that the threats came from Ruby or any specific person. But the homicide captain knowingly made his assertion before Ruby's murder trail. However, when Griffin refers to lying on the Dallas police force he is not talking about innuendo. For instance, he is talking about William J. Newman, a reserve officer on the force at the time of the Oswald murder.

Dallas reserve police officers held day-to-day jobs in the outside business world but were eager to dress up as cops in their spare time. They were given training to assist regular police in routine assignments, but were unpaid volunteers who bought their own uniforms. Newman put on his dark blue uniform, pinned on his badge no. 317 and showed up in the police station basement to stand guard the Sunday morning Oswald was to be transferred. He was in the basement for two hours before Oswald was shot and two days later he filed a report stating he had seen nothing unusual happen before the shooting. But then, like some of the regulars on the force—such as detectives Clardy, McMillon and Archer—Newman began to shift his story so that Ruby appeared as a lone antagonist who had eased down the Main Street ramp.

These stories suddenly emerged during a two-day period: November 30 and December 1—the weekend following the shooting.

It was Sunday, December 1, that Newman radically changed his account. He told two police investigators[4] that "he recalled observing an unknown white male run down the Main Street ramp into the basement . . . approximately one minute prior to the shooting of Oswald. This unknown male disappeared into the newsmen and police officers and was not observed by Newman again."

The story of Ruby supposedly using the ramp entrance into the basement didn't surface in the first written reports of Newman and the three detectives. It was only after the department instituted its own official investigation of how Ruby got into the police basement that Newman and the others adjusted their accounts.

Newman never actually *said* it was Ruby he claimed to have seen but his tardy story came the day after the three detectives belatedly began to tell of hearing Ruby admit, minutes after his arrest, that he had come down the Main Street ramp. Newman's description of an unknown man moving down the ramp about a minute before the shooting fit in exactly with what detectives Clardy, Archer and McMillon claimed they heard Ruby say.[5]

Griffin didn't mince words when he met in late March, 1964, with Newman. The Warren Commission lawyer called Newman a "damned liar" to his face when Griffin found Newman's testimony to be in "direct contradiction" to descriptions of people and events in the police station basement as given by others.

"Newman had no recollection of two automobiles being driven out of the basement [from] the garage and being placed on the Commerce Street ramp [the area where Newman said he was standing] immediately after Lieutenant Pierce's car went up the Main Street ramp," Griffin wrote to Rankin in his April 2 memorandum. "It is inconceivable to me that he could not have seen these cars . . . from where he was supposed to be standing. His failure to recall these movements is understandable—however, his willingness to state positively that these movements did not occur cast doubt on his reliability."

In that same memorandum to Rankin, Griffin wrote disparagingly about Kenneth Hudson Croy, another reserve officer who also waited until December 1 to report for the first time that "he saw Ruby in the basement perhaps a minute before the shooting and that he asked Ruby and another man to move back against the railing prior to the shooting." Croy, who was both a cowboy and a real estate salesman in his outside jobs, told Griffin that "Ruby ran past him, burst through the line in front of him and shot Oswald. This story is inconsistent with the TV films which show Ruby standing still for a few seconds behind officer Harrison and then moving forward quickly to shoot Oswald."

Croy was a reserve sergeant whose duties that Sunday morning were "to check the men as they reported for duty, and much of the time he was free to roam about as he pleased. Nonetheless, he was almost totally unable to tell me anything he did or saw, or any persons he saw between the time he arrived for work Sunday morning and the time that he saw Ruby."

And that wasn't even Ruby he saw, according to the findings of Dallas police investigators. They reported to Chief Curry on December 19, 1963, that Croy's description of "Ruby" in a maroon coat turned out instead to match the description of Robert S. Huffaker Jr., a Dallas television newsman who was in the Main Street ramp area of the basement.

Another television man standing in that same area—Jimmy Turner, a

WBAP producer from Fort Worth, assigned to NBC—told the Warren Commission he definitely saw Jack Ruby walking down the Main Street ramp at about the time Lieutenant Pierce's car went up the ramp. Turner's time-frame for that corresponded with Ruby's own story, but there were three problems with Turner's descriptions of "Ruby."

The most immediately noticeable feature about the man Turner saw was the hat he wore. It was a broad-brimmed Western hat with a sugar-loaf crown. Very distinctive. Turner was very sure about the hat. And Ruby was wearing a snap-brimmed fedora, which was a hat of totally different dimensions. Next, Turner seemed to think the man was wearing an overcoat and "he seemed to be much heavier" than Ruby turned out to be, Turner told Leon Hubert.

As a result, the Warren Report concluded that "Ruby entered the basement unaided, probably via the Main Street ramp, and no more than three minutes before the shooting of Oswald."[6]

To back up its conclusion about the ramp, the Warren Report told the American public that there were three essential witnesses and that one of them, Turner, "testified that while he was standing near the railing on the east side of the Main Street ramp, perhaps 30 seconds before the shooting, he observed a man he is confident was Jack Ruby moving slowly down the Main Street ramp about 10 feet from the bottom. Two other witnesses testified that they thought they had seen Ruby on the Main Street side of the ramp before the shooting."[7]

The two other witnesses—not named in the text of the Warren Report, but identified within the hundreds of cryptic, small-type footnotes on 62 back pages of the Report—turned out to be Newman and Croy, the two reserve officers whose testimony was strongly discounted by the Warren Commission's own lawyer who took their depositions.

Despite discrepancies in Turner's description of Ruby to Hubert, and the inconsistencies in the stories Newman and Croy gave to Griffin, the Warren Report failed to mention specifically what evidence the Commission had—only that "the sum of this evidence tends to support Ruby's claim that he entered by the Main Street ramp. . . ."[8]

Actually, the evidence showed Newman and plain-clothes officers L. D. Miller and William J. Harrison were a lot less than forthright about activities on the morning of Oswald's execution. But the Warren Report never even hinted at that.

Griffin met with detective Miller of the Juvenile Bureau on the first day that Warren Commission lawyers began to question rank-and-file members of the Dallas police. It was March 24, 1964. Griffin held a preliminary interview with Miller and then tried to take a deposition from the police detective. Griffin's notes explain what happened next:

"At the outset I asked him to raise his right hand to be sworn. He declined to do so, stating that he would like me to explain what the deposition was all about. This was after I had previously interviewed him for 15 or 20 minutes and had given a general explanation of what our purpose was."

Griffin decided that Miller was being purposely thick but proceeded anyway to formally read a general statement that Leon Hubert had prepared, outlining the tasks of the Commission. "Miller indicated to me that he still did not understand the purpose of the deposition and I attempted to expand on Mr. Hubert's prepared text," Griffin's notes continue. "When he continued to indicate uncertainty I obtained copies of the Executive Order and the Congressional Resolution establishing the Commission, together with the Commission rules." Miller still balked and was told to return the next day. By then Hubert and Griffin were ready to see that Miller would be subpoenaed to appear before the full Warren Commission, which would have meant a trip for Miller from Dallas to Washington to face an inquisition. Miller decided to raise his right hand.

"The most significant aspect of Miller's testimony was his lack of memory and his original reluctance to testify at all," Griffin noted. After Griffin complained about the detective's lack of memory, Miller volunteered that he had accompanied Blackie Harrison on the morning Ruby shot Oswald to the nearby Delux Diner, "where officer Harrison received a telephone call from an unknown person."

Harrison testified soon after Miller. But Harrison, the officer Ruby stood behind while waiting to lunge at Oswald, showed up in the company of a lawyer, assistant Dallas city attorney Ted P. MacMaster. Harrison "was somewhat slow in revealing the coffee break he had taken with Miller at a diner on Commerce Street," Griffin wrote in his memorandum. "And he had to be prodded to talk about the telephone call which he received there. He explained the telephone call as having come from another member of the police department, officer Goolsby. He said that the telephone call was to summon him back to the department."[9]

Why were Miller and Harrison so guarded, especially about what should have been a routine telephone transaction at the Delux Diner? Griffin did not ask Harrison if he in turn telephoned Ruby with information on the Oswald transfer. The Warren Commission also failed to explore Harrison's relationship with Ruby. And neither side had wanted to summon Harrison as a witness in the Ruby trial, since neither the defense nor prosecution wanted to risk testimony reflecting pre-murder contacts between Ruby and any of the police.

Harrison's two known absences before the murder that Sunday morning, shortly after 9 and again after 10:30—the first time when the basement transfer route for Oswald was established and the second time when the armored van was en route for the planned pickup of the prisoner—

were the two key periods when he could have been in contact with his longtime acquaintance.[10]

Harrison said he had known Ruby at least 11 years, since his days as a motorcycle cop when he would go into Ruby's Silver Spur for a cold one.

Two other Dallas cops arrested Ruby in a brawl that was taking place at the Silver Spur in 1954. They were officers D. L. Blankenship and Edward E. Carlson. In a note written by Ruby to another prisoner and smuggled out of the Dallas county jail after the Warren report came out,[11] Ruby wrote down the names of five Dallas police who were friends of his who he thought could be trusted. Blankenship and Carlson were included. On the afternoon of the day Ruby shot Oswald, the killer encountered Carlson in the Dallas city jail. The two laughed, called each other by first names, shook hands heartily and carried on as though Jack Ruby had just won a good-sized bet and they were celebrating at a bar.

Others on the list of Ruby's special police pals were homicide detective Joe Cody, who worked closely with Captain Will Fritz, and two investigators on the burglary and theft detail—Cal Jones and Buddy Munster.

Another name of those who could be trusted in the Ruby note was "Buddy Turman, prizefighter." Regan (Buddy) Turman was a hard-hitting professional heavyweight out of Tyler, Texas. When he couldn't get fights Turman sometimes worked as a bouncer for Ruby and sometimes Ruby gave him loans, as routinely as Ruby provided loans to certain police. Turman told the FBI that Ruby actually knew several hundred Dallas police and that many of them frequented the Carousel. Ruby's police friends were like an iceberg and the Warren Commission barely noticed the tip. Among those acquainted with Ruby were more than one out of every three Dallas police in the police station basement at the time he shot Oswald.

In one of the sloppiest phases of its assassinations probe, the Warren Commission failed to interview most of those Ruby acquaintances who were in the basement. One was Detective H. L. McGee, who reported that a Dallas lawyer with easy access to the police station walked up to the jail office window from the Harwood Street entrance of the police building—at about the same instant Oswald was brought off the elevator. "That's all I wanted to see," said the lawyer, who turned around and went back out the Harwood Street door. Seconds later, Oswald was shot and the lawyer would have a famous client to defend. The lawyer was Tom Howard. Yet the Commission never questioned Howard, who treated his client Ruby as a hero, and never questioned McGee.

Lieutenant Richard E. Swain, who knew Ruby, was one of those on Oswald's last elevator ride. Swain went ahead of the group and studied the badly confused scene in the basement where Oswald's killer awaited him. Swain turned back to the transfer party and indicated to Captain Fritz that everything was ready.

Standing in the midst of that confused scene was Lieutenant George Butler, normally a hardy man who was seen trembling as Oswald's appearance neared. Butler worked in the same criminal investigation unit with Blackie Harrison and detective Miller. Butler's specialty had been dealing with syndicate criminals, and he had known Ruby a long time. Butler and former Dallas Sheriff Steve Guthrie had trapped one of Ruby's underworld associates, Paul Rowland Jones, in a police payoff scheme in 1946, and Guthrie told the FBI that Ruby was supposed to have been a front-man in Dallas for the Chicago syndicate, as Jones had laid out the scheme in Guthrie's home. The Warren Commission failed to talk to Butler or Guthrie.

And then there was the ubiquitous Sergeant Patrick T. Dean, who was in charge of security in the police station basement the morning Oswald was shot. Dean knew Jack Ruby and was among the first to talk with Ruby after the shooting. Dean's questionable claim that he heard Ruby admit to premeditation and to entering the basement alone, by way of the ramp, was the critical March 6, 1964, testimony that sealed Ruby's fate in the murder trial. Then on the night of March 24 Burt Griffin took Dean's deposition for the Warren Commission, and that confrontation turned into a disaster which contributed largely to the Commission's botch of its whole Ruby probe.

Dean complained vigorously the next morning to District Attorney Wade that he had been treated with disbelief and in a threatening way by Griffin in an off-the-record conversation that followed Dean's deposition. But in a memorandum to J. Lee Rankin on March 31 Griffin said:

> The tone of my conversation with Sergeant Dean was entirely opposite to that which he apparently represented to District Attorney Wade. At the outset I told him that in the two or three hours that he and I had been talking I found him a likeable and personable individual, and that I had believed that he was a capable and honest police officer. I tried to approach him on a basis of respect and friendship while maintaining a certain distance. I said, however, that I did not believe his testimony in some respects but that I thought I understood why it was that he was not making the truthful statement which I believed possible. I then stressed that this investigation by the President's Commission was of extreme importance to the National Security and that I felt that, if there was some way that he could be induced to come forward with a more forthright statement without doing injury to himself, the Commission would probably be willing to explore a means to afford him the protection he deemed necessary. I had in mind protection from disclosure of his identity to his superior officers and the public although I did not say so to him. I pointed out to him that if he had any such inclination to change his story it

would probably be best that he not approach us directly but that he secure an attorney so that the problems that he felt he faced could be worked out without committing him to anything on record.

It is my recollection that, after stating this, he said he didn't understand what I had in mind since he had tried to be extremely truthful and I believe he then asked me to explain what I had in mind. I told him the two particular points in his testimony that I believed to be untrustworthy: that Ruby told him on November 24 that he had entered the basement through the Main Street rampway, and that he thought of killing Oswald on the night of November 22.

In a separate memorandum to Rankin, dated March 30, Griffin analyzed Dean's on-the-record deposition in a six-page battle plan he drew up to pursue the attack on Dean. Griffin suspected the worst of the handsome, nicely groomed, well-spoken sergeant:

> If Dean is not telling the truth concerning the Ruby statement about coming down the Main Street ramp, it is important to determine why Dean decided to tell a falsehood about the Main Street ramp. Dean either actually saw Ruby come down the ramp, heard from homicide detectives or other persons in Captain Fritz's office that Ruby had made this statement, or *told Ruby that he came down the Main Street ramp and Ruby latched on to it.* [Author's italics—ed.] Dean stated to me that he would have no desire to put the finger on officer Vaughn,[12] however, Dean might well do such a thing to protect himself.
>
> Three explanations seem possible to me. One is that Dean's original source of information is homicide detectives and that he continued to insist that Ruby had told him this because he wanted to protect himself against the statement he made in the press.[13] I do not think that this is the strongest possibility because if Dean had actually heard it from homicide detectives, it would have been a simple matter for him to say that that is where he heard it. The second possibility is that Dean did see Ruby come down the Main Street ramp. I do not think he did see him come down the ramp because, if that had been the case, I think that he would have questioned officer Vaughn more forcefully about it. *The third possibility and the one which I consider most likely, is that Ruby came in by another entrance to a point where Dean could have stopped him and that Dean, having been directly responsible for all basement security, is trying to conceal his dereliction of duty.* [Authors Italics—ed.]
>
> For example, the rumor most prominently circulated after the shooting seems to have been that Ruby helped push a TV camera to the basement. This TV camera would have been pushed right past Dean's position and Dean might have recognized Ruby since he had met Ruby in the past. This allegation needs to be explored more thoroughly. If it is true, I am inclined to believe that Dean's purpose in immediately going to the third floor was to find Ruby at homicide, where he would have expected that Ruby was being questioned.
>
> Confronted by Curry first, Dean instead was steered up to the fifth floor where he may have simply stated to Ruby he came down

the Main Street ramp. Ruby being a cultivator of police favor and not being desirous of incurring the wrath of the police department, might well have taken the hint from Dean.

At the end of that Griffin memorandum to Rankin, the Warren Commission attorney suggested an all-out re-examination of Dean's reports and statements, as well as Dean's contacts with others after the shooting of Oswald.

But the Dallas police had an attack of their own under way. Assistant Police Chief Batchelor told Griffin that Dean would take a polygraph test if necessary,[14] and asked if there was hard evidence that Dean wasn't telling the truth.

"I said I couldn't show him what evidence we had without permission from Washington," Griffin noted in his March 31 memorandum, "but that I believed we did have substantial evidence on the question of entry into the basement."

Griffin noted that "from time to time throughout the conversation, Batchelor expressed concern about jeopardizing the prosecution of Ruby.[15] But in any event, I added, I did not have authority to act; nor was the Commission going to make any other statement to the press about our activities in Dallas or take any other action in a precipitous fashion or without careful consideration of the prosecution's problems. I did not give him any assurances but tried to talk in generalities which would convey the impression that we were reasonable people and that there was no need for concern."

But there was need for concern—on Griffin's end of things. There were phone calls to Washington from the offices of District Attorney Wade and U.S. Attorney Sanders. howard Willens, Rankin's chief administrator in Washington, was on the phone with Leon Hubert in Dallas.

"I think I can straighten this out," Hubert recalled telling Willens. "Burt Griffin was doing a great job and I told that to Willens. Burt just got mad because the guy was lying to him, or he thought the guy was lying to him. In any case, several days later I finished the interview with Dean. And I didn't apologize or anything like that. There was just no putting the two of them in the same room, that's all there was to it. I thought I got it straightened out." He didn't.

CHAPTER 10

An Amicable Solution

Whatever the normally curious conjunction was of the stars that guided Jack Ruby's fate, they moved into a mean, wobbling orbit in March, 1964, the month Ruby was sentenced to death. The Ruby family decided defense lawyer Melvin Belli had botched things up, and within hours after the jury verdict the decision was reached to fire Belli and his associate, Joe H. Tonahill. Tonahill refused to be fired and the family (Jack's brother Earl had become the force behind all such decisions) hired Percy Foreman, the flamboyant Houston criminal lawyer, as chief counsel. Four days later Foreman quit in disgust, citing meddling by the Ruby family as the prime reason. All this—from the start of the trial to Foreman's hasty departure—took place between March 4 and March 23, which was the day the disconsolate Jack Ruby turned 53.[1]

On March 24, Burt Griffin and Patrick Dean had their confrontation in Dallas—the showdown that helped doom the Warren Commission's investigation into the steps Ruby had taken to silence Lee Harvey Oswald.

By March 24, Ruby had a new chief counsel, Dr. Hubert Winston Smith, the first person ever to serve simultaneously on Harvard's law and medical faculties. But that spring he was teaching at the University of Texas law school, which wasted no time informing him that unless he got out of the Ruby case there would be no place for him on the faculty that fall. Dr. Smith quickly abandoned Ruby—triggering the arrival of a new parade of several more lawyers who bickered among themselves more effectively than they counseled the caged and desperate figure they represented.

The nation's March 29, Easter Sunday, newspapers were carrying an Associated Press report on the probe into the Kennedy slaying by the Warren Commission, which "has found no evidence the crime was anything but the irrational act of one individual—and the Commission now feels most of the information is in . . . in general the Commission is making the story of John F. Kennedy's death a model of tireless documentation—all in line with its mandate to demonstrate that nothing is covered up, no possible lead slighted." On that same weekend, Burt Griffin was ordered out of Dallas. Vital witnesses remained uncalled and unchallenged. Leon Hubert remembers that Griffin, his partner on the Ruby detail, "felt crushed."

A hint of what was going on emerged a week later on April 5 in *The Dallas Times Herald* in an article by reporter Jim Lehrer,[2] under this headline:

WARREN PANEL PROBER'S TACTICS TRIGGER REMOVAL
A flare-up over the questioning tactics of a Warren Commission attorney resulted last week in the investigator's quiet removal from the Dallas phase of the Commission's probe, the *Times Herald* learned Saturday.

The dispute involved a clash between the investigator-attorney and a witness he was interviewing, a Dallas police officer who was a key witness in the Jack Ruby murder trial.

The officer claimed in protests to District Attorney Henry Wade and other officials that the Commission man had called him a "liar," among other things.

An amicable solution, which included the investigator's leaving Dallas, was worked out through the combined efforts of Mr. Wade, U.S. Attorney Barefoot Sanders and the Commission.

None of the officials involved wished to be directly quoted on any aspect of the incident.

All agreed, however, that it was an "isolated" event and emphasized that it was nipped in the bud before it could disrupt the existing cooperative spirit that prevails between the Commission's men and local authorities.

A factor clearly present in Lehrer's article was the presentation of a major problem in such a way that there would be no public relations harm done to Dallas or the Commission.

Commission staff director J. Lee Rankin had at least two purposes in removing Griffin from the Dallas investigation and one of them was to maintain as smooth a public relations image as possible in the Commission's dealings with Dallas authorities, as well as with the FBI and CIA. The other purpose was an insistence by Rankin that the Commission avoid any appearance of a witch-hunt. The ugly specter of the McCarthy era[3] remained clearly in his mind and Rankin wanted no hint of its return in the way the Commission conducted its affairs. Rankin clearly felt that Griffin had come on too strong in Griffin's March 24 off-the-record talk to Dean.

"Griffin had a lot of trouble believing Dean's account," a Commission colleague said later. "You have to suspect the possibility that Dean at a minimum had seen Ruby enter the basement and had failed to do his duty.

"Dean just totally miscast the nature of that March 24 off-the-record conversation," Judge Griffin recalls now. "My entire approach to him was low-keyed. There was not the slightest threat of intimidation or abuse. Dean admitted this when he testified before the Commission weeks later about the incident."

"Griffin was hurt that we [the Warren Commission management] treated this as a public relations problem, instead of as something we were on to," said the former colleague.

In effect, Griffin had challenged the structure of the prosecution's case against Jack Ruby—as well as the integrity of the Dallas police department—with his open mistrust of Sergeant Dean's statements. That's what it all boiled down to. No wonder authorities in Dallas fought back so hard. Rankin yielded immediately.

A trickle of people on the Commission staff indicated privately they were appalled that Griffin had been withdrawn summarily from Dallas. Fellow assistant counsel David W. Belin was one. He would complain again privately, too, when Hubert and Griffin were excluded from the Warren Commission's interview with Jack Ruby. A few others on the staff felt that Rankin had caved in too easily to outside pressures in the Griffin-Dean matter.

Griffin feared he would be fired from the Commission staff at the very worst, or at best assigned to some menial tasks in Commission headquarters. But even though he clearly was in Rankin's doghouse, neither of these things happened or was contemplated. He was left alone. He was free to pursue his investigation of Jack Ruby's movements in Dallas—just so long as he did it from Washington, where he couldn't talk to Dallas police. Griffin would be stuck in Washington for weeks. It was a strange way to conduct the Ruby probe.[4]

Maybe Burt Griffin's assumptions about Sergeant Dean were right, or maybe not. But his opportunities to prove it either way were at an end. It was all done "amicably," according to The Dallas Times Herald of April 5.

On April 21, Lyndon B. Johnson was meeting on a warm spring afternoon in the White House rose garden with a group of out-of-town editors and broadcasters, when he was asked if he could tell "when we might expect a complete report from the Warren Commission."

"No," the President answered indifferently. "I don't think that they have a particular deadline. It is a very thorough commission, made up of the most able men in this country. A very patriotic group. They are taking testimony today."

They were taking testimony that day from Texas Governor John B. Connally, who told Commission members it was "inconceivable" that he had been hit by the same bullet that had gone through John Kennedy. Connally refused to believe the single-bullet theory that had been developed within the Commission staff by assistant counsel Arlen Specter. Tests had shown that both Kennedy and Connally could not have been hit by separate bullets from the same rifle in the short amount of time between the two hits[5] unless they had been wounded by the same bullet—the barely dented so-called "magic bullet" that was found on a stretcher at Parkland Hospital after both wounded men were brought there.

President Johnson did not like the portent of Governor Connally's dissent, since without substantiation of the single-bullet hypothesis the Warren Commission's case against Lee Harvey Oswald as the lone gunman would collapse.

While the President casually made it sound as if the Commission were free to amble through as much time and testimony as were needed, the White House had begun to exert private pressure on Earl Warren to wind up everything. A June 1 deadline was expected.

Did this kind of pressure from the White House, through Warren and Rankin, discourage the Warren Commission's Ruby detail from broadening its investigation into still other questions that demanded answers?

"They clearly discouraged us," says Judge Griffin. "In fact they more than discouraged us. They told us in no uncertain terms to stop messing around with things that weren't so important—the peripheral things that weren't going to lead us any place."

An example of one of "the peripheral things," Griffin says, was the charge by former Dallas County Sheriff Steve Guthrie that Jack Ruby had been designated to serve as a front in Dallas in 1947 for Chicago mobsters who planned to control the area's gambling and police payoffs. The Commission decided to skip all that.

CHAPTER 11

May Day

It was early May, 1964, when J. Edgar Hoover decided to go for the Warren Commission's jugular.

The FBI director still was resentful that the Warren Commission was not accepting his bureau's reports on events surrounding the Kennedy assassination without further layers of questions. He retaliated by seeing to it that derogatory information on Norman Redlich reached a group of reactionary congressmen. Redlich had been serving five months as special assistant to Commission staff director J. Lee Rankin. Redlich was a hard-driving man, on leave from his post as law professor at New York University and in a position of particular power on the Commission staff because he was to shape much of the writing in the Commission's ultimate Warren Report.

On May 5, Ralph F. Beermann, an alfalfa processor from Nebraska who had become a Republican congressman, took the floor of the House to charge that communists were trying to distort evidence in order to blame anti-communists for the President's murder. Beermann then got to the point of his prepared text:

Considering these circumstances, it is amazing—shocking—incredible, to find that although competent and unimpeachable legal and investigative counsel can be found in any community in the land, the Warren Commission has on its staff as a $100-a-day consultant a member of the Emergency Civil Liberties Committee—an organization cited by both the House Committee on Un-American Activities and the Senate Internal Security Subcommittee.

Prof. Norman Redlich, on the national council of the Emergency Civil Liberties Committee—cited by House and Senate committees as an organization "to defend the cases of Communist lawbreakers"—is currently employed at $100 a day, for the Warren Commission. And as recently as April 13, 1964, just a few weeks ago, this "consultant" had his name listed in an advertisement appearing in *The New York Times* with other members of the cited Emergency Civil Liberties Committee—an advertisement condemning the Un-American Activities Committee.[1]

Using innuendo and a hint of conspiracy, Beermann pointed out that the "subversive" group with which Redlich was affiliated "has unexplained connections and associations with the very Fair Play for Cuba Committee to which the accused assassin Lee Oswald belonged." Beermann's prepared remarks added:

Strangely, little has been said or written about the Redlich hiring, although it certainly impresses me as one of the greatest miscarriages of appointive judgment in the history of American Government. I call upon those in responsible positions to dismiss this patently unqualified "consultant" from the Warren Commission staff and to investigate and make public facts concerning how Redlich managed to get hired and keep his job despite his known Communist-front affiliations.

Beermann stuck the knife in, but it was Senator Karl E. Mundt, Republican from South Dakota and a chief spokesman for hybrid rightwing emotions, planted and raised in the nation's farm-belt, who twisted it.

"I think this is a great disservice to President Kennedy's memory," Mundt intoned. "We want a report from the Commission which Americans will accept as factual, which will put to rest all the ugly rumors now in circulation and which the world will believe. Who but the most gullible would believe any report if it were written in part by persons with Communist connections?"

Mundt predicted "with certainty that Communist leaders around the world will have a detailed report on such testimony long before it reaches the American public—since once a Government body is infiltrated by one with Communist sympathies or connections, history has shown that the pipeline to Moscow is fast and it is filled with classified material."

Finally Mundt demanded that the Warren Commission suspend the taking of all further testimony and hold up on all writing of its report to the American public until Redlich and others on the Commission staff faced the challenge of obtaining "complete security clearances."

Mundt's demand was unobtrusively slipped into the body of the May 11 Congressional Record and no public notice was taken of it. But members and staff of the Commission certainly noticed that the ranking minority member of the Senate Government Operations Committee was insisting that they dump Redlich. They could see an orchestrated attempt beginning on Capitol Hill to embarrass the Commission into conforming with the way the FBI said things happened in Dallas on the weekend of November 22-24, 1963. Three days after Mundt's demand, Beermann was back on the House floor to step up the attack on Redlich—leading off with pointed praise for J. Edgar Hoover. Beermann quoted from passages on page 89 of Hoover's book, *Masters of Deceit*, which said that the Emergency Civil Liberties Committee championed by Redlich was typical of communist-front organizations, where "behind scenes there is a Communist manipulator." This time, five other Republican congressmen joined Beermann on the House floor to intensify the cry for Redlich's scalp.

Redlich was a self-important but prodigious worker and his role on the Commission staff was significant because of his command of the substantive issues that had to be investigated and then assembled to create the packaged conclusions. Redlich hadn't concealed his Emergency Civil Liberties Committee connection when Rankin had hired him. In fact, he had impeccable connections with the academic community, and Rankin was impressed with Redlich's credentials.

But Chief Justice Warren made no immediate move to cut off criticism from the rightwing sharpshooters in Congress and the beleaguered Redlich offered to resign under the growing pressure. The sharpshooters included Commission member Gerald R. Ford's day-to-day associates in Congress, and he pleaded their case to fire Redlich in at least one closed-door session of the Commission. According to August E. Johansen, a Republican colleague who represented a nearby Michigan district in Congress, Ford sponsored the motion that would have sacrificed Redlich up to the critics.

While the Ford motion was failing, Rankin was in the midst of several private discussions with his chief administrator, Howard Willens, who kept urging Rankin not to yield by any means to this kind of pressure. Rankin agreed. He had not wanted the Commission to appear in any way—as Burt Griffin had appeared to some in Dallas in the Patrick Dean affair—to be using the bullying tactics of the McCarthy era. But now the Commission was being bullied, and for political reasons similar to those that Senator Joe McCarthy had used a decade earlier. Two weeks after the concerted attacks began, fronted by Beermann and Mundt, Chief Justice Warren advised Redlich that his security clearance had been granted. That was the end of the witch-hunt, except for a final shot from Ford's colleague, Johansen, on the House floor, May 25.

"The Commission cleared Redlich on the grounds that there was no evidence of actual Communist Party membership," grumbled Johansen. "Standard government security criteria include many other disqualifying factors—among them, 'unsuitability and pressure risk,' and 'sympathetic association with subversive individuals or groups.'² . . . By it hiring and retaining Norman Redlich, the Commission has shown about as much concern for public confidence as a clumsy and careless baggageman does for the 'handle with care' labels."

Johansen's sour grapes underscored the fact that the outcome of the Redlich controversy had been no victory for the bulldog-like man in the background, J. Edgar Hoover. But neither would it be a victory for the Warren Commission's Ruby detail.

Leon Hubert and Burt Griffin had found somewhat of an ally in Redlich in their attempts to widen the Ruby investigation into a number of unexplored areas. But after getting his clearance from Chairman Warren, and maybe because of an accommodation that resulted, Redlich seemed to lose his patience for further detective work by the Ruby detail. Warren wanted conclusions written and Redlich became anxious to write them.

On May 14, in the midst of the controversy over Redlich, Rankin received a petulant 11-page memorandum from Hubert and Griffin. In it they chastised the Commission management for failing to authorize a meaningful Ruby probe. The May 14 memorandum established for the record an itemized number of areas not gone into and people not interviewed. The purpose of the harsh memorandum from the Ruby detail was, according to Griffin, to tell the Commission's power center that "you're going to write a report, maintaining you did a job. Then here's the record. You either deal with this record or not, but we're not going to be the ones that bite the bullet on this. We want the record clear that these are the things we're very concerned about."

"We wanted to protect ourselves against any accusation later on that we had not gone far enough," Hubert explained.

But the scolding tone of the May 14 memorandum of course annoyed Rankin and Willens. "I think they thought we were sandbagging them," recalls Griffin. "It's just that they were in a different ball game than we were. They thought ours was psychotic. They really thought that ours was crazy and that we were incompetent. But they finally said to us, all right, we'll look at most of this stuff. Quit bellyaching. Go do it."

Rankin made the policy decisions but Willens had the responsibility of budgeting time, resources and emphasis on staff projects, to make sure that the total Warren Commission investigation went forward. With it, Willens says, he had a "strong intellectual commitment" to make sure that the Commission completed an honest investigation that was as thorough as possible.

"I was also aware, however, that we had to proceed in a unified way and you don't proceed antagonistically in order to achieve that end," Willens adds. "I didn't fault Hubert and Griffin for pressing the investigation, because that is what they were there to do. But at some point we had to come to an end."

Willens complained about the crabby ways of the May 14 memorandum but, style aside, it laid out numerous FBI and Commission failures after five months to perceive what Ruby was all about. For instance, the memorandum said Ruby "had time to engage in substantial activities in addition to the management of his clubs. Ruby's nightclub business usually occupied no more than five hours of a normal working day, which began at about 10 a.m. and ended at 2 a.m. It was his practice to spend an average of only about one hour a day at his clubs between 10 a.m. and 9 p.m. Our depositions were confined primarily to persons familiar with Ruby's club activities. The FBI has thoroughly investigated Ruby's nightclub operations but does not seem to have pinned down his other business or social activities."

Another question raised in the memorandum was that "in 1961, it is reported, Ruby attended three meetings in Dallas in connection with the sale of arms to Cubans and the smuggling out of refugees. The informant identified an Ed Brunner as Ruby's associate in this endeavor. Shortly after his arrest on November 24, Ruby named Fred Bruner as one of his expected attorneys."

Transmitted at a time when Earl Warren was seeking final conclusions, the memorandum said "substantial time segments in Ruby's daily routine from September 26 to November 22 have not been accounted for," and the Commission had yet to disprove that "Ruby killed Oswald at the suggestion of others."

The memorandum complained that FBI reports on known associates of Ruby had failed to evaluate the information it received: "In every case where there was some evidence implicating others, those other persons were interviewed and denied the incriminating allegations. Further investigation has not been undertaken to resolve the conflicts."

About 46 persons who saw Ruby on the weekend of the assassinations, November 22-24, were interviewed by the FBI but Rankin had not authorized Hubert and Griffin to talk to any of them. The memorandum also named four people who spoke to Ruby that weekend as being particularly necessary to question. The memorandum listed the names, and commented:

> *Henry Wade.* This person can testify to the development of the testimony by Sergeant Dean and detective Archer against Ruby and of seeing Ruby on November 22 in the police department building.[3]
>
> *Tom Howard.* This person is one of Ruby's original attorneys and is reported to have been in the police basement a few minutes before Oswald was shot and to have inquired if Oswald had been moved. He

filed a writ of habeas corpus for Ruby about an hour after the shooting of Oswald. He could explain these activities and possibly tell us about the Ruby trial. We should have these explanations.[4]

FBI Agent Hall. This person interviewed Ruby for two and a half hours on November 24, beginning at approximately noon. His report is contradictory to Sergeant Dean's trial testimony. He also interviewed Ruby on December 21, 1963.[5]

Seth Kantor. This person was interviewed twice by the FBI and persists in his claim that he saw Ruby at Parkland Hospital shortly before or after the President's death was announced. Ruby denies that he was ever at Parkland Hospital. We must decide who is telling the truth, for there would be considerable significance if it were concluded that Ruby is lying. Should we make an evaluation without seeing Kantor ourselves?[6]

The May 14 memorandum prepared by Leon Hubert and Burt Griffin renewed an appeal for answers from the CIA to questions first posed to that agency by the Ruby detail on February 24. The questions had been framed within a 13-page document about Ruby's activities and associates. On March 12, J. Lee Rankin had met with Richard Helms, the CIA's deputy director for plans, and personally handed over the questions drawn up by Hubert and Griffin. At that meeting Rankin asked Helms for helpful information from the CIA files. There had been no response. On May 19, Rankin again asked Helms for the answers, this time in writing. Rankin stressed the need for particulars on Ruby's "alleged associates and/or activities in Cuba."

On June 8, Helms replied to Rankin in a memorandum which the CIA kept classified in its files as Document No. 730-326 for the next 12 years. "Examination of CIA records has failed to produce information on Jack Ruby or his activities," the memorandum began.

Hubert and Griffin had asked the CIA for specific information on 22 other people. One of those was Alex Gruber, an exact contemporary of Ruby's, born in Chicago in 1911. Gruber had a police record and West Coast mob associates. His sudden appearance in Dallas for meetings with Ruby a few days before the Kennedy assassination, and his long-distance telephone conversation with Ruby minutes after Kennedy was pronounced dead at Parkland Hospital, had aroused the interests of Hubert and Griffin. This is what the CIA told them on June 8:

"CIA records contain a number of references from usually reliable sources to an Alexander Gruber, born on 13 April 1905. This person was identified as an Austrian policeman and a Communist.

"We also have a report from other usually reliable sources that one Alexander Gruber, a Hungarian national, born in about 1907, had arrived by air in Rio de Janeiro, traveling to Brazil, on 4 September 1960. In Rio he stayed at the Hotel Natal."

H. L. Hunt was well known as one of the world's richest men, who lived in Dallas and sponsored rightwing political causes. Hubert and Griffin had reason to suspect that Ruby might have had some dealings with Hunt or a member of his family. They asked the CIA about him, too.

The CIA came up with an H. L. Hunt who, in 1943, had been editor of an antifascist bilingual newspaper on the Texas-Mexican border, *El Tiempo de Laredo*, which had a daily circulation of 10,638.

No wonder the CIA kept its June 8, 1964, report to the Warren Commission a secret for 12 years. After all, it was revealing the 1943 circulation figures of a newspaper. That ranks right up there with the report that had been turned in to the Warren Commission four months earlier by the FBI—revealing the 1938 dental chart of Jack Ruby's toothless mother in Chicago.

On June 8, the day of the CIA's secret report to the Warren Commission, Patrick T. Dean, the Dallas police sergeant, appeared before the Commission in Washington to formally protest the treatment he had received from Burt Griffin in their March 24 off-the-record confrontation.

Dean was accompanied into the Commission hearing by Texas Attorney General Waggoner Carr. Even though Carr was there to testify on additional matters, his juxtaposition with Dean lent unspoken but obvious official Texas support for the police officer who had been the state's most damaging witness against Jack Ruby. The Commission more than encouraged this show of support for Dean by failing to ask either Griffin or Hubert to be present at the accusatory session.

Hubert had been allowed to resign his regular duties as head of the Ruby detail the week before. Hubert was unhappy with the lack of meaningful progress in the Ruby probe. Back in New Orleans both the small law firm Hubert headed and his marriage appeared to be in trouble,[7] and he felt it necessary to leave the Commission—with an understanding Hubert put into writing to Rankin that he would be available for the Commission's essential interview with Jack Ruby. Hubert departed for New Orleans on June 6. Rankin and Warren staged the interview with Ruby in Dallas on June 7, without advising Hubert. On June 8, back in Washington, they were meeting with Patrick Dean and "that kind of griped me, too," Hubert recalls, when they didn't give him the opportunity even to observe the session. They would call on Hubert frequently in the weeks to come to help handle the lesser Commission interviews, but the exclusion of Hubert from the June 7 and 8 sessions said quite a lot about the intent of the Warren Commission.

Present at the Dean interview were Chief Justice Warren and one other panelist, Allen Dulles. But only Warren and chief counsel Rankin questioned Dean. Griffin was in his office a few doors down the hall, unaware in advance that Dean would be coming to testify.

The session provided no new information and principally it was cosmetic in nature, creating a means for the Dallas police sergeant to put his strong objections on the record to Griffin's off-the-record statements and questions.

Warren and Rankin treated the witness gingerly and when Dean protested that he had been wronged by the Warren Commission's Burt Griffin, Warren answered, "Well, sergeant, I want to say to you that, of course, without knowing what your conversation was with Mr. Griffin, I have never talked to Mr. Griffin about this. I didn't know that you had this altercation with him, but I want to say this: That so far as the jurisdiction of this Commission is concerned and its procedures, no member of our staff has a right to tell any witness that he is lying or that he is testifying falsely. That is not his business. It is the business of the Commission to appraise the testimony of all the witnesses, and, at the time you are talking about, and up to the present time, this Commission has never appraised your testimony or fully appraised the testimony of any other witness, and furthermore, I want to say to you that no member of our staff has any power to help or injure any witness."

More than two months had passed since the Griffin-Dean run-in in Dallas, and if the chairman of the Warren Commission still did not even know there had been such a run-in—which had caused a major behind-scenes furor in the Commission and the recall from Dallas of Griffin—then communication within the Warren panel was incomprehensibly bad. More than likely Chairman Warren was signaling the most dominant Texan of all, the President of the United States, through Dean and Carr, that the Commission would absorb its losses here and forget the matter. Warren picked the most agreeable way of saying it that he could.

As a result, the on-the-record portion of Dean's controversial Warren Commission testimony in Dallas never was appraised by the Commission. There was not one word in the Warren Report about: 1) Dean's decision to withhold highly incriminating evidence against Jack Ruby in his police department reports until just before the Ruby trial; or 2) the contradictions involving Dean as spelled out by assistant Commission counsel Griffin; or 3) the encounter between Dean and Griffin.

Despite the June 1 deadline that Earl Warren had imposed on the staff for writing its conclusions, only two of the Commission's lawyers managed even to get drafts of their chapters completed by then. Griffin and others were in no way ready.

In his 1966 book, *Inquest*, Edward J. Epstein wrote that Commission members apparently were not made aware of the situation and, as the planned June 30 date approached for releasing the Report, "Willens and Redlich went over Rankin's head and told Warren that some of the lawyers still had not completed their investigations and that it was impossible for the Report to be completed by June 30. Warren then reportedly lost his temper and demanded that Willens close down the investigation immediately. The deadline, however, was extended to July 15."

A few of the important interviews of the Commission's Ruby detail had not been undertaken by July 15. More importantly, in their critical May 14 memorandum, Hubert and Griffin had said it was essential for the Commission to view video tapes and movie films made in Dallas throughout the weekend of the assassinations. As a result, Commission historian Alfred Goldberg assembled about 1,500 pounds of these films and tapes in cans flown largely from Dallas and Fort Worth. In mid-July, Goldberg, Griffin and others were spending up to nine hours a day in a Pentagon screening room, viewing scenes in search of bits and pieces of evidence that would support or disprove critical portions of testimony.

Goldberg and Redlich shared the heaviest responsibility for redrafting and rewriting chapters. "It was very depressing," Epstein quoted Redlich. "It seemed as if it would go forever." Warren fitfully granted one time extension after another as the summer wore on—past the Republican national convention in July, which nominated Barry M. Goldwater, and the Democratic convention in late August, which performed under the heavy hand of President Johnson. The Johnson White House was keeping a close and narrowed eye on Warren. The Warren Report had to be produced substantially before the November elections, in order to remove it as a political issue. McGeorge Bundy, the President's special assistant for national security affairs, made that abundantly clear to the embattled J. Lee Rankin several times in telephone conversations.

One of the final people Griffin interviewed was Eva L. Grant, Jack Ruby's loquacious sister. At one point in the interview Mrs. Grant resented an innocent-appearing question by Griffin[8] and began to shout angrily at him. She shouted so loudly that U.S. Attorney Barefoot Sanders came in from the next office to see what had gone wrong now.

"Look, you don't even have to go into this as far as I'm concerned," Griffin said defensively to the witness as Sanders hurried in. "Let me say this, that the testimony we have been taking today, I don't think there has been any suggestion of accusations—I have simply been trying to find out from you what you did." It had become a very tough summer for Burt Griffin.

CHAPTER 12

Man's Best Friend

For Jack Ruby, too, it had become a very tough summer. Almost at the instant the jury returned the verdict that Ruby was to be electrocuted, he seemed to lose all hope. There was no talking to him about a carefully structured appeal through the courts. He grew frantic instead about the genocide of American Jews in the streets that he envisioned. He became taunted by sexual and global political fantasies. He was certain he never again would see the dogs he had kept at home and at the Carousel, the pets he thought of as his wife and children. He expected at times that he simply was to be taken out within hours and incinerated by the authorities, and he tried in different ways to destroy himself first.

The possibility that Jack Ruby might commit suicide was not something that arose for the first time in the post-trial period. A dozen years earlier, 1952, when Ruby was 41, he got into desperate financial straits. He lost control of two Dallas clubs, including the Silver Spur, which had been a mob hangout. He lost a stake of up to $25,000 in the clubs from shadowy investors, and owed federal taxes. "I hibernated and became panicky for a couple of months," he said later.[1] "I had no desire for anything and did

not care if I lived or died. I thought about my being a complete failure."
After hiding out in a small, walkup hotel in Dallas for two months, Ruby
then slipped into Chicago, where he languished for another three months
in the YMCA.

Not long after Ruby's arrest for the Oswald murder and his subsequent transfer from city jail to the custody of Sheriff Bill Decker, there
was concern that Ruby might be overtaken again by severe despair. During that period, I remained on assignment as Scripps-Howard staff correspondent in Dallas, investigating the story of the assassinations for two
weeks, and filing one or two pieces a day back to my Washington bureau.
These articles were then distributed on the bureau's overnight wire to
Scripps-Howard newspapers in a number of cities across much of the nation. One such article began:

> DALLAS, Nov. 30—Police officials fear that Jack Ruby, the
> slayer of President Kennedy's alleged assassin, Lee Harvey Oswald,
> might try to take his own life or become the target of another Dallas
> assassination.
>
> Dallas County Sheriff J. E. (Bill) Decker has Ruby confined in a
> solitary cell under 24-hour guard.
>
> Ruby's attorney, Tom Howard, complained that his client had
> not been allowed to see any of his mail after six days in jail.
>
> Last night Decker personally delivered a batch of letters and
> telegrams to the prisoner.
>
> "Some of the mail was in praise of him," said Decker, "but some
> of it contained insults."
>
> Decker said mail had been withheld from Ruby because "there's
> stuff in there which could depress him." One letter, however, had a
> check made out to Ruby for $100.
>
> Ruby is given a special guard at mealtime when he uses eating
> utensils. He is wearing coveralls and has no belt with which he could
> injure himself. He has been given no newspapers and the letters he
> got last night were the first tangible evidence for Ruby that he is "not
> a hero to the world," the sheriff said.
>
> Reliable police sources also indicated today that threats on
> Ruby's life mailed to Ruby in the county jail have been turned over
> to the FBI.

Ruby's post-trial suicide efforts were crude but he had limited opportunities and they appeared to be spontaneous. The first time, he rammed his head against the wall of his cell. He stood back about 20 feet and
ran as hard as he could headlong into the wall, hoping to split his skull.
When attorney Joe Tonahill visited him the next day, Ruby had a knot as
round as a silver dollar on his head. Another time Ruby tried to hang
himself, but there was not enough time for him to rip his clothing and
fashion a sturdy knot out of a pants leg because there always was a guard
assigned to watch him.

One reason for Ruby's overwhelming despair after the trial was that Ruby felt one of those assigned guards, the psalms-saying, hymn-singing deputy sheriff Jess Stevenson, had gained his confidence through prayer and piety in order to strip him of information that could be used against him by the prosecution. Stevenson was alone with him the evening Ruby tried to beat the state's electric chair at Huntsville by electrocuting himself.

Describing what happened, Stevenson said[2] Ruby appeared to be asleep, sitting up in his chair in the large enclosure outside his cell where Ruby and his guards could sit at a table and play what Stevenson says is "that Las Vegas game of cards." (Gin rummy. Ruby had taught it to him in kind of a cultural exchange wherein Stevenson discoursed on the Bible.) Ruby's head was slumped; his eyes closed. Stevenson got up from his chair at that point and went off to get a glass of water. Ruby moved fast. He unscrewed the overhead light bulb, dumped water from his own glass onto the floor as a conduit, but then couldn't reach the socket with his finger while standing in the water. Ruby began jumping up and down, fitfully trying to make foot and finger contact somehow match. It was "something nearly comical," Stevenson smiles maliciously. Stevenson says he also thinks Ruby's suicide attempts and delusions of Jewish persecution likely were put-ons inspired by Ruby's attorneys.

Ruby had a "kind of hysterical interest in religion."[3] When he received a leather-bound Bible as a gift a month after his murder trial, he inscribed it to himself on the front page: "Presented to Jack Ruby by the will of God, April 15, 1964." Several months later he was reading the Old Testament portion of that Bible and came to a part about "the persecution of the Jews," according to Ray Pennington, another of the sheriff's deputies assigned to guard Ruby.[4] "He became mad and disgusted and started to tear it up. I asked him not to tear it up—just hand it to me. He gave it to me and wrote a note inside it." Ever the man of outer appearance, Ruby was anxious not to seem irrational and the note he wrote to Pennington said: "May you always remember me as you have always known me and most certainly if anyone should know that I haven't changed, you would be the one person to know it. Sincerely, Jack Ruby."

Feelings of hopelessness drifted in and out of Ruby's consciousness in jail, and he began to keep his hands and mind occupied with "doodles" that he created with a ferocity. They were crowded, intense designs, each line done stridently straight. Doodles tend to be people's casually drawn inner expressions, but in Ruby's hands these were meticulous statements of anguish.

The prisoner used a well-worn wooden 12-inch ruler as his straightedge and, according to Pennington, he would draw with his right hand while turning the paper quickly with his left to achieve the angles of his lines. He would keep his pencil finely sharp by rubbing the flat sides of the point over and over on a separate piece of paper.

Ruby considered these to be highly personal drawings and he prided himself in the design work. As a result he gave away a number of them as gifts within the jail as treasures of friendship. In particular he awarded several, along with a lengthy biographical letter about himself, to a fellow prisoner—a 27-year-old trusty who had befriended him—and these have been in the private possession of Dr. John Lattimer since shortly after Ruby's death in 1967. Dr. Lattimer, a prominent New York surgeon and Columbia University medical school departmental chairman, is also a widely recognized collector of historical memorabilia. As Lattimer's interest in Ruby grew he assembled some private analyses of Ruby's handwriting and "doodles" from experts in the fields of psychology, psychiatry and graphology.

The draftsmanship of these drawings revealed another side of Ruby. Here are some comments acquired by Dr. Lattimer from the experts on Ruby's writings and drawings:

"I think it is significant," according to one analyst looking at Ruby's jumbled letter to the fellow prisoner, "that he writes Nazis as *nazi's* with a small *n*. But whenever he speaks of Jews, he always spells the word with a capital and not the small letter he uses in *negroes*. All through the letter he portrays a phobia about the Nazis and Germans, accompanied by a fear and hatred that was one of the contributing factors in shooting Oswald. It is interesting to note here that although Oswald had a Russian wife and possibly was a communist, the writer never equates Oswald with the communists but vicariously substitutes the Nazis—showing positively when he killed Oswald he was avenging the Jews in the gas chambers and not JFK."

The analysts found "a good deal of constriction" in style and an overcrowding of detail in both the drawings and the writing.

"His overall identification seems to be more feminine than masculine, with its delicacy and conventional form," wrote one expert, enlarging then on that:

"He is becoming rigid in his functioning. In fact almost to the point of pathology. If just a little stiffer, I would worry that he is heading toward pathology. There are impulsive moves toward the environment, then a holding back. The more you look at his writing, the worse it gets. He seems to have assumed a defensive cover for his sexuality and other impulses which he cannot handle, such as his femininity. His ethical emphasis may be a defense."

The drawings showed Ruby to be "fantastically obsessive-compulsive," said another. "There is always something at the center—the symbol of the door or the vulva (the external parts of the female sex organs)—

speculatively interpreted as ruminative attempts to cope with pre-Oedipal incestuous attachments to the mother. Attempts are all blocked off. He can't move forward or backward. If drawings are taken in order from light to dark, they present greater despair at the end."

Aside from the straight-line "doodles," attorney Joe Tonahill had Ruby do some free-form sketches on subjects that just came to mind. Tonahill then sent the sketches to one of the defense psychiatrists, whose comments Tonahill just kept quiet. The psychiatrist said the sketches showed Jack Ruby was a latent homosexual.

It was not difficult for Ruby's defense psychiatrists to detect quickly that the prisoner—a bachelor at 52, who spoke with a slight lisp and loved to soothe himself with oils and creams—had apparent homosexual tendencies. In their written reports to Tonahill and chief defense counsel Melvin Belli, the psychiatrists seemed almost to be presenting the lawyers with a sex-murder case.

Ruby's conversational description of President Kennedy's "charm and manner cannot be reproduced in words here," Dr. Bromberg noted. "Essentially it was the speech of a man in love with another man. It was a love that passed beyond a rational appreciation of a great man, coming out of the unconscious. The prisoner said, 'This is the end of my life' when the President died, and in so doing he expressed more than mourning."

During the Ruby trial Belli put Dr. Guttmacher, Ruby's defense psychiatrist, on the stand and asked what Ruby had said to the psychiatrist about President Kennedy.

"Well, he uses such terms as, 'I fell for that man.' It's the kind of term one uses really for someone that really one is in love with," Guttmacher replied.

Belli asked him if such a term by Ruby would convey any "latent homosexual pathology," and Guttmacher replied that "there are suggestions of it."

Ruby lived with a succession of young men who sometimes worked as bouncers at the Carousel or at least kept themselves physically tough. An exception was George Senator, beer-bloated and almost Ruby's age. In the first week of November, 1963, the week George Senator moved in, Ruby was sharing his apartment with a 25-year-old baseball player from Iowa, according to Nancy Powell, who stripped at the Carousel under the name of Tammi True.

Senator, who enjoyed the company of men, sometimes used the term "boy friend" to describe Ruby, according to a report by FBI agent Kenneth C. Howe, the day Ruby murdered Oswald. Senator told Howe that day that Ruby "has never been married and has never shown any special interest in girls."

Later, Senator met with Leon Hubert of the Warren Commission.

Their conversation about Ruby bore the traces of an old Abbott and Costello routine:

HUBERT: What was his attitude toward women?
SENATOR: Like any other man.
H: That is to say, any other normal man?
S: Any other normal man.
H: Have you ever observed any traits which suggested to you the possibility of homosexuality?
S: Never.
H: On his part?
S: Never.
H: Did he have any peculiar mannerisms which might have suggested such a thing to other people, even though it was not so?
S: I never noticed it.
H: Did he lisp?
S: Yes. So do I.
H: Jack has a lisp?
S: He has a lisp. He has always had it to my knowledge.
H: In your opinion he was not a homosexual at all?
S: No. Just as normal as any human being.
H: He was single?
S: He has got a brother older than he is and single, never been married—Hyman.
H: Did he have any girl friends?
S: Yes; he went out with various girls.
H: What I am getting at is what you know about his sex relationships.
S: His sex relationship, you know I'm not there to watch wherever he may be.
H: Still you may have some knowledge of facts which would throw light upon that.
S: He likes women.
H: How do you know that?
S: How do I know he likes women?
H: Yes.
S: I like women.
H: Did he ever tell you that he liked them?
S: Did he ever tell me? In any normal conversation I'm certain [pause] anybody here [pause] who doesn't say they don't like women? I think this is a normal thing to say.
H: What I am trying to get at is simply this. Very naturally as you pointed out a moment ago, it is very rare that there are any eyewitnesses to acts of sexual intercourse. On the other hand, there are other facts and circumstances from which one may judge if a man is having sexual intercourse with a particular woman, and that is what I am trying to get at. Do you know of any such things?
S: This here I'm never around.
H: What?
S: You mean when he is having sexual intercourse with a woman?

H: Yes; of course you wouldn't be around, but do you have any opinion as to whether or not he was having any affairs of a sexual nature with anybody? If you are reticent about naming names, perhaps we can leave that off.

S: I have no names to name, but I am certain that he likes women. I know he talks to them like I talk to them or anybody else talks to them.

H: Did he ever bring any to the apartment that you know of?

S: I am certain he has them up for coffee when I have been there, such as that or a drink or talk, conversation. He has had even the help [the strippers] up there, you know. Once in a while we have a party. This is when I turn out to be the cook.

H: But you can't tell us then of any particular person that you would think Jack had intimate relationships with?

S: No.

At one of those parties, according to testimony given to the Warren Commission by a former Carousel bartender, Ruby peeled off his clothes to his shorts, while one of his strippers slowly undressed and gyrated in front of him. As he reached for her she smiled and pulled away, but Ruby "in a loud and excited voice said, 'Come on, man or woman. I'll take anyone on.' "

Dr. Guttmacher, the psychiatrist, noted that Ruby had "at a deep unconscious level, intense psycho-sexual conflict, leading the patient to be constantly asserting his masculinity by fighting, sexual promiscuity, bodybuilding exercises, etc."[5]

Ruby told Dr. Guttmacher that homosexuals were repulsive to him; however this is the way he worded it: "I won't be belligerent or hit them but if I go into a bus station toilet I won't even let them know I am interested."

There was something else, revealing perhaps, that Ruby told Dr. Guttmacher when asked for some self-evaluation. "I can't tolerate people who are undesirable," he said. "I want to get rid of them like a cancer. I don't want to be a sucker for a girl. I'd rather help a fellow out."

John C. Jackson of Lafayette, Louisiana, who had lived with Jack Ruby in Dallas during the 1950s, told the FBI that Ruby would be scornful of any woman after she went to bed with him, and he would not date her again. Jackson's account matched what several Carousel strippers said about him—that Ruby had no use for any employee who succeeded in getting him to compromise her. Jada, the stripper who received twice as much pay from Ruby as any of the other girls because he considered her to be a supreme sex object, was highly insulted when Ruby offered to move her into his apartment. Ruby wanted to install her there as a sex symbol he would show off to the neighborhood. He assured Jada that she would have her own bedroom and their relationship would be platonic.

That's what burned up Jada. She enjoyed the rhythm of sex off the stage as well as on, and she turned down Ruby in salty language.

Most women were commodities to Jack Ruby, who'd had an unbearable relationship with his mother, who pushed and shoved his sister around, and who once threatened to permanently cripple a cigarette girl at the Carousel by throwing her down a flight of stairs. They were commodities. He procured some for use of out-of-town promoters who would come to Dallas to get the local disc-jockeys to plug certain songs. He employed some to establish himself as a second-rate downtown impresario. He used some to maintain the outer appearances he wanted. But even so, they could manipulate him easily.

For instance, Ruby boasted that he was "very clever about protecting myself" from the diseases of sexual intercourse. He said he used contraceptives, referring to them as fish skins, and frequently carried his own syringe and medicine. Since Ruby had been afflicted by gonorrhea several times even after passing the age of 40, Dr. Guttmacher asked him how it was possible to take so many precautions and still fall prey to venereal disease so often.[6] Ruby shrugged. The girls would tell him they were clean, he said.

Apparently the safest way for Ruby to have relationships with women was by telephone. That was his style with Elaine Rogers, a telephone company employee who met Ruby through one of his strippers, Marylin Moone. Ruby began telephoning Miss Rogers, at first reading her suggestive poetry. The calls became progressively obscene, to the point where she became certain he "obtained some sexual gratification from the conversations," according to FBI report No. 44-1639, filed in Dallas four days after Ruby shot Oswald. Ruby would begin some of the telephone conversations with "a detailed description of his privates," said the FBI report. "He told her he had been circumcised and this would enable him to give her greater pleasure. Ruby would then describe in minute detail how he would have sexual intercourse with her and . . . the pleasure she would derive from this act. Miss Rogers indicated that the longer Ruby talked the more excited he became. . . ."

Women ranked third with Ruby among those who meant most to him. His closer bonds were with men and he often used the term "love" to describe his feelings for the Dallas police. But his special companions were his dogs. His relationships with them had grown bizarre, as Rabbi Hillel E. Silverman testified.

Rabbi Silverman, who had seen Ruby infrequently at the synagogue when the nightclub operator would attend a service, appeared as a defense witness at the Ruby trial, and told about one day when Ruby had dropped by the Silverman home to visit:

We were standing on my lawn and the dogs were running around, he was telling me about his Chicago background, and I turned to the dogs and made a remark about them, and suddenly he began to cry for no reason at all. And he began to tell me, "I'm unmarried, I have no children, this is my wife"—and he pointed to one of the dogs—"and these are my children," and he began to sob and to cry and to moan, and then in five or 10 minutes he forgot about it completely and went on to another subject.

Later, the Warren Report stressed in one paragraph that "Ruby was extremely fond of dogs. Numerous persons stated that he was constantly accompanied by several of the dogs he owned. Testimony at Ruby's trial in March, 1964, indicated that he referred to his dogs as his 'children.' He also became extremely incensed when he witnessed the maltreatment of any of his dogs." Word for word, that was the total paragraph and the caption above it read: "Affection for Dogs." Critics of the Warren Report say the paragraph supported an unjustifiably saccharine view of Ruby, especially in conjunction with a questionable conclusion three pages earlier in the Report that there was no "significant link between Ruby and organized crime." But the most transparent failure in its brief paragraph on Ruby and his dogs was the Commission's decision to cast an apple-pie normal outlook on the relationship between the man and his pets. Not only was it brought out at the trial that one dog was his wife, but also that the children were undisciplined. The witness was William G. Serur, an upholstery salesman whom Ruby had telephoned to bring seat covers for Ruby's car. Serur said:

He opened the [car] door and when he did I burst out laughing. And he looked at me as he said, "What are you laughing about?" He kind of tilted his head that time. I said, "I want to know what did this. I've never seen seat covers like this."

They were all eat out. All the upholstery was all over the back floorboard, and all over the front floorboard. The only thing left of the seat covers was the outer shred of the seat covers. They were nylon material that Oldsmobile usually puts on, but they ate out the pockets. I called it pockets. The only thing they left was the outer edges. If I could describe it to you, they left the outer edges but they ate out the whole thing and you could see the springs protruding. I said, "Jack, what did this?" He said, "My children." He said, "anything wrong with that." He kind of tilted his head and I said, "I can't figure this out. You mean the dogs?" And he said, "My children did it." He said, "What do you want to do, cause an argument out here?" He said, "I asked you to come down here and give me a price on those seat covers, and now you want to criticize my children."

. . . Jack used to always tell me, "I don't want you to refer to them as dogs." He said, "Those are my children." He said, "Don't you have children?" He said, "Don't you respect them?" He said, "I respect my kids." He said, "They go wherever I go and I want you not

> to call them dogs any more." . . . [and then on another occasion when
> Serur came to visit Ruby in his apartment] the first thing I noticed,
> the baseboard was all eat up, and the couch was all eat up, part of it.
> And I said, "Jack, what in the world happened?" And he said, "My
> children." He said, "Anything wrong with that?" He said, "My chil-
> dren eat it up."

Ruby had as many as 10 dogs at a time, and the one he referred to as
his wife was Sheba, a dachshund. She provided Ruby with a litter of six
pups in 1963 and he housed them in a back room at the Carousel. Sheba,
meanwhile, went everywhere with Ruby. He took her to work and then
back home again. She rode with him to all-night restaurants and waited
unquestioningly in the car while he went into the police station and shot
Lee Harvey Oswald. It was the last time she would see him.

Aside from seeking out Ruby, to hear what he sounded like, the psychiatrists probably should have examined the contents of the two-door,
1960 Oldsmobile he left parked in the 2000 block of Main Street that Sunday. Besides Sheba, he left a glimpse into his volatile, uneven mind. There
were two sets of lightweight metal knuckles for hitting people, one set of
them worn with use, in the locked car. There was a holster for his snub-
nosed pistol—unpaid parking tickets, a wallet that was empty but a paper
sack that was stuffed with $837.50 The surrealistic scene on wheels in-
cluded one white bathing cap; a left golf shoe, size 10-1/2 D, with a one-
dollar bill in it; a grey suit; several hundred photographs of Jada, the
stripper he was no longer speaking to; a jar of dietary food; a can of paint;
several new, unused men's white handkerchiefs; copies of Fort Worth and
Dallas newspapers from November 20, showing what President Kennedy's proposed motorcade routes would be in those cities on November
22; the names, addresses and phone numbers of dozens of people who
held passes to the Carousel or were contacts; and a roll of toilet paper.
Ruby didn't care about the inside look of his car, so long as the outside
was washed. Caring for outside appearances steadily was one of his special characteristics—and that became clear in the way Ruby and Oswald
handled themselves as each was arrested for murder and put in the Dallas
jail.

Oswald shouted out in the boisterous third-floor corridor that he
wanted John J. Abt, and Ruby shouted out for Gordon McLendon. Abt
was a New York lawyer who did not know Oswald but who had a reputation for defending unpopular political prisoners. McLendon operated
KLIF, the gimmicky Dallas radio station. McLendon was an outspoken
supporter of Dallas police policy and used his station to read politically
conservative editorials in launching an abortive campaign for the United
States Senate. The KLIF disc-jockey known as Weird Beard recalled later
that Ruby "greatly admired McLendon." From almost the moment of his

arrest Jack Ruby attempted to interest McLendon in publicizing the story of his murdering Oswald as the act of a national patriot. Oswald thought in terms of getting an experienced lawyer. Ruby went for the publicist.

Public image was Ruby's priority. When another man bit off a portion of one of Ruby's fingers in a brawl in Dallas, Ruby said he was upset because he had hoped to become a Mason, and understood that Masons wouldn't accept people who were missing any part of their anatomy.

Ruby had a lot of strange ideas. He wore a woman's silk stocking pulled down tightly over the crown of his head when he swam in his apartment house pool, in order to prevent particles in the water from reaching his scalp.

He had stopped taking C.R.D., a weight-loss medication, because he had become convinced it made the sparse hair on his head deteriorate. C.R.D. had a stimulating effect on him, but the way he worded it was, "It takes out your procrastination."

Ruby had a jumbled way with words which was intriguing to the psychiatrists. They found his speech patterns to be "an indication of actual intellectual disorder which is not readily visible on the surface, since in a rapid flow of speech he can cover it up." In talking to the psychiatrists about how his sister's mourning for President Kennedy caused them to cry together, Ruby said, "She was contagious to me."

As he lay dying as a prisoner in December, 1966, his body ravaged by cancer, Ruby weakly called his sister, Eileen Kaminsky, to his bedside. "Do me a favor," he whispered. He handed her a shopping list in which he asked for pastrami, corned beef, kosher dill pickles, rye bread, lox, bagels, cream cheese and green onions. He was too frail to hold any of it down. But for Jack Ruby it was as grand a meal as any condemned man could ever hope to order.

CHAPTER 13

The Truth, The Whole Truth & Other Fables

Over the protests of his family, Jack Ruby could hardly wait to be put into the electric chair on July 18, 1964. Actually it was an *electronic* chair, especially configured as a testing seat for the Model 22500 Stoelting Deceptograph, a lie-detector machine. The chair was angled in ways to support Ruby's arms comfortably and to discourage him from slouching or crossing his legs while hooked to instruments that simultaneously measured his heart rate, breathing patterns and skin sensations as he answered the Warren Commission's questions. One of Ruby's attorneys threatened to sue the Commission for violating Ruby's rights by subjecting him to the test.

But Ruby had been alternately begging for and insisting on taking the test for about seven months. He had sought a shot of truth serum or to be hooked to a polygraph machine in order to prove both that he was telling the truth and was sane—especially when a clinical psychiatrist in Dallas, Dr. William R. Beavers, examined Ruby in the weeks following the Ruby murder trial and reported that Ruby had become psychotic. Dr. Beavers said the prisoner needed to be removed from a cage-like setting and hospitalized.[1] Ruby resented any inference that he was a mental case.

Typically he clung to every outer image that would show him to be as sane as any other patriotic Texas killer.

However, most of those in the band of 18 defense lawyers who tramped out of step through Ruby's trial and the various motions for a new trial were against Ruby taking the lie-detector test. Some didn't want him on the witness stand and others didn't want him hooked up to an electronic device since they maintained he had emotional problems and they didn't know what he might say to incriminate himself further. The Warren Commission, too, was against giving Ruby the test.

Essentially the Commission was basing its findings on about 26,500 interviews conducted by FBI and Secret Service agents without the use of lie-detector devices. In addition, the Commission and its staff picked out 489 witnesses to question and only twice was there serious consideration given to administering a polygraph examination to any of them. The first time was in January, 1964, when the staff got into a heated argument over whether Lee Harvey Oswald's widow, Marina, should be asked to submit to such an examination as a backup to her regular testimony. Assistant counsel David Belin felt there were many murky facts about what the widow knew and had seen, and led the fight to have the test made available to her. Belin insisted in a memorandum that a test conducted by a highly skilled polygraph operator not only could produce investigative leads, but if "it were to be shown that Marina Oswald had not been truthful in her testimony, it could throw an entirely new light on aspects of the investigation." Belin argued that the young Russian woman ought to be confronted with the challenge of a lie-detector test as a means for her to show the American public she had told all there was to tell about the complete story. Belin failed to convince superiors at the Commission. They decided that since polygraph findings were inadmissible in courts of law, many people would construe the test to be used as a weapon to intimidate the witness.

Belin smarted over the argument he lost. He was convinced a lie-detector test for Marina Oswald was an intrinsic investigative tool the Commission had failed to use. When the prospects of such a test for Jack Ruby came along, Belin decided he wouldn't confront his superiors at the Commission head-on a second time. He would outmaneuver them.

Belin was aware that Ruby was seeking a lie-detector test as a means of backing his story that he was innocent of conspiracy, and Belin also became aware that Rabbi Hillel Silverman had become a regular visitor to Ruby, to comfort the prisoner scheduled to become the first Jewish prisoner in Texas history to go to the electric chair at Huntsville. Belin and Silverman had met by chance as travelers abroad in the summer before the Kennedy assassination, at a time when Belin was a lawyer in Des Moines and the rabbi was spiritual leader of Congregation Shearith Israel, the synagogue that Ruby attended only sporadically.

In the course of a couple of meetings with Silverman in Dallas, Belin easily got the rabbi to agree to a plan. The rabbi would convince Ruby to insist on taking a polygraph test as a condition to his being questioned by the Commission as a witness. Ruby had to be convinced to buck his own attorneys who for the most part were dead set against their client submitting to the test. The rabbi agreed because he didn't think Ruby had been a conspirator and the test would prove it.

On June 7, 1964, when Chief Justice Warren and Congressman Ford confronted Ruby in the Dallas county jail to question him as a sworn witness before the Warren Commission, Ruby laid down his demand. Lawyer Joe Tonahill was at Ruby's side and Tonahill didn't agree with other Ruby lawyers who thought a lie-detector test was all wrong for their client. Tonahill supported Ruby's demand, and the Chief Justice agreed to the condition. "Any kind of a test you want to verify what you say, we will be glad to do," said Earl Warren. Belin had engineered the only polygraph test the Warren Commission consented to give.

Shortly after Warren and Ford returned to Washington from their meeting with the jittery prisoner in Dallas, another in the parade of chief defense attorneys was named to aid Ruby. He was Clayton Fowler, president of the Dallas Criminal Bar Association. The selection of Fowler had been made of course by Earl Ruby in Detroit, since that's how the system worked, and brother Earl was being guided by Sol A. Dann, a Detroit lawyer. Dann was a wizened, argumentative man who had made his reputation by filing charges of corruption and incompetence in the highest management levels of the Chrysler Corporation, foreshadowing the resignation of Chrysler's president. Dann was a battler, a distrustful man who injected himself into every area of the Ruby defense, even though he was not a criminal lawyer. At one point he filed a 35-page memorandum with the court, which charged Texas with an outpouring of anti-Semitism that led to a situation where "Ruby is now a 'number,' tho it is not tattooed on his arm. What irony that Ruby, who concerned himself with fighting anti-Semitism, became a further victim of it during the trial and may be executed because of this hate and prejudice. . . . The jury tried Jacob Rubenstein—the Jew." Dann in Detroit and Fowler in Texas more than once had discussed their mutual determination to keep Ruby from taking a lie-detector test, just as David Belin had anticipated. So the Warren Commission showed up with two expert FBI polygraph operators late on the morning of July 18, 1964, a Saturday, without notice. Fowler was notified by Sheriff Decker after the polygraph team already was in the jail and by then Fowler felt it was too late to find a judge on a Saturday who would issue a restraining order against the test.

Assistant counsel Arlen Specter had arrived from Washington to represent the Warren Commission. With him to direct the test was Bell P. Herndon, polygraph supervisor at the FBI laboratory in Washington. Herndon had given thousands of these tests.

Fowler hurried to the room on the seventh floor of the county jail and found another of Ruby's attorneys, Tonahill, had been summoned, too. Tonahill had survived several attempts by the Rubys, including Jack, to have him removed as part of the defense team, but he refused to leave and remained an advocate of the lie-detector test. Fowler met privately with Ruby and tried one last time to dissuade him from taking the test, but the prisoner excitedly said he was determined to take it. The first chance he had, when there was a break in the proceeding, Fowler got to a telephone, dialed Ruby's sister, Eva Grant, and told her what was going on. She was able to reach Sol Dann in Detroit. Dann called the Dallas jail and told Fowler he was fired as chief counsel for not having kept the lie-detector test from happening. Fowler countered that Dann was fired. But by then Dann was shouting that he would file assault and battery charges against the Warren Commission and everyone else involved, for subjecting his client to the truth.

Sol Dann was especially upset because his grand strategy was to get Jack Ruby into a sanity hearing and convince a jury that his client was not sane. But his strategy would be in deep trouble if his client performed as a reliable person on a lie-detector test.

The problem was just that simple. People with psychotic problems are not considered reliable enough to be recorded with accuracy on the polygraph charts. If the Warren Commission found Ruby to score credibly in the examination then it would be that much harder for Dann to convince a jury that Ruby had lost his marbles.

So it was significant that among those present in Room 7-M of the Dallas county jail during the several hours involved in the testing of Jack Ruby was Dr. Beavers, the psychiatrist who three months earlier had told Judge Brown that Ruby was acutely mentally ill.

This time Dr. Beavers was on hand as official medical observer during the test. When it was over he told Arlen Specter that Ruby continued to appear to be a "psychotic depressive," but to a "less obvious" degree than in April, and that Ruby appeared to comprehend most of the questions, answering them realistically.

The answers Ruby gave supported both his own claims and the Warren Commission's ultimate conclusions that Ruby had been personally innocent of any conspiracy to kill President Kennedy.

For instance, Ruby was asked if he had known Oswald before the day President Kennedy was assassinated, had he assisted in the assassination or did he shoot Oswald in order to keep the assassin from talking? Ruby answered no to these questions and the polygraph charts indicated Ruby was not lying.

But there were times during the test when the mechanical

pens moved excitedly on the charts, reflecting physiological changes in the prisoner when he was asked certain questions. Those changes indicated Ruby could have been lying, and they occurred when he was asked about entering the Dallas police station on the weekend of November 22-24, 1963.

He was asked, for instance, if he had appeared in the police station more than once on November 22, the day the President was shot, and Ruby answered, "No." Ruby always clung to his story that he had gone to the station just once that night—a simple errand to deliver sandwiches, which had led to the chance opportunity for him to participate in Oswald's abortive press conference. Ruby denied the insistent testimony of detective Mike Eberhardt and two Dallas reporters that he had been encountered in the vicinity of the room where Oswald was being interrogated several hours earlier that evening. But the so-called cardio pen—the pen that recorded Ruby's blood pressure changes—literally plummeted as far as it could go when Ruby made that denial during the polygraph test. Bell Herndon, the highly skilled FBI polygraph supervisor, later told the Warren Commission that the drop in the line made by the cardio pen was so severe when Ruby said no, it could have been caused "by a body motion that I failed to detect during the actual response." Herndon said it would have required a "sudden, rapid shift" in Ruby's body position to make that pen line plunge like that, if the plunge hadn't been caused by a deep physiological change inside Ruby. It was unlikely that Herndon, a top man in the polygraph field, would not have noticed something as fundamental as a quick change in Ruby's sitting position. He was trained to look for that. Another FBI observer, agent W. James Wood, was there to watch Ruby's movements, too.

One more witness to the Ruby test, lawyer Tonahill, says now that Ruby "may not have been responding truthfully" to that question. "He may have been there [in the police station when he said he wasn't]. He was moving so fast after that assassination. He just went from place to place. It really did turn him on—had him going around like a wild man."

Then, when Ruby was asked relevant questions about the steps he had taken before shooting Oswald, Herndon noticed so much irregular breathing and involuntary body movements that the chart became "relatively difficult to interpret." The questions were:

"Were you on the sidewalk at the time Lieutenant Pierce's car stopped on the ramp exit?" (Ruby answered, "Yes.")

"Did you enter the jail by walking through the alleyway?" (Answer: "No.")

"Did you walk past the guard at the time Lieutenant Pierce's car was parked on the ramp exit?" ("Yes.")

"Did you talk with any police officer on Sunday, November 24, prior to shooting Oswald?" ("No.")

Herndon reported that all through those questions Ruby "took several deep breaths [and] could not refrain from moving his left foot and the rest of his body," which Herndon chose to interpret as signs of fatigue, and he gave Ruby a recess in the questioning. Herndon had no trouble recognizing body movements at that point.

Rather than get into a description of Ruby's reactions to certain questions involving a pattern of possible evasiveness when it came to his police station movements that weekend, the Warren Report ignored his specific reactions to any of the questions—even to those which supported his claims of murder without malice and premeditation. Instead, the Warren Report sidestepped all interpretations of the Ruby test by stressing J. Edgar Hoover's official FBI viewpoint on the results:

> The FBI feels that the polygraph technique is not sufficiently precise to permit absolute judgments [*sic*] of deception or truth without qualifications. The polygraph technique has a number of limitations, one of which relates to the mental fitness and condition of the examinee to be tested.
>
> During the proceedings at Dallas, Texas, on July 18, 1964, Dr. William R. Beavers, a psychiatrist, testified that he would generally describe Jack Ruby as a "psychotic depressive." In view of the serious question raised as to Ruby's mental condition, no significance should be placed on the polygraph examination and it should be considered nonconclusive as the charts cannot be relied upon.

Consequently, "the Commission did not rely on the results of this examination in reaching [its] conclusions," the Warren Report said in the end. By casting doubt on the quality of Ruby's answers, the Report shifted the entire emphasis away from the quality of the Commission's questions. For example, on behalf of the Commission, Herndon asked the prisoner, "Did any foreign influence cause you to shoot Oswald? . . . Did you shoot Oswald because of any influence of the underworld? . . . Did you shoot Oswald because of a labor union influence?" Ruby answered no to each of those three successive questions, and there was nothing reflected on the charts to indicate important physiological changes as he gave his answers.

But he never was asked the fourth and perhaps most essential question: Did any Dallas police influence him to shoot Oswald?

The key questions asked of Ruby were drawn up by the Warren Commission. They were asked over a course of nearly six hours[2]—but Herndon made sure there were periods for Ruby to relax, including a recess of more than an hour and a half, so that the time of the actually recorded questions and answers amounted to only about 33 minutes during the span of Saturday afternoon and evening.

By normal standards the test conditions were terrible. Normally only examiner Herndon and Ruby would have been in the testing room, to avoid external pressures. But a number of people said they had to have a piece of the action. There was Arlen Specter, of course, to handle the Commission's interests, and there had to be an official court reporter in the room. Then there were two defense lawyers—Tonahill, who wanted Ruby to be tested, and Fowler, who didn't.[3] Bill Alexander, the severe assistant district attorney who had prosecuted Ruby, demanded to be there on behalf of the prosecution since Ruby's trial appeal was pending. Herndon required that an associate, FBI agent Wood, remain to help as observer, and under clinical conditions Wood would have been stationed in an adjoining room, observing through a two-way glass. In addition to the others, chief jailer E. L. Holman was on hand to maintain custody of the prisoner, and Dr. Beavers was there as official medical observer. That meant there were eight times as many people in the room than there should have been under prescribed conditions.

Herndon kept the eight arranged behind Ruby so that the prisoner couldn't see them. Yet there were constant conflicts in the room, between the rounds of Herndon's questions. For instance, Ruby quarreled with Tonahill and wanted him out of there. Tonahill fumed because Ruby wanted Alexander to stay, even though Alexander had treated Ruby contemptuously in court. Beavers tried to calm Tonahill by explaining that psychologically Ruby wanted Alexander in the room so the prosecutor could see and hear firsthand what the truth was. All this tension was going on over Ruby's shoulder, and Holman's presence in the room could not have soothed Ruby either. Holman was supervisor of deputy Jesse Stevenson, the guard who Ruby felt had tricked him into making incriminating statements against himself. Ruby's lawyers felt Stevenson had been a plant to turn the prisoner against defense counsel.

Stevenson believed Ruby's suicide attempts were ploys encouraged by those same lawyers, and Holman had told Dr. Beavers privately that he was sure Ruby tried to appear that he was having delusions.

Dr. Beavers said he, too, thought Ruby was trying to put on the delusions at times—while "on the other hand, at times it is quite obvious that he is trying to seem sane and becomes quite truculent and angry at people who imply that he was in fact of unsound mind."

Psychiatrist Beavers told the Commission that Ruby's delusions of torture to his family and to the Jews in the streets seemed to come and go—possibly on time cycles or how close he was to the people he was with.

In other words, during Ruby's June 7 appearance as a witness before Earl Warren and Gerald Ford, he became delusional after dealing at length with topics that he presented with a good memory and in a rational framework. As Ruby grew frantic in repeated attempts to get the Chief Justice to remove him from the hands of Texas jailers and transfer him to federal protection in Washington, the delusions of Jewish extermination rushed through the gullies of his mind.

There was clear evidence as far back as 1952—when he suffered the severe depression overcome in the course of time without medical help— that Jack Ruby's post-trial delusions in 1964 would "wax and wane," as Dr. Beavers put it.

Did that mean Ruby was mentally competent or not during the lie-detector test? According to Dr. Beavers, Ruby likely was waxing and waning during the test, but "in the greater portion of the time that he answered the questions, I felt that he was aware of the questions and that he understood them, and that he was giving answers based on an appreciation of reality."

Herndon agreed. He said that "during the first several series of questions, and based on the presumption again that Mr. Ruby was rationally sound and competent during this phase of the examination, he responded very normally, and the polygraph examination proceeded without any technical difficulties."

One of the questions Herndon asked during an early series (there were 11 series of questions and this came in the third series) was: "Are you married?" It produced a strange reaction on the lie-detector charts.

There was, according to Herndon, "a rather significant rise in his relative blood pressure," his skin tingled and his breathing pattern changed when he said he wasn't married.

It wasn't supposed to be a significant question. Polygraph operators call it a control-type question—one of several interspersed to test the reactions of the person being examined.

Ruby later explained that when he answered no to the "are you married" question, he thought of Alice Nichols and wished he had married her.

But Ruby and Mrs. Nichols, the divorcee, never had seen each other more than twice a week on dates, according to Mrs. Nichols, and stopped dating in 1959—five years before Herndon asked Ruby the question.

Was it Alice Nichols or was it Sheba—the dog Jack had described to Rabbi Silverman as his wife—that Ruby was thinking about?

Or did he have that peculiar reaction to the control question because it occurred between two other questions that might have caused him anguish? Those two questions were: "Between the assassination and the shooting, did anybody you know tell you they knew Oswald?" and, "Aside from anything you said to George Senator on Sunday morning, did you ever tell anyone else that you intended to shoot Oswald?" Ruby knew both those questions were coming.

Before he asked each series of questions on the record, Herndon went over them with Ruby—an accepted procedure in polygraph testing. The idea was to prepare Ruby so that he wouldn't be hit with surprise questions, and when he heard them again he would have to be ready to answer truthfully or to deceive.

The tenth series of questions was the last cluster of significant questions. It began at 8:27 p.m. Herndon used words such as "weary" and "tired" to describe Ruby's condition by then. He said Ruby could have become immune to the testing at that point, which was more than six hours after Ruby first had entered the testing room.

It was in that series that the prisoner was asked, "Have members of your family been physically harmed because of what you did?" He also was asked, "Is Mr. Fowler in danger because he is defending you?"

Ruby would not or could not answer either one of those.

Dr. Beavers explained that "there was so much hesitation and uncertainty which resulted in no answers, that we were seeing a good deal of internal struggle as to just what was reality."

The two questions tapped the "underlying delusional systems" of the prisoner, Dr. Beavers determined.

Both Dr. Beavers and examiner Herndon said results on the charts of the tenth series were jeopardized because Ruby appeared both psychotic and tired at that point. Another of the questions in that tenth series was: "Were you at Parkland Hospital at any time on Friday?" Parkland was the place where I had talked with Ruby shortly after the President was shot that Friday. His answer was no.

CHAPTER 14

Faster Than A Speeding Magic Bullet

Part I—The Hendrix Connection

In the hours after Jack Ruby shot Lee Harvey Oswald, I set up my portable typewriter on a desk in the auto theft bureau of the Dallas police station and wrote a piece for the next day's papers that went, in part:

> DALLAS, Nov. 25—In disbelief, I watched a friend of mine, Jack Ruby, gun to death the man charged with killing President Kennedy.
>
> It happened less than 10 feet from where I was standing in the basement of the Dallas police station. . . . The last time I had seen Oswald's killer, Ruby, was two days earlier. It was at Parkland Memorial Hospital, moments before the news was official that President Kennedy was dead. I had come to Texas, covering the President's trip.
>
> I felt a tugging at the back of my coat. I turned. It was Ruby, putting out his hand. I shook hands numbly, having minutes earlier witnessed the tragic event of the President's assassination.
>
> "This is horrible," Ruby said. "I think I ought to close my places for three days because of this tragedy. What do you think?" His places are a downtown strip joint and a saloon.
>
> I agreed that he should shut them temporarily but I spent no

more time talking to him because I was hurrying behind the pale and shaken Malcolm Kilduff, White House press aide, who was on his way to make the historic announcement that the President was dead.

Before Friday I hadn't seen the 52-year-old unmarried Ruby for nearly two years, since leaving Texas to be a reporter in Washington.[1]

I saw much of Ruby when I had lived in Dallas. He was someone who came to me frequently with an idea for a newspaper story.

There was a snake charmer he knew—a suburban Dallas housewife who kept large snakes in crates in her house. Her husband was studying to be an engineer. At night, while he babysat with their children, she performed in Ruby's nightclub, stripping off her clothes while a snake coiled around her arms and legs.

I did another story about the male West Indies limbo dancer who Ruby brought here as a performer, had taken a liking to and was sponsoring for U.S. citizenship.

That's the way he was. When he liked you, he wanted to do anything and everything he could to help you. If he didn't like somebody, he would curse them and fight them, and he has had a few arrests here because of the passionate ways in which he has expressed his feelings about people.

"I came up the hard, tough way in Chicago," he once told me.[2] "I've been around real thugs. I can handle myself." . . . But Friday I saw tears brimming in Jack Ruby's eyes when he searched my face for news of the President's condition . . . Ruby was a non-political man as I knew him. But he was always emotional.

How was the emotional man able to walk into the police station basement yesterday morning and murder the unemotional man charged with killing the President?

I couldn't believe my eyes. The precautions taken by Dallas police appeared to be thorough.

They even searched the elevator shaft, leading from Oswald's upstairs cell to the basement, to make sure nobody had found a hiding place.

Ruby knew and was known by many Dallas police. He was allowed in, somehow. He was Jack Ruby the kibitzer in the jail basement, just as he had been Jack Ruby the kibitzer at the hospital where President Kennedy died. He was a constant face at all kinds of events in this city.

But yesterday he stopped being the kibitzer.

I remained in Dallas for two weeks after the Kennedy assassination, covering news developments and investigating the prior movements of Oswald and Ruby. Meanwhile, my article on having encountered Ruby at Parkland appeared in Scripps-Howard's newspapers in New York City, Washington and throughout much of the country, and among its readers was the FBI. As a result, special FBI agent Vincent E. J. Drain interviewed me in Dallas, December 3, about the encounter. "Kantor states he would place the time at about 1:28 p.m., when Ruby tugged the back of his coat and talked with him," Drain wrote in his FBI report.

Remembering that kind of detail at the time was not so difficult. For instance, Dallas police authorities also questioned me about the encounter and I told them that my recollection of it had been freshened on Saturday night, November 23, the night before Ruby killed Oswald. I had been walking through downtown Dallas, trying to put my head back together after the events of the assassination, when I came to Jack Ruby's Carousel. The crudely lettered "closed" sign was posted there, and I thought about the weird conversation I'd had with him the day before, when I had been anxious to keep pace with Kilduff. "Well, he did it," I thought. "He did close his place." A couple of doors away, the strip-show music was playing at Abe's Colony Club, where "Chris Colt and her 45's," the feature act, was under way. Other saloons were open downtown, too. I was very aware of Ruby's concern to be closed.

On December 21, 1963, virtually a month after my talk with Ruby at Parkland, FBI agents C. Ray Hall and Manning C. Clements interviewed Ruby for three hours in front of his attorneys at the Dallas county jail. He denied having been at Parkland at any time on November 22.

The first I learned of Ruby's denial was on January 2, 1964, when Washington-based FBI agents Richard W. Kaiser and Albert B. Miller advised me of it. I was almost as shocked when they told me that as I had been at seeing Ruby pull the trigger.

"Kantor was told that he might be called upon to testify in this case [the Ruby murder trial]," Kaiser and Miller wrote in a report of their interview with me that day in the conference room of the Scripps-Howard Washington bureau. "He was asked what he would say if under oath and on the witness stand in a court of law . . . Kantor stated he fully realizes the importance of what he has said. . . . He knows a man's life is at stake . . . Kantor speculated that perhaps Ruby has said he was not at Parkland as part of his reported plea of temporary insanity. Kantor stated he is not acquainted with all the facets of such a plea but felt it might help Ruby's cause for Ruby to deny being at the hospital when he knows he was, and that Kantor would have to testify that he saw him there. Then, too, Kantor stated, Ruby might have been in emotional shock and cannot recall being at the hospital."

Soon after agents Kaiser and Miller completed their questions I wrote a letter to Ruby, asking to meet with him in the county jail. I had been trying to interview him almost from the moment he shot Oswald. The day of the shooting, I handed a note to Art Hammett, an officer who worked in the executive offices of the Dallas police station. The note was addressed to Ruby and asked if he would see me. Hammett said he could make no promises that the note would get through to the prisoner. After Ruby was transferred the following day to the county jail, I tried to reach him again with notes that I gave to Ruby's attorney Tom Howard and to Sheriff Decker. There were no responses until I wrote to Ruby from Washington, seeking to question him. This time I received two answers. The first was from San Francisco, from Ruby's new chief counsel, Melvin M. Belli. The Belli letter got right to business:

> Dear Mr. Kantor:
>   Jack Ruby forwarded me your letter with inquiries for reply. I know upon reflection, you will appreciate that for Mr. Ruby to answer such inquiries as yours would be most unusual and prejudicial, perhaps, to his defense. I am happy that Jack forwarded me your letter as I have instructed him to do just this in case of any inquiries such as yours. Jack asked me to express his best regards to you. That I do, freely and unhesitatingly.
>   Best Wishes,
>   (signed) Melvin M. Belli

Approximately at the same time I received the letter from San Francisco, I received another from Dallas, written in a delicate hand by pencil on three pieces of note-sized paper. The return address on the envelope was 505 Main Street—the county jail. Dated January 26, 1964, the letter said:

> Dear Seth:
>   Thank you for your very nice letter and your good wishes.
>   Please, I hope you do understand that when there are letters with questions they are forwarded to Mr. Melvin Belli in S. Francisco.
>   However, I did mention to him what a nice person I thought you were and of our friendship while you were working here in Dallas. Also that he shouldn't fail to answer your letter.
>   Well, Seth, I've been keeping up with your wonderful work; before all this I would frequently get the Ft. Worth papers[3] and would always make certain to look for your column.
>   It would really be nice if I could hear from you again.
>   Sincerely,
>   Your friend,
>   Jack

The two things I mostly got out of those two letters were that Ruby didn't structure his thoughts or sentences like an unbalanced person, and that the real message was in what Belli was saying to me—that any conversation about what I had seen of Jack Ruby's actions could be "prejudicial, perhaps, to his defense."

The Ruby trial began five weeks later.[4] Had I been sent back to Dallas to cover it for my papers, I would have continued to seek even a brief interview with Ruby, as others were doing. But once the FBI showed up at Scripps-Howard to talk to me, and there was conflict between what I had written and what Ruby was saying, Scripps-Howard lost all interest in turning me loose on the story ever again.

Nor did *The New York Times, The Washington Post* and other major news organizations show any desire to do independent digging on the

Kennedy assassination story. They just stayed out of the way. Ruby's denial that he had been at Parkland Hospital within an hour after the President was shot, and my insistence that I had seen Ruby there, led the Warren Commission's Leon Hubert and Burt Griffin to write in their May 14, 1964, memorandum to general counsel J. Lee Rankin that "we must decide who is telling the truth, for there would be considerable significance if it were concluded that Ruby is lying."

As a result, Ruby was asked essentially one question: Did he go to Parkland Hospital? Warren Commission member Gerald R. Ford asked him the question three weeks after the Hubert-Griffin memorandum:

> RUBY: No; I didn't go there. They tried to ask me. My sisters asked me. Some people told my sister that you [sic] were there.[5] I am of sound mind. I never went there. Everything that transpired during the tragedy, I was at the *Morning News* building.
> FORD: You didn't go out there subsequent to the assassination?
> RUBY: No; in other words, like somebody is trying to make me something of a martyr in that case.[6] No; I never did.

But the distraught Ruby left the *News* offices at about 1:10 p.m., some 40 minutes after the President was shot, according to the Warren Commission testimony of *News* advertising salesman Richard L. Saunders, and was not accounted for again until after 1:40 p.m., when he walked into the Carousel Club still distraught.

In a span of 30-35 minutes, Ruby had ample time to drive from downtown Dallas to Parkland and back—a round trip of less than eight miles—and spend about 10 minutes at the hospital.

Kilduff's announcement of the President's death was made officially at 1:33 p.m., and if Ruby promptly left the hospital then to launch into the flurry of calls he undertook, Ruby would have been back at the Carousel a minute or two before the first of the calls was made. Phone company records showed the first call was placed by 1:45 p.m. That was when Ruby's helper, Andy Armstrong, dialed the stripper known as Little Lynn at her Fort Worth home. Acting under Ruby's instructions, Armstrong told her not to be at work that night because the Carousel would be closed. At the same time Ruby must have been into the first of his numerous local calls, probably to his sister, Eva Grant. During it, Armstrong said his boss was crying heavily over the death of the President. Ruby would have used the pay phone at the Carousel for that call. The first long-distance call placed by Ruby then was at 1:51 p.m., a minute after assassin suspect Lee Harvey Oswald had been captured, when Ruby telephoned his business backer Ralph Paul in nearby Arlington, and told Paul the Carousel would be closed.

While some people that day may not have driven to Parkland Hospital, spent less than 15 minutes there—perhaps even less than 10 minutes there—and then driven off quickly at the news of the President's death, it was logical for Ruby to have done it. The Carousel was his only true domain in Dallas. It was the one place he could feel secure. It would make sense for him to head there quickly when faced with the realities he found at Parkland.

And remember that Joe Tonahill, Ruby's attorney, described Ruby as "moving so fast after the assassination. He just went from place to place. It really did turn him on—had him going around like a wild man."

After shooting Oswald two days later, Ruby subsequently denied having been at Parkland on Friday, just as he denied having made multiple trips to the Dallas police station on Friday and Saturday. It was a month later before federal authorities asked him for the first time if he had been to Parkland, and by then Ruby was not admitting to anything that might have showed a network of special interest on his part before he gunned down Oswald on Sunday.

A month after Congressman Ford questioned Ruby about the trip to Parkland, that same basic question was asked of Ruby again in his lie-detector test. Question: Were you at Parkland Hospital at any time on Friday? Answer: No. But medical and FBI experts said the answer came at a time in the test when Ruby appeared to be psychotic and tired, his answers not accurately measurable.

No one asked Ruby if he knew me, if he recalled having talked to me during the weekend of the Kennedy assassination, or where we had talked, what had we talked about—and could he account for some 30 missing minutes after the assassination? At close to the center of those missing minutes was 1:28 p.m.—the time I had reported seeing Ruby at Parkland.

Meanwhile, Warren Commission lawyers Griffin and Hubert interrogated me extensively over a two-day period in the week before Commissioner Ford put the question to Ruby. Their questions and my answers, which centered on an exchange between Ruby and me that had taken no more than 30 seconds, covered 25 pages of Warren Commission testimony.[7] In an additional 88 pages, the Commission photographed and published most of my written notes on the Dallas trip.[8]

When Commission attorneys Hubert and Griffin were interrogating me, and after I had twice described for them the setting of my brief encounter with Ruby near a small doorway at Parkland, Burt Griffin asked, "Well, do you have any question in your mind that you did see Ruby out at Parkland Hospital?"

"If it was just a matter of seeing him," I replied, "I would have long ago been full of doubt. But I did talk to the man, and he did stop me, and I just can't have any doubt about that."

But in the end the Commission decided to discount my testimony and to believe Ruby, after the Commission asked the FBI to obtain records of my long-distance telephone calls from Dallas on the day of the Kennedy assassination, and to check the automobile driving time between Parkland

Hospital and two downtown points. These two points were the *Morning News* building, which Ruby left after the President was shot, and the Carousel Club, where Ruby arrived about 10 minutes after Kilduff's announcement that the President was dead.

Both the phone checks and the time studies by the FBI failed to alter the facts I had given about encountering Ruby at approximately 1:28 p.m. In fact, records obtained from the telephone company by the FBI showed I had placed a call to my Washington bureau at 1:02 p.m. from a phone in the hallway of Parkland's emergency treatment area, and had concluded the call at 1:27 p.m.

Despite the consistencies between my account and what the FBI discovered, the Warren Report concluded that I "probably did not see Ruby at Parkland Hospital in the few minutes before or after 1:30 p.m., the only time it would have been possible for Kantor to have done do." Instead, said the Report:

> Since Ruby was observed at the Dallas police department during a two-hour period after 11 p.m. on Friday, when Kantor also was present, and since Kantor did not remember seeing Ruby there, Kantor may have been mistaken about both the time and the place that he saw Ruby. When seeing Ruby, Kantor was preoccupied with the important event that a press conference represented. Both Ruby and Kantor were present at another important event, a press conference held about midnight, November 22, in the assembly room of the Dallas police department. It is conceivable that Kantor's encounter with Ruby occurred at that time, perhaps near the small doorway there.[9]

In other words, the Warren Commission concluded without corroborative evidence that my memory of the encounter may have been 11 hours off and set in the wrong location—although my reporting of nothing else that weekend was disoriented or challenged as being wrong.[10]

But what would the reason have been for Jack Ruby's visit to Parkland Hospital in the early afternoon? Or, maybe more to the point, what wouldn't the reason have been?

For one thing, he didn't go there to place the "magic bullet" on the stretcher. The so-called magic bullet, otherwise known as Warren Commission Exhibit 399, was a barely rumpled bullet that was determined by the Warren Commission to have come from the wounded Governor John Connally's stretcher at Parkland. It was the crucial bullet upon which the Commission built its case that Oswald had been the lone assassin. The Warren Report said the single bullet passed through both Kennedy and Connally, smashing rib and wrist bones in the governor and exiting from his left thigh. If one bullet had not gone through the two men, then they were hit by separate bullets, fired almost simultaneously from two sources. Oswald's weapon could not have gotten off two shots that quickly. Two major questions about Exhibit 399 have continued ever since the Warren Report was published: How could this bullet have inflicted such terrible damage to both men and have emerged in such good shape; and which stretcher did the bullet really come from? After Ruby had left Parkland, Darrell C. Tomlinson, the hospital's chief engineer, moved a stretcher out of the way, bumping it against a wall and the magic bullet fell from it to the floor, in a public hallway. Tomlinson said he never was sure whether 399 came from the stretcher used for Connally or for somebody else.

There are those who have insisted that Ruby had gone to Parkland for a purpose—to put the magic bullet on the stretcher. But in order for that to have happened, there would have had to be a sort of central assassination command post, where the impact of the shots fired into the President's car could be quickly analyzed, with orders relayed then for a messenger to head straight to Parkland with a slightly damaged bullet, which could be matched to the rifle that could be traced to Oswald. That kind of thing would have been questionable even on the TV series, "Mission: Impossible." But had there been such a supersmooth organization, capable of operating such a push-button conspiracy, it would have been too smooth to have selected Jack Ruby—with his propensity for reckless driving, his craving for publicity and his mood swings—for the role of messenger on that job. No. He went to Parkland because of his own compulsions to go.

These were the compulsions of "a news hound," frequently seen circulating at local public happenings, ranging from sporting events to court trials, where he "would endeavor to be interviewed by newsmen," according to statements to the FBI by Wes Wise, the Dallas TV reporter who was among several reporters intruded on by Ruby that weekend. And when the Warren Commission asked what occurred at Parkland when I first saw Ruby there, I said, "I very well remember my first thought. I thought, well, there is Jack Ruby. I had been away from Dallas for 18 months and one day at that time, but it seemed just perfectly normal to see Jack Ruby standing there, because he was a known goer to events."

The only other person ever to come forward with information about Ruby at Parkland was Mrs. Wilma M. Tice (see footnote 5.), a 38-year-old housewife who said she had stood about three feet away from Ruby—a man she didn't know, never talked to, and had never seen before—outside the hospital that day. She also failed to discuss the episode with authorities until the following spring. Wilma Tice then told the FBI and the Warren Commission that she had been threatened by an anonymous male telephone caller "that it would pay me to keep my mouth shut" and not testify about having seen Ruby at Parkland. Mrs. Tice had a flare for the dramatic. It was as if she had become a witness sent by Central Casting.

Under questioning by Burt Griffin of the Warren Commission, Mrs. Tice said she hurried in her car to Parkland about a half hour after the President was shot:

> GRIFFIN: Do you think you could have been mistaken about the man you saw?
>
> MRS. TICE: It could have been somebody else that looked just like Jack, named Jack; yes.
>
> GRIFFIN: If you had been really sure of it, that you saw him out there, wouldn't you have reported it to the FBI or the police in late November or early December?
>
> MRS. TICE: Now this is where my husband's part comes in. He doesn't like for me to go out of that house unless he is with me. He goes down to the farm every weekend, and I was home alone. My children were in school and everybody in Dallas was looking and listening. And I decided that I would jump in the car and run over there, too. It is only 15 minutes from my house.
>
> GRIFFIN: You mean when you went to Parkland Hospital?
>
> MRS. TICE: When I went to Parkland Hospital.
>
> GRIFFIN: Did your husband object to the fact that you had gone to Parkland Hospital?
>
> MRS. TICE: Yes.
>
> GRIFFIN: Has this disturbed you, his objection to that?
>
> MRS. TICE: Yes; it disturbs me all the time, because he doesn't want me to go out of the house while he is gone, because he says my place is in the house. . . . And he is so unreasonable, and he is just— my husband is kind of jealous and you can't hardly talk to him.

In the spring of 1964, after the Ruby trial, Mrs. Tice said she decided to telephone Ruby's sister, Eva Grant, whom Mrs. Tice also didn't know:

"Well, I called Eva. It was no more than a sympathy call. And when I called her I didn't get her on the phone. I got Eileen on the phone. And I felt sorry for them because they had been so deserted for something their brother had done. They had been rejected by everybody, and I felt sorry for them. I mean just like I try to teach my children, right is right and wrong is wrong, and I try to abide by the same thing."

The Eileen she got on the phone was Eileen Kaminsky, a sister visiting from Chicago. Mrs. Kaminsky subsequently told the Warren Commission about this lady who claimed Ruby had appeared at Parkland. The FBI contacted Wilma Tice and filed a report which said, in part:

> Her attention was drawn to this man as he had a hat . . . in his left hand, hitting it against his leg. . . . He was heavily built. She thought by hitting his hat against his leg he would ruin it. He was alone.
>
> She stood about three to four feet from this man when he was approached by another man who stated, "How are you going there, Jack?" Mrs. Tice said that some other individual in the crowd had made the remark that Governor Connally had been shot in the kid-

ney and, when this remark was overheard, the man identified as
Ruby stated, "Couldn't someone give him a kidney?" The man who
approached Ruby then stated, "Who the hell would give him a kidney?" To which Ruby replied that he would.

Mrs. Tice said . . . she forgot about this incident until seeing the
shooting of Oswald on television, at which time she believed the man
hitting his leg with his hat at the Parkland Hospital was the same man
who shot Oswald. She then subsequently saw his pictures in the paper
and still believed it to be the same individual.

It was not like Ruby to stand outside the hospital, which is where Mrs.
Tice said she saw him, when he could have gotten inside, which is where I
encountered him—at the base of a stairway, in an area where there were
medical attendants. Ruby was a classic name-dropper, and one of the names
he might have dropped that day was Judy Smalley's. A secretary, Miss
Smalley had lived at 223 South Ewing Street, in the same apartment building as Ruby. She once had cared for his dogs when he had gone off on a trip.
But Miss Smalley told the FBI that she regularly kept her distance from him.
Nonetheless, Ruby had learned enough about her to use her name for an
entry into Parkland, because her boss was Dr. George T. Shires, who conducted part of the major surgery on Governor Connally that day. Dr. Shires
was chairman of the department of surgery at the University of Texas Southwestern Medical School, which adjoined Parkland.

So far as Wilma Tice and her husband James were concerned, the
Warren Commission might as well have been a domestic relations court.
The Tices bickered the whole time they were involved as FBI and Commission witnesses. Tice complained to the FBI that his wife refused to tell
him any details about her being called to testify. "Hell, nobody tells me
anything around here. I guess all I'm supposed to do is chase prowlers and
buy groceries," he grumbled.

A number of Warren Commission critics have counted Mrs. Tice's
testimony as significant corroboration that Ruby had been to Parkland after the President's shooting. That's either because these critics have not
read in detail what Mrs. Tice had to say, or perhaps it's because they
wished the lady had been on firmer ground.

On August 7, two weeks after Wilma Tice's appearance as a witness,
a rough draft of chapter six of the Warren Report was turned in by the
Commission's analysts on Ruby. It recognized there was "speculation
about Ruby's role in a possible conspiracy to assassinate the President or
to silence Oswald" as a factor in "Ruby's alleged presence at Parkland
Hospital."

But that was no obstacle for the Ruby analysts. After all, aside from a
secretive housewife and a harried reporter, there were no other witnesses
who said they had seen or spoken with Jack Ruby during his emergency

emotional run to and from Parkland Hospital. There was no hard evidence of him being there, such as pictures.

They avoided the obstacle by ignoring the housewife and by referring to the reporter as "the witness who believes he saw Ruby at Parkland [and] has reported a conversation which most probably occurred after Ruby decided to close his clubs at about 4 p.m."

But everything Ruby had said to me could not have been said that late. A new draft, dated August 10, eliminated the sentence involving 4 p.m. and generally was more flexible, even allowing that Ruby might have made a stop at the hospital, although "he would have stayed no longer than a few minutes before driving to the Carousel Club." In the final Warren Report, completed a month later, even that crumb of flexibility had disappeared.

Twelve years went by then before I next saw the Ruby investigators, Burt Griffin, who had become a judge in Cleveland, and Leon Hubert, the courtly law professor in New Orleans. In my separate conversations with them, they both brought up the Parkland Hospital episode and both volunteered that they continue to feel certain that Ruby's conversation with me had to have taken place somewhere else and hours later. They reasoned that my account of the conversation limited it to somewhere within a four-minute period, between 1:28 and 1:32 p.m.—after I got off the telephone and before Kilduff's announcement that John Kennedy was dead. And they reasoned that Ruby would not have weighed closing his places for three days to mourn the late President until there was a late President. Judge Griffin and Professor Hubert were logical and honorable men. But they were wrong on this matter for three reasons.

First of all, even before Ruby left the *Morning News* building that day, Dallas business operators had begun calling in orders for Saturday ads that would announce store closings for the weekend, out of respect for the wounded President. A number of the callers made it clear they had been ashamed to see the full-page rightwing ad, hateful to Kennedy, that *The Morning News* had run that day. Ruby agreed with those calls coming in, and told advertising salesman John W. Newnam he was considering shutting his places, too. This conversation between Ruby and Newnam occurred about 30 minutes before Ruby brought up the same possibility with me.

Secondly, Ruby's trip to Parkland was emotional, but it was based on economics, too. The regular deadline for the next day's ads in *The Morning News* was passed. The deadline had been at noon. Now it was after 1 p.m. The deadline time was being extended awhile because of the tragedy but Ruby knew that if the President was dead or dying, he would have to make up his mind quickly about any changes in his ad to appear in the next day's paper.[11] At stake would be Saturday night revenues—the key night of the week in the strip business. He didn't know what to do because there were all kinds of reports: by 1 p.m., United Press International was quoting Secret Service agent Clint Hill as saying the President was dead.[12] At 1:18 p.m., the Associated Press carried an unconfirmed report that Lyndon Johnson had been "wounded slightly by gunfire." Another piece of misinformation being broadcast was that a Secret Service agent had been shot and killed when Kennedy was hit.[13] Ruby needed answers when he talked to me, so he could make a decision.

Thirdly, my conversation with Ruby could not have taken place 11 hours later in the police station (where I never saw Ruby), as the Warren Commission decided out of the blue that it had. The central point of Ruby's questions to me was whether or not he should close his places for three days.

Since he made the decision at about 4 p.m. to go ahead and close them, there would have been no purpose in his telling me seven hours later that he was thinking about doing what he already had done.

Following my testimony before the Warren Commission, the Commission asked the FBI in Dallas to check out the driving time and distances that would have been involved in a roundtrip by Ruby to Parkland Hospital.

Agents Robert M. Barrett and Ivan D. Lee drove from the *Morning News* parking area to the rear entrance at Parkland in 10 minutes, at 1 p.m., Tuesday, June 9, 1964.

Then the agents returned from Parkland to the parking facility next to the Carousel over two different routes. The first route covered 3.7 miles and again took 10 minutes, using the most direct street channels (Harry Hines Boulevard to Cedar Springs; then down Ross and Griffin to Commerce). The second route covered more ground, but took less time—4.1 miles in nine minutes—because it involved the use of Stemmons Expressway. Stemmons was wide, with multiple traffic lanes, frequently driven at speeds of more than 70 miles an hour, and was the logical course for Ruby to have covered that day.

Carousel stripper Tammi True (her real name was Nancy Monnell Powell) told the Warren Commission she drove from downtown Dallas to Parkland at about 1:30 p.m. on the day of the Kennedy assassination, and used Stemmons. She said she heard the 1:34 p.m. bulletin on her car radio that the President was dead, as she approached Parkland.

"How was the traffic on Stemmons Expressway?" Burt Griffin asked Tammi True.

"It didn't seem too bad on the expressway," she replied.

"Did you make normal time?"

"I drove very fast."

The Warren Report concluded that "at a normal driving speed under normal conditions the trip can be made in nine or 10 minutes. However, it is likely that congested traffic conditions on November 22 would have extended the driving time."

But just the opposite probably was true, where Ruby was concerned. Often a speeding driver under normal circumstances, Ruby had plenty provocation that day to gun his way to Parkland and back. If he made the trips in nine or 10 minutes, he still had ample time to lurk inside the hospital. Chances are he made the trips in seven or eight minutes, while the two FBI agents drove moderately.

Then, in another investigation for the Warren Commission in June, 1964, the FBI checked into telephone company records of my long-distance calls that day, to help establish my movements at given times on November 22. As a result, a log of my calls was published on pages 236-237, Book 25, of the Warren volumes, labeled as Commission Exhibit No. 2301. The log showed the times and duration of eight collect calls I placed that day to my Washington bureau, and the numbers from where my calls originated. Okay. No problem. The years go by.

On October 15, 1975, Mrs. Mary Ferrell, a Dallas researcher who has been devoting her life to a thoroughly professional exploration of the Kennedy murder, contacted me and asked why the FBI was keeping Warren Commission Document No. 1133 sealed from public view at the National Archives.

"What on earth is Document 1133?" I asked.

"A record of your phone calls from Dallas on November 22—12 years ago," she said.

"Naw. There must be some mistake. The Warren Commission printed all that in 1964 in the volumes."

"Oh, no they didn't," said Mrs. Ferrell. "The FBI has held back something in there, under a provision which says that public disclosure 'might reveal the identity of confidential sources of information . . . .' "

There was nothing routine about what the FBI had done. The bureau had ordered Document 1133 sealed in 1964 and, in periodic reviews in 1965 and 1970, had ordered the document to remain sealed. Ninety percent of all FBI documents relating to the Kennedy assassination had been made public, but Document 1133 was locked up in that 10 percent of stuff considered too sensitive to be seen. Why, for crying out loud? I told Mrs. Ferrell I would find out why.

The next day, October 16, I hand-carried a request to FBI headquarters, asking that the document be made public immediately, under the federal Freedom of Information Act. Twelve days later, FBI Director Clarence M. Kelley signed a reply to me, saying the bureau would not take immediate action and my patience would be appreciated. On October 30, I filed a formal appeal with Attorney General Edward H. Levi, asking him to overrule Kelley on grounds that "any decision to keep me from knowing what information the FBI developed from a phone call which I placed 12 years ago is both ludicrous and illegal." At the same time, I began making a series of phone calls and personal visits to the Justice Department, to inquire about Document 1133, and I wrote to Burt Griffin, the Cleveland judge who had originally requested the FBI probe of my phone calls. He wrote back on November 21 that "I can recall nothing in the Commission's Ruby materials that I ever saw which, in my judgment, should be or was intended to be withheld from the public." A high-ranking FBI official looked at the sealed document and telephoned me. He said, "I can't understand why such a thing has been kept secret." By mid-December, 1133 was made available to me, and I couldn't understand why the secrecy, either.

Document 1133 had exactly the same information in it that had been publicly printed in the Warren Commission's Exhibit 2301 in 1964—except it identified the places I was calling from, by name. In other words, I had placed the calls from three different Dallas phone numbers, listed in the Warren exhibits as 748-9711, 351-9072 and 631-5050.

And then the FBI purportedly decided to keep secret from the American public the fact that 748-9711 was Dallas City Hall—one of the most commonly called numbers in Dallas. Another of the FBI-kept secrets (631-5050) was the main number for Parkland Hospital, and the other (351-9072) was a pay phone at Love Field, where Lyndon Johnson had been sworn in as President.

That's all there was to it, the FBI advised me. One of those bureaucratic blunders that happen in Washington.

But that's not all there was to it. During the two months the FBI made me cool my heels, waiting to see Document 1133, I began reviewing everything I could for a clue to what might be in that document, and I found it in my notes of November 22, 1963. Here's what happened.

At 3:23 p.m. that day I telephoned Charles Egger, managing editor of the Scripps-Howard bureau in Washington, with details of the Johnson swearing-in at Love Field. By then, Air Force One, bearing the shaken mix of new and former presidential parties, was trying to outclimb a storm over Arkansas. Egger told me the wire services had just identified the murder suspect as Lee Harvey Oswald, and told me to get back downtown to the police station, and begin covering the story from there.

The next time I telephoned him with information, at 5:43 p.m., Egger told me to call Hal Hendrix in the Miami area, because Hendrix had some background to give me on Oswald. I wrote down Hendrix's home phone number on my note pad—MO5-6473, in Coral Cables—and called him right away.[14]

Harold V. (Hal) Hendrix had won the Pulitzer Prize earlier in 1963 as Latin American affairs reporter for *The Miami News*, for his insightful coverage of the Cuban missile crisis of October, 1962. On September 1, 1963, he joined Scripps-Howard, to cover the Latin American beat. Instead of moving to Washington, he continued to be home-based in Miami, where his contacts were. These contacts were so good that, in an article for

Scripps-Howard on September 24, 1963, Hendrix was able both to describe and justify the coup that toppled the leftist, pro-Kennedy Juan Bosch in the Dominican Republic. The coup took place on September 25—24 hours *after* Hendrix described it.

All this insight by Hendrix was not a matter of happenstance. Some of the more disrespectful reporters in Scripps-Howard's Washington bureau referred to Hendrix as The Spook, because of the handouts he reputedly took from the CIA.

Some years later, information received by the Senate Subcommittee on Multinational Corporations was that Hendrix had been into "black propaganda" during the late 1950s and early 1960s, when Castro was establishing and strengthening his power base in Cuba. Black propaganda is a CIA term for political stories, not necessarily supported by fact, floated to hurt "the other side."

Perhaps Hendrix was not a black propagandist, but here is an example in an article he wrote, November 11, 1964, of his approach. The article dealt with the success of "spontaneous" sabotage "which increases Castro's inability to cope with communist Cuba's steady economic disintegration." In the article, Hendrix quoted unnamed Cuban escapees who were praising the work of saboteurs smuggled into Cuba, but "they add bitterly that considerably more could be done to make life increasingly miserable for Castro if infiltration and raiding parties were not harassed by both British and United States authorities."

It was about 6 p.m., November 22, 1963, when I telephoned Hendrix at his Coral Gables home, apologizing because I had to place the call collect from the Dallas police station. He said that was no problem, and he was preparing to embark immediately on a trip into Latin America; otherwise he would be writing the information he was about to give me himself.

The information he gave me, according to my notes, concerned details of Lee Harvey Oswald's past, particularly Oswald's time span in Russia and his later connection with the Fair Play for Cuba Committee in New Orleans. Hendrix gave me a bunch of knowledgeable background on Oswald's appearance on New Orleans radio station WDSU, the previous August. In a show moderated by William Kirk Stuckey, Oswald had debated Carlos Bringuier, an anti-Castro activist and Cuban refugee. On the show, Oswald had been sharply critical of U.S. intolerance of the Castro government.

I didn't use any of the Hendrix information in my piece for the next day because much of it was emerging through the news services during the evening, and also because I held off writing anything until the end of the anguished news conference set up for Oswald in the police assembly room at midnight, where the news was freshest.

During the next two weeks, Hendrix wrote pieces out of Venezuela and the Dominican Republic which were singularly unusual because they never once mentioned the reaction of people in those countries to the murder of President Kennedy and the accession of power of the lesser-known Johnson. The story was Topic "A" everywhere in the world, but Hendrix's daily story out of those countries primarily dealt with the projected threat of Cuban military influence in Latin America.

Three years later, at a time when the use of U.S. domestic organizations as CIA conduits began to surface, Hendrix and Scripps-Howard parted company. He went to work for the International Telephone & Telegraph Corporation, as director of inter-American relations in Buenos Aires. Later, he wound up in ITT's world headquarters in New York, and then he went to Chile at a critical time.

Chilean leftist leader Salvador Allende narrowly defeated conservative presidential candidate Jorge Alessandri, September 4, 1970, for control of the country. Allende's margin of victory was so narrow (he got 36.3 percent of the vote, Alessandri got 35.3 percent and a third candidate got 28.4 percent) the election was thrown into Chile's congress, where the winner was to be chosen by October 4. Hendrix had a job to do there because it was expected Allende, the socialist, would expropriate $150 million worth of ITT properties if he won.

September 7, Hendrix sent a coded, confidential message that reached William R. Merriam, ITT vice-president in charge of the Washington office. The message told of a "very confidential and private session" between Hendrix and Dr. Arturo Matte, brother-in-law of Alessandri and Alessandri's closest adviser, in which Matte described a strategy for Alessandri to pull out a victory. Hendrix said he "inferred it would require some money and influential pressures, perhaps from Washington."

Hendrix's messages to ITT headquarters in New York were routinely being made available to aides of William C. Broe, who was in charge of clandestine services in the western hemisphere for the CIA, according to investigators for Senator Frank Church's multinational corporations subcommittee.

The subcommittee held hearings in 1973 on actions by the CIA and ITT in that 1970 election won by Allende. On March 20, 1973, Hal Hendrix denied under oath to the subcommittee that he ever had been a paid agent of the CIA, but he was not asked if he ever had worked for the CIA on a non-paid basis. Even so, Hendrix lied under oath.

Hendrix was asked under oath, March 21, 1973, to name the source of information he had cabled from Chile to ITT Senior Vice-President E. J. Gerrity, in what became known as The Green Light Message. It had been sent on September 17, 1970, and it said: "Late Tuesday night [September 15] Ambassador Edward Korry finally received a message from the State Department giving him the green light to move in the name of President Nixon. The message gave him maximum authority to do all possible—short of a Dominican Republic-type action—to keep Allende from taking power." That message was sent at a time when President Nixon publicly was keeping hands-off in Chile. When Hendrix was asked to name the source of his cable, he replied that the person "was a Chilean who was a personal friend of mine . . . very highly placed in the Christian Democratic Party organization."

Not long after the Senate hearings concluded, Hendrix left ITT and became director of development in the Caribbean area for Inter-Continental Hotels, an operation of Pan-American Airways. But Attorney General Levi pursued the ITT-CIA Chilean affair and Justice Department lawyer Walter May went into federal court in Miami, November 30, 1976, with fresh evidence against Hendrix.

May told the court that CIA cables revealed Hendrix's source for The Green Light Message "came from the CIA station chief [in] Santiago and to some extent from the American ambassador himself." May's evidence showed the CIA knew in advance that Hendrix would testify falsely before the Church Senate subcommittee in 1973. As a result, Hendrix pleaded guilty to a charge of withholding information from the subcommittee.

Hendrix was allowed to plead guilty to a misdemeanor—which cost him a $100 fine and a one-month suspended sentence—in return for his cooperation with the Justice Department in its pursuit of perjury charges against higher-ranking ITT and CIA officials in the Chile matter.

Of course, it had been my telephone call to Hal Hendrix, the friend of the CIA, that had been left off the public record by the FBI.

At the time of the FBI reviews in 1964, 1965 and 1970 of my telephone calls on November 22, 1963, there had been no public link between Hendrix and the CIA. Sam Papich, who was the FBI's liaison with the CIA during the time of the Kennedy assassination investigation, said "sometimes the CIA would pass on information it felt was pertinent to us. Sometimes in writing. Sometimes orally."[15]

In turn, the FBI furnished me nothing about Hal Hendrix in writing. Not even his phone number.

Part II—The Greater Weight of Evidence

In the preceding section of this chapter it was reported that Judge Burt Griffin volunteered during my taped interview with him for this book in his Cleveland chambers in 1976 that he continued to feel certain my conversation with Ruby had not taken place at Parkland Hospital less than an hour after President Kennedy had been brought there—but must have taken place hours later; somewhere else.

However, in the spring of 1977, after reading a copy of that whole section of this chapter, the judge reversed his 1964 opinion—which had appeared in the Warren Report. Griffin now says he no longer believes his 1964 conclusion on page 336 of the Warren Report that "Kantor probably did not see Ruby at Parkland Hospital in the few minutes before or after 1:30 p.m., the only time it would have been possible for Kantor to have done so." Instead, Judge Griffin said in a prepared statement to me on May 2, 1977:

> Having read your analysis of the Warren Commission's evidence on Jack Ruby's alleged trip to Parkland Hospital, I am persuaded that the greater weight of the evidence supports your claim that you saw Ruby there on Friday afternoon, November 22, 1963.
>
> I find especially persuasive your observation that, in fact, the Warren Commission's evidence showed that traffic conditions were such as to have made it possible for Ruby to return to the Carousel Club before 1:45 p.m. and that Ruby's employee, Andrew Armstrong, testified that Ruby mentioned closing his clubs as soon as he returned shortly before 1:45 p.m. Thus, in separate conversations within approximately 15 minutes to two different people (neither one of whom knew about the other's conversation with Ruby when each first reported his conversation), Ruby's mind was on closing his clubs.
>
> And the reason for Ruby's going to Parkland Hospital is most plausibly set forth in your analysis—to get quick first-hand information on what to do about his nightclubs after the shooting of the President. It was fully consistent with Ruby's personality, as you suggest, for him to leave the *Dallas Morning News* office and follow the action to Parkland Hospital.

So far as is known this is the first time a key member of the Warren Commission staff has determined that one of the Warren Report's judgments in his area was not valid.

Griffin intended for his colleague on the Warren Commission's Ruby detail, Leon Hubert, to read this chapter, too. Griffin felt Hubert, the Tulane law professor, would agree that the 1964 judgment should be reversed. But Hubert, in frail health, died of congestive heart failure in the spring of 1977 before he could read it.

What seems especially meaningful now is a segment of the May 14, 1964, memorandum prepared by Hubert and Griffin and sent to their boss, J. Lee Rankin, the Commission staff director. It was a paragraph in the memorandum which said Kantor had been "interviewed twice by the FBI and persists in his claim that he saw Ruby at Parkland Hospital shortly before or after the President's death was announced. Ruby denies that he was ever at Parkland Hospital. We must decide who is telling the truth, for there would be considerable significance if it were concluded that Ruby is lying."

The significance was, of course, that if it were shown that Ruby lied about having been at Parkland, he would have lied about other movements he made during those hours that led him to silence the President's accused assassin.

CHAPTER 15

A Matter Of Conspiracy

May I also suggest that every effort be made to determine why Oswald was headed in the general direction of Ruby's house at the time he was intercepted by officer Tippit.—Texas Attorney General Waggoner Carr in a private advisory to J. Lee Rankin of the Warren Commission, May 26, 1964.

Jesse Curry, the former Dallas police chief, leans back in an easy chair in his living room long after the Kennedy assassination and discusses the route of Oswald's getaway attempt that Friday afternoon in Oak Cliff.[1] "I can't in my mind firmly make myself believe that he might not have been trying to get to Ruby's apartment," Curry muses. "You know he was in close proximity to it, and I know he didn't leave his house with the idea of going to the Texas Theatre. There again, after he shot Tippit I think in his fright he just thought the movie house was the place to hide." Curry says he hasn't tried to figure out what Oswald might have done at Ruby's apartment had Oswald reached it, "because I never really seriously admitted that there was a conspiracy. But there's been coincidental things that have happened here to lead one to believe that there could have been a conspiracy after all. . . . There might have been a connection there between the two that we never established. And if there was it was more than a local thing, I believe. I think if there was collusion between those two, it involved probably an international conspiracy." Curry says he thinks Castro could have been involved. Curry says the whole story was not learned.

Small wonder Curry has begun to acknowledge a concept of a conspiracy entwined in the murders of Kennedy and Oswald that weekend. It's because the whole story was not learned, including Ruby's relations with some of Curry's police. As a result Curry and countless others have changed their views over the years, at least in shadings, as the weight of evidence appears to grow or shrink in different directions. Some of my views have changed. For instance, just to the opposite of Jesse Curry, I started thinking Oswald probably had been heading on purpose directly toward Jack Ruby's apartment as he, Oswald, sought refuge. But now I am a believer in the "Belin Theory." Devised by assistant Warren Commission counsel David W. Belin in the summer of 1964, the theory I think explained a more likely direction in which Oswald was trying to head when he was stopped by officer Tippit.

Needless to say, the Belin Theory was so sound, and made so much sense, it appeared nowhere in the Warren Report. Belin completed it on July 11, 1964. It got as far as the Commission's August 7 draft of chapter six of the Report, but no further. Here's what Belin produced for that draft:

> The Commission does not believe a substantial inference connecting Ruby and Oswald can be drawn from the fact that Oswald was headed in the general direction of Ruby's apartment, two-thirds-of-a-mile away, when he shot Tippit. Perhaps Oswald was fleeing elsewhere or, perhaps, he was just walking, frightened and aimless. To ascertain another possible destination, the Commission has examined other evidence for significant signs.
>
> One item of evidence that may be more significant than the location of Jack Ruby's apartment is that, when Oswald was arrested, he had in his shirt pocket a bus transfer from the Marsalis bus. After the Marsalis bus left the downtown Dallas area, the only transfer point was at Jefferson Avenue, barely three blocks away from the scene of the Tippit shooting. At the time Tippit was shot, Oswald's bus transfer, marked for 1 p.m. in the downtown area, was still valid, expiring in Oak Cliff at 1:15 p.m., or when the next scheduled bus arrived after the time of issue, if the arrival time was after 1:15 p.m. By walking to the transfer point Oswald could save the bus fare by using his transfer, a not unlikely course of action based on his living habits. There were a number of buses which Oswald could have boarded at the Marsalis and Jefferson transfer point. Walking east on East Tenth Street at the time Tippit approached him, Oswald was taking a direct route to that transfer point, particularly if he wanted to avoid the main thoroughfare of Marsalis as much as possible.
>
> Barely a block away was another bus which could have been

boarded by Oswald at Jefferson and Ewing. This particular bus, Route 55, traveled south on Ewing and eventually on Lancaster Road. Since the first Route 55 bus to arrive after 1 p.m. at Jefferson and Ewing came at 1:40 p.m., Oswald's transfer would have been good for that bus. Had Oswald boarded that bus, it would have taken him to a point on Lancaster Road where the first southbound Greyhound bus was scheduled to stop for passengers around 3:30 p.m.

That Greyhound bus could be taken directly to Waco, Austin and San Antonio, Texas, where connections could be made for Corpus Christi, Brownsville and Laredo, Texas, and Monterrey, Mexico. Oswald had just enough money on his person when arrested to pay for such a trip.

The Belin Theory was that the city bus transfer in Oswald's shirt pocket might well have been his basic "passport" to Mexico. Oswald had been reported to have been in Mexico two months earlier and having gotten there by bus. Belin also was aware of the Warren Commission testimony given by Nelson Delgado, who had served in the Marine Corps with Oswald. Delgado had recalled Oswald once telling him that the best way to escape from authorities in the United States to Russia was by way of Mexico, where a plane could be caught to Havana, and then another plane to Moscow.

The Belin Theory was innovative and extremely logical but suffered a fatal axing within the Warren Commission when Belin figured out that Oswald probably was in the act of escaping to Mexico when encountered by officer Tippit on Tenth Street. That injected a foreign connection into the escape which blew the Warren Commission's mind. Mexico. Cuba. Russia. Belin had practically invented World War III.

It was Norman Redlich who put the ax to the Belin Theory. Redlich had a great deal of control over what would appear in the Warren Report. Redlich, remember, had survived the communist witch-hunt aimed at him on Capitol Hill three months earlier when the granting of his security clearance had been threatened. And now Redlich wanted to keep from stirring up any more problems for Earl Warren, so he argued that Belin had come up with nothing more than supposition, which had no place in the Warren Report. Belin argued in return that the Commission had a public obligation to disclose the existence of Oswald's possible escape plan, even if it were removed from chapter six of the Report and relegated to the 31-page section in the appendix of the Report, entitled "Speculations and Rumors." But Redlich instead saw to it that the Warren Report made no attempt to explain why Oswald, the fast-moving young man on the lam, appeared to be heading directly toward Jack Ruby's apartment with a gun. Instead, the Warren Report simply said, "There is no evidence that Oswald knew where Ruby lived."

There is no evidence, either, that Ruby and Oswald even knew each other, despite claims by several people over the years that the two had been seen together.

Example: Bill DeMar (real name: William D. Crowe Jr.) a stand-up comic, ventriloquist and impressionist, was doing a "memory act" at the Carousel Club in November, 1963. Within a couple hours after Ruby shot Oswald, DeMar began telling reporters he had seen Oswald seated in the audience of the Carousel in the week before the shooting. DeMar couldn't remember what night it might have been.[2]

As soon as DeMar's recollection of Oswald became public, comedian Wally Weston complained in an FBI interview that the spotlight shining into DeMar's eyes at the Carousel would have made it nearly impossible for DeMar to have recognized the faces of strangers in the audience. Weston had preceded DeMar as master of ceremonies that month at the Carousel. The FBI report[3] said Weston "felt DeMar had made the claim he saw Oswald in the audience because of DeMar's desire for publicity."

Example: Thirteen years later in an exclusive story for *The New York Daily News*, Weston claimed Oswald had been in the Carousel "at least twice" before the Kennedy assassination. Weston identified Oswald as a heckling patron who "walked up in the middle of the club, right in front of the stage [where Weston was performing] and for no reason he said, 'I think you're a communist.' I said, 'Sir, I'm an American. Why don't you sit down?' He said, 'Well, I still think you're a communist,' so I jumped off the stage and hit him. Jack was right behind him when I hit him. He landed in Jack's arms and Jack grabbed him and said, 'You ----, I told you never to come in here.' And he wrestled him to the door and threw him down the stairs." Weston had not burdened the FBI with that information.

Weston told the New York newspaper in 1976 he had waited so long to come forward with information because he had been concerned about his "personal safety. So many people connected with it [the assassination investigation] died or disappeared." But Weston originally had been questioned by the FBI late on November 24, 1963, the day Ruby shot Oswald, and before any of those people could have died or disappeared.

Example: That same *New York Daily News* article, dated July 18, 1976, reported that "Dallas lawyer Carroll Jarnagin told FBI agents he saw Oswald and Ruby together in the Carousel on the night of October 4, 1963, and overheard them discussing plans for Oswald to assassinate Texas Governor John Connally, who was wounded in the fusillade that killed Kennedy."

The *Daily News* did not say how Jarnagin told FBI agents about the Ruby-Oswald meeting. He waited until after Ruby shot Oswald and then furnished the FBI with a complete dialogue, in script form on December 3, 1963, of the conversation he said he had overheard two months earlier. Jarnagin told the FBI he had overheard the governor referred to by name as "Shivers" (an earlier Texas governor, Alan Shivers) in the assassination plot.

Jarnagin said he had been sitting in the Carousel, at the next table to Ruby and Oswald, while accompanied by Shirley Mauldin, a stripper known professionally as Robin S. Hood. According to what Jarnagin told the FBI,[4] he and Miss Hood had been drinking heavily and were drunk that night. Jarnagin told the FBI he regularly had a drinking problem and his ex-wife had divorced him for that reason. The FBI located Miss Hood in the county jail at Omaha, Nebraska, December 8, 1963. She said she had accompanied Jarnagin to the Carousel on October 4, but that there had been no conversation about murder at the next table by anybody.

Example: In 1975, two men who had been deputy constables in Dallas at the time of the Kennedy and Oswald killings said they had seen papers in a carboard box linking Ruby and Oswald together. The deputies said one of the items in the box had been a photocopy of what was supposed to be an old press card for the communist newspaper, *The Daily Worker*, with Jack Ruby's name on it as Chicago correspondent. The deputies, Billy J. Preston and Ben Cash, also reported they had seen a receipt from a motel near New Orleans, with Ruby's and Oswald's names on it, dated several weeks before the assassination of President Kennedy. They said the receipt showed several phone calls had been placed to Mexico, to numbers identified as the Cuban and Russian embassies. Preston said he and the late Constable Robie Love personally had turned over the box of papers to Dallas District Attorney Henry Wade.

Love died in 1973, never having mentioned any such transaction to his wife. Wade said he may well have been handed a cardboard box, "but I know whatever they had didn't amount to nothing. You can see how much it would have helped us in the [Ruby] trial if we could prove Ruby and Oswald were together. We never found any substantial proof that they knew each other."

Example: On March 28, 1977, the select House Assassinations Committee—plagued with inner turmoil and the threat of a vote on the House floor, March 31, that would abolish the committee—hinted that it had uncovered a witness who had been introduced to Oswald by Ruby at the Carousel, with Ruby confiding that Oswald was a CIA "agent." The witness's identity was being protected, but there was a promise of significant testimony to be made public at a later date.

The witness, it seems, was Beverly Oliver McGann Massegee of Hooks, Texas. As Beverly Oliver she had been an entertainer at Abe's Colony Club, and had come over to the Carousel to have coffee with Jack Ruby one day, when she was introduced to Oswald, according to the story the congressional committee was keeping concealed until The Right Moment. Beverly was a beautiful young woman, a professional singer, who fell in with bad company. Her husband, George McGann, was a top figure in organized crime in Dallas at one point and was gunned down in Big Spring, Texas. Afraid that both the police and hoodlums were after her, Beverly got religion and married an evangelist. In the spring of 1977 she was being hidden out in Missouri until her testimony about Ruby and the CIA-connected Oswald could be made public. More than a year later, The Right Moment still had not arrived.

In fact, is the connection proved—either Oswald's connection with the CIA or with Ruby? Other people have come forward over the years, claiming they had seen someone they said was Oswald in the half-light of the Carousel, or saw him with Jack Ruby in cafes that were located in different parts of southern and western states. In the aftermath of Oswald's shooting death, I began to investigate possible links between Oswald and his killer, and filed this story to my newspapers:

> DALLAS, Dec. 3—Events in the life of Lee Harvey Oswald two months ago today may be the key to the murder of President Kennedy.
>
> On Oct. 3 Oswald, the President's presumed assassin, checked into the downtown Dallas YMCA, which was frequented by Jack Ruby—the man who was eventually to be Oswald's executioner.
>
> Oswald spent two nights in the YMCA. Then he checked out.
>
> Two months ago today Texas Gov. John B. Connally was in Washington, conferring with President Kennedy. Was it the same day that a plot against them was being hatched in Dallas?
>
> Oswald had just returned from a hasty, myterious trip to Mexico. The President's trip to Texas, including Dallas, already had been announced.
>
> The route of the Presidential motorcade through Dallas was not yet announced, but dignitaries could be expected to be driven past the Texas School Book Depository building on the western edge of downtown Dallas in any downtown procession.
>
> Any veteran Dallasite knows that. Oswald himself did not know Dallas customs intimately.
>
> Did he meet with one or more persons Oct. 3 and 4 to plan where he would be when the President came to town?
>
> Eleven days later, Oct. 15, Oswald was hired by R. S. Truly, manager of the Texas School Book Depository.
>
> If the paths of Oswald and Ruby did cross in the YMCA, was the encounter a coincidence or was it intentional?
>
> Investigators are marching through fields of question marks left over from Oct. 3 and 4.
>
> The YMCA is 13 stories high. Federal probers are checking out every guest registered there during those two days. Did any of them ever happen to be in the same place at the same time as Oswald, in New York or New Orleans or elsewhere over the past three years?
>
> One thing already is known about Oswald's two-day stay at the YMCA. He set the stage for mail to be delivered to him there and he continued to get letters, mailed in his name to the YMCA for several

weeks thereafter. Meanwhile, other mail came to him at other addresses.

Oswald was jobless on Oct. 14 when he rented an $8-a-week bedroom in the rooming house at 1026 North Beckley, about a mile from the apartment into which Ruby had recently moved.

The next day Oswald approached Truly and got his job in the Texas School Book Depository building. Investigators are trying to learn if Oswald already knew that a job would be available in the building.

The company pays its salaries twice a month. Oswald applied for a job precisely on the mid-month payday. Truly told him there was an immediate opening and he could begin working the next day.

Oswald lived friendlessly in the rooming house as "O. H. Lee." Was this meant to give him a chance to escape after the Nov. 22 assassination, under an alias and from an address unknown to the police?

He was heading in a straight line, with a gun in his pocket, toward the street on which Ruby lived, when Dallas police officer J. D. Tippit challenged him and was slain by Oswald, according to witnesses. This changed the direction of Oswald's escape attempt.

Truly has told authorities that Oswald was "a very good worker." Oswald's previous working records indicate he had not been competent.

Could this job—the last one Oswald ever held—have been much too important to him to lose, until the afternoon of Nov. 22?

Had Ruby and Oswald rendezvoused at the YMCA on October 3, and then plotted a killing in the Carousel, as lawyer Jarnagin had said, on October 4? Had Oswald been heading straight to Ruby's apartment for a purpose on November 22?

There might have been a reason to think so, in the beginning. But Jarnagin was a drunk and he provided no information to the FBI about Oswald until after the same information about Oswald already had been made public through other channels. Then, too, the Warren Commission's David Belin produced a more logical reason for Oswald's route on foot than the supposition that Oswald had been heading toward Ruby's place.

And in the end there is no reason—not a shred of proof—to think that Ruby and Oswald even knew each other.

Ruby and Oswald probably didn't know each other; yet both could have been used as separate parts of a conspiracy to commit murder in Dallas on the weekend of November 22-24, 1963. Oswald on Friday. Ruby on Sunday. Two men separately manipulated by the same power.

After they were arrested and jailed, both men said they had been manipulated. "I'm a patsy," said Oswald.[5] "I've been used for a purpose," said Ruby.[6]

But how would they have been manipulated, and by whom?

As in any universe, there is a sun, with planets moving around it. And in the universe of the Kennedy assassination, the mob loomed as the sun. Call it by any name: The mob, Cosa Nostra, organized crime, or by the name its enemy, Attorney General Robert F. Kennedy, had hung on it, The Private Government. Orbiting around it were components of the Teamsters, the CIA, the Dallas police force, the rightwing paramilitary, and Cuban interests.

It would have been no problem for the mob to reach out through its CIA contacts and then, in turn, through their Cuban connections to find Oswald. Oswald never even needed to see the dark light of the sun to become involved.

"The peculiar overlapping of interests that existed among the anti-Castro exiles, organized crime and the Central Intelligence Agency amounted in the autumn of 1963 to a tripartite pact," wrote Robert Sam Anson in 1975.[7] "Each had individual motives: the mob, greed and revenge; the exiles, a longing for their homeland; and the agency, a twisted kind of patriotism. Cuba fused those motives in a common cause. Each group helped the other. In their free-floating association, members drifted out of one group and into another and then back again. When it came to Cuba, the demarcation between organized crime, the exiles and intelligence was fuzzy, if not meaningless. An offense against one was an offense against all. The President's Cuban policy offended all of them." Identified with them were the conspirators of the extreme right—such as the Minutemen who secured weapons in Dallas late in 1963 for the most violent of Cuban exile groups, Alpha 66.

A man who used the name Morris Bishop and was connected with Alpha 66 is listed prominently in the files of the House Select Committee on Assassinations. A mysterious figure said to have been associated with the CIA, Bishop reportedly operated out of Alpha 66 headquarters, in a house on Hollandale Street, Dallas, and dealt personally with Oswald. Richard A. Sprague, who had served six months in late 1976 and early 1977 as chief counsel and staff director of the House Assassinations Committee, reported on April 11, 1977, that Bishop may have been responsible for rigging a phony story for the CIA, making it appear that Oswald had been in Mexico City in late September, 1963, supposedly dealing with the Cuban and Russian embassies—when actually Oswald had been in Dallas at the time.

If it were no problem for the mob to locate a militant like Oswald through its universal connections—and then leave Oswald to dangle out there as both triggerman and victim in its conspiracy—the mob also would have had no problem finding itself a Jack Ruby to silence Oswald. Ruby had been preparing most of his life for the job, running errands for the mob one way or another since he was the 16-year-old Chicago streetfighter who delivered sealed envelopes for the Capone people and kept his mouth shut about it. Ruby had gotten a coded message delivered to Lewis McWillie, his mob ally in Havana, in 1959, and then appeared before the feared narcotics and gambling don, Santo Trafficante Jr., in a Cuban prison.[8]

Trafficante, identified in Washington FBI files as No. 482531B, "has information that is important to the investigation of President Kennedy's murder," according to Sprague, the chief counsel who had Trafficante sub-poenaed March 9, 1977, to appear before the House Assassinations Com-mittee. The subpoena ordered Trafficante to bring with him any documents he had, relating especially to attempts to assassinate both Fidel Castro and John Kennedy—as well as to the workings of Alpha 66.

"Perhaps the most feared mobster in the underworld is Florida's Mafia chieftain, Santo Trafficante," columnists Jack Anderson and Les Whitten wrote in their syndicated column later that month. "House inves-tigators approached his Miami hideaway, therefore, with some apprehen-sion.

"He appeared at the screen door to accept their subpoena. 'Shove it under the door,' he said softly. They peered through the screen. The sinis-ter Trafficante was pale, and his hands were shaking.

"He may have had reason to shake. The House Assassinations Com-mittee had taken a sudden interest in the murder last July of mobster John Rosselli. Before he died, the flamboyant Rosselli hinted that he knew who had arranged President John F. Kennedy's assassination. Carefully hedg-ing, he told an incredible story that implicated Trafficante."

Over the years Rosselli had taken columnist Anderson into what the underworld figure said was his confidence. Rosselli told Anderson that he had reason to speculate that Trafficante had become a double-agent, first assigned by the CIA to knock off Castro, and then by Castro agents to hit Kennedy. The Trafficante organization "may have lined up Lee Harvey Oswald as the assassin or may have used him as a decoy while others am-bushed Kennedy from closer range. Once Oswald was captured, the mob couldn't afford to let him reveal his connection with the underworld. So Rosselli speculated that Jack Ruby, a small-time hoodlum with ties to the Havana underworld, was ordered to eliminate Oswald," Anderson wrote in 1977.

Rosselli in 1976, like Chicago mobster Sam Giancana a year earlier, was found murdered gangland style—at a time when U.S. Senate investi-gators were anxious to talk to both about their connection with the bizarre CIA plots to assassinate Castro in the months before and after Kennedy became President. The Senate investigators said they couldn't locate Trafficante, the third Mafia leader involved in the CIA contract on Castro.

Presumably Trafficante turned "pale" and began "shaking" when the subpoena drafted by Sprague reached the front door of his Miami hideaway, because he feared the same killers who had stalked Giancana and Rosselli would find him, to keep him from talking.

As a result, Trafficante's lawyers met privately with Sprague and refused to let their underworld client testify in a closed session with the congressional committee. They demanded an open hearing, in order that Trafficante could be seen and heard taking the fifth amendment and refusing on other constitutional grounds to say anything.

In the public hearing, March 16, Trafficante was asked about his connections with Jack Ruby, the CIA and what foreknowledge he might have had about plans to assassinate President Kennedy. Trafficante answered nothing, and then left brusquely.

But a source inside the House investigation of the Kennedy murder later told me that the whole episode involving the handling of the Trafficante subpoena and his appearance on Capitol Hill had been staged by Trafficante to throw off suspicions that it was he who'd had Giancana and Rosselli killed.

In other words, the Anderson-Whitten column had served to make Trafficante's point. Trafficante only wanted to appear intimidated by the delivery in Miami of the summons from Washington. After all, Trafficante had a long history of not turning pale and not shaking. The mob kind of smiled and winked when Trafficante returned to Florida from the questions on Capitol Hill.

Among the questions that went unanswered was this one by Sprague: "Mr. Trafficante, did you ever discuss with any individuals plans to assassinate President Kennedy prior to his assassination?" The witness replied, reading the words from a card, "I respectfully refuse to answer that question pursuant to my constitutional rights under the first, fourth, fifth and 14th amendments." Translated, the answer was, "Drop dead." And, translated, the question had been, "When are you going to tell us what happened at Carlos Marcello's meeting at Churchill Farms in September, 1962?" That was the meeting of select mafiosi in which Marcello, the New Orleans boss of bosses, had demanded blood-letting revenge against his sworn enemy, Bobby Kennedy, and the Kennedy power base. Within days, Trafficante was confiding in Miami that President Kennedy was to be hit. There is no doubt that Marcello and Trafficante were tough enough and close enough to make such plans. They were seated next to each other in a private basement room of La Stella, a New York restaurant in Queens, with 11 other mobsters, including the leaders of the Genovese, Gambino and Colombo Mafia families, when the police raided the business meeting, three years after the Kennedy assassination. They were arrested for consorting with mobsters. No longer threatened with deportation or jail by "little Bobby son of a bitch," as Marcello had referred to the former attorney general, Trafficante and the rest had no problem putting up $1.3 million in bail, and going about their business the next day.

Sprague got nowhere when Trafficante appeared before the House Select Committee on Assassinations, March 16, 1977, but was getting nowhere with the House even faster.

Sprague, a Humphrey Bogart kind of Philadelphia lawyer who had been a tough public prosecutor, had been hired soon after the committee was formed in the fall of 1976.

Carl Albert, the House speaker who had lost the confidence of many House Democrats, found it expedient to retire at the end of 1976. But before he did, he named Thomas N. Downing of Virginia to be chairman of the new committee. Not only was Downing a conservative who had blended quietly into much of the upholstery on Capitol Hill in nearly 20 years there, but he also was retiring from Congress at the end of 1976. So Albert picked a lame duck to head a committee which he structured with a number of relatively powerless junior members and some considered by their peers to be lightweights. Albert's weak move was taken as a sign by those inside the influential House establishment, such as B. F. Sisk of California, that the new committee was not meant to be taken all that seriously. As a veteran member of the powerful Rules Committee, Sisk drew significant support in the House when he tried to block formation of a committee to investigate assassinations. Sisk asked, "What difference does it really make at this point whether Oswald did it alone or not at all?" He compared the search for truth to recent information that Abraham Lincoln's Secretary of War, Edwin M. Stanton, had conspired to assassinate the President, which Sisk said "may be figments of chance." Sisk then cited the impressiveness of the Warren Commission members and a "need for this country to get over the sackcloth and ashes repentence we have for Watergate." It was time for the country to concentrate on the challenges of the future, Sisk said, and "not keep going over the past." Sisk didn't succeed in killing the new committee but it was given no more than a tentative charter just to get organized before the 94th Congress adjourned at the end of 1976.

Given that kind of backhanded endorsement, Downing, a retiring man in more ways than one, took an immediate back seat. He never had ruffled feathers in Congress and wasn't going to start in his final days. He brought in the tough Sprague as both chief counsel and staff director, and in that vacuum Sprague seized power.

By January, 1977, with Downing gone and Sprague in firm command, the staff director didn't know and didn't care that Congress expected him to be subservient. He demanded that the House establishment furnish him with what would amount to a $13-million budget for the two-year run of the 95th Congress, and a more imposing staff than any other congressional committee was allowed to have. At this kind of affront by Sprague, one congressman, Henry B. Gonzalez of Texas, sniffed, "Staffers should be on tap; not on top."

What Gonzalez had to say became enormously important because he was next in line to become chairman of the new committee. But Gonzalez found he would be arriving too late to gain real control. Sprague already had filled key committee slots with his own people, told to take orders from him alone, and he would not relinquish this kind of power. By the end of January the two men were not even speaking. By February 10 Gonzalez fired Sprague. Other members of the committee felt Sprague was more important to them than this new chairman with a noted, fiery Latin temperament, and they mutinied—refusing to support any such unilateral firing. Angry as a hornet, Gonzalez lined up what offstage support he could among House leaders but could not get rid of Sprague in what had become an armed camp. Committee doors were locked and Gonzalez could not or would not go there. Gonzalez resigned, on the point of nervous exhaustion, March 10. In retaliation, members of the House establishment threatened to derail the committee which was running headlong now, like a train out of control, unless Sprague resigned, too.

Sprague insisted his staff already had uncovered enough "startling information" to keep the committee alive, but two weeks after the Trafficante piece of show business, March 39, 1977, Sprague quit—when he learned that there were ample votes in the House to kill the committee. Later that day, with Sprague out of the way, the House voted grudgingly, 230 to 181, to keep the committee going through the end of 1978, but at a far less dollar amount than Sprague had insisted was necessary. Even so, the House authorized a significant sum, $2.5 million, for the investigation into two assassinations, those of John F. Kennedy and Martin Luther King, to continue.

Louis Stokes of Ohio became the new chairman and for a while the circus atmosphere of this weird committee continued. By June 20, however, the search for a new staff director and chief counsel ended with G. Robert Blakey, a Cornell law professor who found some sound advice in Sprague's angry, parting shot at Washington, "Congress is not the proper agency or branch of government to investigate any crime, much less murder. There is continual pressure for public hearings—titillating headlines. That is not the way to investigate."

Blakey undertook the job by getting rid of the Assassinations Committee's two press information people. Press conferences and meaningful, public sessions of committee investigative business were ended. Committee panelists and staff members were pledged to maintain silence. The probe continued through 1978 in deepest, darkest silence, with the possibility that a series of public hearings could be held late in 1978.

Before it winds up its business, the committee has to look at 10 central facts in the Jack Ruby case, unless the Stokes-Blakey phase of the investigation is to fail behind closed doors as did the Warren Commission in its examination of the secretive, enigmatic role played by Ruby in the action surrounding President Kennedy's murder:

1.   Leading up to the assassination, Ruby was in debt and seeking money.

2.   On the afternoon of Kennedy's assassination, Dallas bank officer Bill Cox saw Ruby with several thousand dollars in hand at the bank, but Ruby moved none of it into or out of his account.

3.   Ruby's best sources of money were in organized crime and he met privately with crime syndicate paymaster Paul Rowland Jones just before suddenly signing that power of attorney, only hours before President Kennedy reached Texas.

4.   Organized crime had a known history of control inside the Dallas police department.

5.   When Ruby sprang at Lee Harvey Oswald, he came from behind a policeman—from behind plain-clothes officer Blackie Harrison.

6.   Harrison had been in position at two different times that Sunday morning to let Ruby know by telephone precisely what the plans were for moving the prisoner Oswald.

7.   Ruby left his apartment on the route which led to the silencing of Oswald, after Harrison was in position to make the second and final telephone call to the apartment.

8.   Harrison and his partner, detective L. D. Miller, became strangely reluctant witnesses. Miller acted more like a suspect than a policeman, refusing at first to become a sworn witness—when all he had done was to have coffee with Harrison on the morning of Oswald's murder.

9.   The evidence shows Ruby lied about his entry to the police station basement.

10.   Ruby then tried to conceal his private meeting with police officer Harry N. Olsen soon after Oswald was arraigned as a cop killer.

Armed with subpoena powers, the House committee also must look deeper into Ruby's motivations for having shot Oswald than did the Warren Commission. For instance, there were five conceivable motivations:

A.   *Ruby acted alone and was not mentally competent.* That was attorney Melvin Belli's defense for Ruby. Privately, the Warren Commission never bought that as being the truth.

B.   *Ruby acted alone. But his actions were planned and murder was premeditated.* The Warren Report vaguely supported this concept, but did it in obscure footnotes and drew no such conclusion in its text.

C.   *There were separate murder conspiracies, wherein Ruby was not involved in the Kennedy assassination but then became the operative to kill Oswald.* The Commission's Ruby probers, Hubert and Griffin, began to check this out but became thwarted by Commission policy. Hubert and Griffin looked at certain members of the Dallas police force in terms of working parts of the plot to kill Oswald, using Ruby as the hit-man. But Hubert and Griffin didn't look deep enough or far enough.

D.   *There was a single conspiracy in which Ruby and Oswald worked together.* The Warren Commission ruled this out.

E.   *There was a single conspiracy in which Ruby and Oswald did not know each other, and Ruby was manipulated into killing Oswald.* Amazingly, the Warren Commission did not check this out.

Point "E" looms as one of the most significant possibilities, yet the Warren Commission ignored it even after Ruby told the Commission, "I have been used for a purpose." Either the police or the underworld, or a combination of both, could have activated Ruby. It is an area congressional probers should examine now.

Point "C" is especially important, because of the role of a limited few members of the Dallas police department. The probers particularly ought to take a look at the composition of the Dallas police department's Juveneil Bureau at the time of the Oswald slaying.

Assigned to the bureau were lieutenants George E. Butler and Cecil C. Wallace; detectives Roy L. Lowery, W. J. Cutchshaw and Miller; and patrolman Harrison.

Butler, who admits he was acting apprehensively in the police station basement just before Ruby shot Oswald, never was questioned by the Warren Commission. He not only knew Ruby over a long period of years but he knew and had dealt with the crime syndicate's Paul Rowland Jones, whom Ruby had dealt with over those same years.

Lowery and Cutchshaw immediately reported seeing Ruby enter the basement from a direction other than the Main Street ramp. Remember, it was after some delay that Ruby came up with the ramp story. Both detectives were ignored by members of a special Dallas police panel set up to investigate how Ruby had entered the basement. Lieutenant Wallace was a key member of that panel.

The panel saw nothing suspicious in the movements of Miller and Harrison on the morning of Oswald's murder, and did not pursue the foggy results of the lie-detector test given Harrison within the police department.

On December 1, 1963, three Dallas police—lieutenants Jack Revill and F. E. Cornwall, and inspector J. H. Sawyer—interviewed Ruby in the Dallas County jail. It was seven days after Ruby had shot Oswald. During the interview, according to a memorandum by the three officers to Chief Curry on December 4, "it became apparent that [Ruby] was not going to cooperate in any way as he stated that he did not want to get any police officers in trouble and also anything that he might tell us might be used against him in his forthcoming trial for murder. . . . During the interview, Ruby became very emotional and was almost to the point of hysteria in his effort to protect any police officer from being implicated into his entrance into the basement of the City Hall."

Other areas for the House investigation ought to include certain movements by Ruby's roommate George Senator, and by Ruby's onetime chief counsel Belli. Senator could not account for about six hours of his time on the day before Ruby shot Oswald. Ruby could not account for large chunks of time that day, too.

At the moment Oswald was shot, Senator was having coffee in the nearby Eatwell Cafe. The moment a waitress at the Eatwell excitedly said there was a news report about Oswald getting shot, Senator went right to a phone and called Jim Martin, a Dallas lawyer who knew Ruby and would become one of Ruby's first lawyers, along with Tom Howard, after the shooting. The only strange thing about what Senator did is that he telephoned Martin *five minutes before* there was any public announcement that Ruby was the person who had shot Oswald.

In Belli's case, immediately after his client Ruby was sentenced to die in the electric chair, in March, 1964, Belli was fired by the Ruby family and the lawyer made a hurried trip to Mexico City. He stayed there one night, meeting with Victor Velásquez. Then Belli flew to his home in San Francisco.

Velásquez was a noted Mexican trial lawyer, described in a CIA report as a former pro-communist Falangist party member in Mexico, who, in 1942, "directed drug-smuggling for the party, proceeds being used for Falangist propaganda." The report (Document No. 616-790) was held in the CIA's secret files until mid-1976, along with another (CIA Document No. 635-798) that quoted two agency sources in Mexico City as saying Velásquez's "reputation among local lawyers is shabby."

The Warren Commission never found out to its satisfaction the exact nature of Belli's quick meeting with the Mexican lawyer, although the CIA reported in its confidential file that "Velásquez issued [an] innocuous press statement for him."

That's not all the Warren Commission never found out from the CIA. The agency was a leading factor in the Commission's failure to investigate Jack Ruby properly.

Beginning with a 13-page request on February 24, 1964—early in the life of the Warren Commission's Ruby detail—Hubert and Griffin attempted to pry information from the CIA about Ruby. There were several followup requests.

On September 15, 1964—after the Warren Report already was into a final printing stage—the CIA stiffly told Commission Chief Counsel Rankin that "an examination of Central Intelligence Agency files has produced no information on Jack Ruby or his activities."

How much information the CIA really was holding back from the Commission still remains for House Assassinations Committee probers to dig out.

Just one of the items withheld from the Commission by the CIA on

Ruby was Document No. 150-59, the one reporting Ruby had visited American mobster Santo Trafficante in prison in Havana. The document was kept secret by the CIA for nearly 13 years.

Another example of the CIA coverup was its "ignorance" of the Warren Commission's request for information on a man identified as Leopold Ramos Ducos, who the Commission believed to be an anti-Castro gunrunner, possibly connected with Ruby.

The CIA gave no indication it ever had heard of such an individual— although there was a Leopoldo Ramos *Duclos*, and the CIA knew about him. Duclos had been installed by Teamsters boss Jimmy Hoffa as head of a violence-ridden local in Puerto Rico.

Eleven days after the CIA said it had been unable, in seven months, to locate information on Ruby or his associates, the Warren Report was issued on September 26, 1964, to the waiting nation.

In the end the Commission succeeded in delivering a dispassionate report so that America could put a great tragedy behind it and go forward. The idea must have seemed practical to at least one member of the Warren Commission, Congressman Gerald R. Ford. Ten years later he would use the same principle to deal with the issue of Watergate, and thus help America put a great tragedy behind it and go forward. He would pardon Richard M. Nixon. In the matters of both the Warren Report and the Nixon pardon there are those who say a great deal was not laid to rest.

Notes

CHAPTER 1   Los Foxes And El Songbird

1. In an August 9, 1976, interview at his residence in New Orleans where, at age 65, Hubert was professor of civil and criminal procedural law at Tulane Law School. Hubert died of a heart attack, March 26, 1977.

2. Preserved in Hubert's memoranda file among Warren Commission documents assembled in the National Archives, Washington, D.C.

3. Willens had been with the Justice Department's criminal division before the Warren Commission and now is with a major Washington law firm. He talked with Kantor, September 1, 1976, in a rare public interview on internal Commission functions.

4. Others were as concerned as Griffin was. More than two years later, October 5, 1966, the Texas Court of Criminal Appeals granted Ruby a new trial, growing out of Dean's disputed testimony.

5. In August 27, 1976, comments from his Des Moines law office to Kantor.

6. Tonahill to Kantor, July 15, 1976. There was no public feud between Ford and Warren but even from the beginning, when the investigation into Oswald and Ruby had just begun, Ford confided to the FBI that he was "disturbed about the manner in which Chief Justice Warren was carrying on his chairmanship of the Presidential Commission," according to a high-level internal FBI memorandum written December 12, 1963, but not made public by the FBI until January 18, 1978.

7. Griffin to Kantor, July 12, 1976, in Cleveland court chambers, where Griffin serves as Cuyahoga County common pleas judge.

8. From a letter written by Ruby in his cell and smuggled out by a confederate in 1964.

9. Olsen's reputation was borne out by his departmental records, according to former Dallas Police Chief Jesse E. Curry.

10. Jack Ruby to psychiatrist Manfred S. Guttmacher, in Dr. Guttmacher's Ruby trial testimony.
11. From a 17-page memorandum to Ruby's chief defense counsel Melvin Belli, January 11, 1964, from Dr. Walter Bromberg, based on a two-day psychiatric examination of Ruby.
12. To Ed Reid and Ovid Demaris, authors of *The Green Felt Jungle,* in a privately taped interview regarding conditions leading into Jack Ruby's arrival in Dallas from Chicago in 1947.
13. Description James M. Underhill Jr. and James P. Morgan Jr., June 26, 1964.
14. Description of Civello's power, on page 1098 of a report by the U.S. Senate Permanent Subcommittee on Investigations, July 30, 1964.
15. Report by Peace Justice David L. Johnston, December 11, 1963, to FBI agents Edmund C. Hardin and Robert J. Wilkison. On August 7, 1976, Johnston told Kantor that he had been acquainted with several top Dallas banking officials and top echelon police when he talked to the FBI.
16. Report by detective H. M. Hart, December 3, 1963, to Captain W. P. Gannaway of the Dallas police department's Special Service Bureau.
17. Ruby's statement in his December 21, 1963, interview by the FBI.
18. Davis preferred to put "Jr." at the end of his name, even on legal documents. But his name was identical to his father's and grandfather's, and was recorded on his death certificate as Thomas E. Davis III.
19. U.S. passport authorities refused for more than two months in 1976 even to admit Davis had been issued a passport. Their intransigence was overruled by officials of the State Department's Bureau of Security and Consular Affairs on November 23, 1976. These officials however continued to refuse to confirm or deny that Davis's passport was revoked after the Algerian episode.
20. A year earlier, QJ/WIN himself had to be rescued through CIA efforts when he faced smuggling charges in Europe. QJ/WIN's actual identity has been kept secret by the CIA.

CHAPTER 2   The Private Government Of Jack Ruby

1. Page 801, the Warren Report.
2. Jones told the FBI, June 26, 1964, in Charlotte, N.C., outlining his relationship with Ruby in Chicago and Dallas.
3. Pages 370-371, the Warren Report.
4. The Jones-FBI interview, June 26, 1964.
5. In a 1976 interview in Dallas with Kantor.
6. Not a unique event in Dallas. The Chicago mob earlier had sent a team of "marketing" experts to Dallas to make a businesslike appraisal of projected police-payoff conditions and vice distribution methods, the McClellan Senate rackets committee had been informed.
7. The FBI kept the location of these two phone calls concealed from the public record until March 16, 1976.
8. The FBI-Jones interview, June 26, 1964.
9. Separate reports filed December 3, 1963, by FBI agents James E. Doyle, Arthur N. Barrett and Donald M. Holland in Las Vegas.
10. Interview with Kantor, August 7, 1976.
11. Ruby made the comment July 18, 1964, in off-the-record remarks during the polygraph test he was taking, administered by the Warren Commission.
12. Interview with Kantor, August 3, 1976, at Greenville Avenue Bank & Trust where Cox, a former major-league baseball player, is senior vice-president.
13. Bank records show Ruby made a $31.87 withdrawal from the Carousel account that day.
14. Attorney General Robert F. Kennedy's remarks, before the U.S. Senate Permanent Subcommittee on Investigations, September 25, 1963, less than two months before the murder of his brother.
15. From the CIA Inspector General's Report, 1967, page 62.
16. Giancana was gunned down in his home, shot seven times in the head by highly profes-

sional assassins, June 20, 1975, virtually on the eve of his scheduled closed-door appearance before the Senate Select Committee on Intelligence. He was to be questioned about the CIA-Mafia project to kill Fidel Castro. Rosselli did testify, June 24, 1975. Rosselli (real name: Filippo Saco) was born in Italy and entered the United States illegally. He used the aliases "John Rawlston" and "J. A. Rollins" in his CIA role, posing in his dealings with Cuban exiles in Florida as a representative of Wall Street business enterprises that had financial interests in overturning Castro's government. Before he could testify again in 1976 in front of the Senate committee, Rosselli disappeared from his Florida home, July 28, 1976, and his body was found decomposing in an oil drum afloat in the ocean near Miami several days later.

17. Trafficante's customary alias has been "Louis Santos." In the CIA-Mafia project he served as a courier to Cuba, to make arrangements there for the Castro assassination plans.

18. "The attorney general was not told that the gambling syndicate operation already had been reactivated, nor as far as we know, was he ever told that CIA had a continuing involvement with U.S. gangster elements" (from the CIA Inspector General's Report, page 65).

19. From former President Johnson's 1971 interview with Leo Janis, which later appeared in the July, 1973, *Atlantic*, in an article entitled, "The Last Days of the President."

20. CIA Inspector General's Report, 1967, page 29.

21. July 29, 1975.

22. Newsman Clark Mollenhoff once asked Hoffa why two Teamster officials in Tennessee were allowed to maintain their positions of power after it was disclosed that one had used $20,000 to bribe a judge while the other (with several criminal convictions already) had beaten a Nashville trucking executive senseless. Hoffa told Mollenhoff: "We need somebody down there to kick those hillbillies around." Another Teamster official, Joey Glimco of Chicago, like many hoodlums in Hoffa's union and like Ruby in Dallas, disdained the use of a bank account for day-to-day personal business. Instead, Glimco channeled thousands of dollars for his own use out of his Teamsters taxicab drivers Local 777. Once when Glimco was charged with extortion, he spent $3,840 in Teamster funds to hire a private detective, Maurice Adler, to investigate Chicago police, who had listed him among the top 19 crime bosses of the city.

23. Not every picture of Ruby was out of focus. Sometimes the Warren Commission simply managed to get its thumb in front of the lens. For instance, the Commission reported (Vol. 5, page 200 of the Commission hearings) that Ruby said he contacted "Deutsch I. Maylor" of the "American Federation of Labor," instead of properly identifying the contact as M. W. (Dusty) Miller, director of the Southern Conference of Hoffa's Teamsters.

24. Commission Exhibit No. 2344.

25. From a confidential report on Dr. Jacobson's medical file on Ruby, provided January 15, 1964, to Dallas Police Chief Curry by Captain Gannaway; and from a report by Dr. Bromberg to Ruby's chief defense lawyer Belli, January 11, 1964.

26. The Gannaway Report to Chief Curry, January 15, 1964.

27. From the files of the Texas Attorney General's *Report on President Kennedy's Assassination*: Dr. Guttmacher's account of his psychiatric interview with Ruby.

28. Telephone logs show 70 instances of contact between Judith Campbell (who in a subsequent marriage became Judith Exner) and the White House. A friend of Frank Sinatra's, she developed frequent contacts with President Kennedy through the first 16 months of his administration, at a time when she was "also a close friend of Rosselli and Giancana, and saw them often," according to findings of the Church Senate Committee in 1975. Kennedy is supposed to have broken off his relationship with her on March 22, 1962, the day FBI Director Hoover privately informed him that she was a consort of hoodlums. Sinatra's friendships with the underworld proved to be more durable than his friendships with the White House.

29. Nelson B. (Bunker) Hunt told the FBI on May 15, 1964, that he had been glad to contribute to the advertisement which he characterized as "a criticism of President Kennedy in a dignified way." The FBI never asked Bunker Hunt if he was acquainted with Brading and Brown. On December 17, 1964, the FBI met with Bunker's brother, Lamar, who said in the terse interview that he "has had no contact whatsoever with Ruby to the best of his knowledge." Hunt's name appeared in a book of contacts that Ruby possessed.

30. The interview occurred January 29, 1964, conducted in "Braden's" investments office by FBI agents Chester C. Orton and John K. Anderson.

31. Commission Deposition Exhibit No. 5226: interrogation of Curtis LaVerne Crafard.

CHAPTER 3   The Weekend

1. Ruby's description, given by him to the Warren Commission, June 7, 1964.
2. The fatal shooting of officer J. D. Tippit.
3. Gonzalez became chairman on February 2, 1977, of the new House Select Committee to Investigate the Assassinations of President Kennedy and Martin Luther King. By March 8, he resigned in the midst of a power-struggle for control of the committee.
4. He was a town character and would come to my desk occasionally in the city room of the *Times Herald* with ideas for stories about other characters in his circle. There had been Jimmy Lacoune, operator of a dilapidated, walkup professional boxing gym near the Dallas County Courthouse. And there had been Bernard Vincent Ferguson, barely five feet tall, who could contort himself to walk under desks, bent backwards, his shoulder blades touching the floor. And a suburban housewife named Mrs. William Leavelle, who kept three blue indigo snakes, each of them six-footers, in her laundry room enjoying having them wind around her when the children were in school. She said she intended to use the snakes in a striptease act, to earn money to pay for her husband's education in engineering school. Ruby was self-seeking and publicity hungry; but I never mentioned him or his clubs in any story, and never visited his places.
5. Ruby told FBI agents C. Ray Hall and Manning C. Clements, December 21, 1963.
6. The same edition of the *Mirror* carried columnist Jack Anderson's account of Joe Valachi, referred to in Chapter One.
7. In a tape-recorded interview with Kantor in Jasper, Texas, July 15, 1976.
8. From the private collection of Ruby letters in the possession of Dr. John K. Lattimer, Columbia University College of Physicians and Surgeons.
9. Subsequently Wise served as mayor of Dallas in the 1970s.
10. In a tape-recorded interview with Kantor, July 27, 1976, in Curry's Dallas home. Curry retired from the force as chief in March, 1966.
11. Harrison was a patrolman on plain-clothes assignment.
12. James Andrew Putnam was fired in 1970 from the Dallas police department after 17 years on the force, for general negligence. Then just before Christmas, 1973, Putnam's wife was shot three times. She identified him as her killer to police and ambulance attendants before she died. Putnam was arrested while hiding from police and sentenced to 11 years in prison in 1974.
13. Page 461 of Belin's book: *November 22, 1963: You Are the Jury.*
14. Tonahill's public position during Ruby's murder trial was much different. Tonahill and chief defense counsel Melvin Belli argued that Ruby acted on impulse and as a helpless victim of psychomotor epilepsy. However, on October 14, 1976, three months after Kantor's interview with him, Tonahill, who still must deal with Dallas law-enforcement officials on behalf of clients, wrote Kantor that he wanted to add these words to his views on the conspiracy: "But emphatically there was no conspiracy between Ruby and the police—just plain Texas homicide."
15. Cutchshaw interview by Kantor, July 29, 1976.
16. Ruby confided to Tonahill in a handwritten note, early in 1964, that Howard had furnished him the idea of sparing Mrs. Kennedy the painful trip back to Texas as the reason for the shooting.

CHAPTER 4   A Stillness On The Fifth Floor

1. Ten days later Assistant FBI Director Cartha DeLoach wrote an internal memorandum (not made public by the FBI until Jan. 18, 1978) about a conversation he'd had with Nicholas Katzenbach, the deputy attorney general: "Katzenbach mentioned that Waggoner Carr, the Texas state attorney general, would like very much to see the Director [Hoover] on Friday, 12-6-63. I asked him what for. He stated that Carr had no particular motive in mind other than to indicate to the press later on that he had discussed matters with the Director. I told him I could see no percentage in the Director's seeing Carr . . . Katzenbach indicated that the White House might think otherwise. He stated that the President was most anxious for Carr

to be given attention in Washington in as much as Carr was running for office next year. I told Katzenbach I knew this. However I still felt that the Director should not be injected into this matter. Katzenbach stated he would attempt to disuade Carr from seeing the Director. However, Carr was quite persistent." At the foot of the memorandum, DeLoach made this recommendation: "In view of the close friendship which Carr obviously has with the President, the Director may desire to just shake hands with Carr without sitting down and discussing facts concerning our report." Hoover looked at it and wrote in longhand: "If he calls I will see him." Eventually they settled on posing for a quick picture together and Carr was ushered out immediately.

2. Shortly after his appointment to the Commission, Dulles told *New York Post* columnist Murray Kempton that he was certain no evidence of a conspiracy would be found, according to Kempton in a private interview with author Robert Sam Anson on April 12, 1975.

3. The pattern in Washington is familiar. Ten years later another seven-member group would be formed—the Senate Watergate Committee. One of its members, Democratic Senator Herman E. Talmadge of Georgia, repeatedly stressed two themes as a guideline for the investigation into misconduct in the Nixon White House: "We don't have to prove anything, and we shouldn't try unless we've got the evidence. And let's not drag out this investigation too long." (From *Chief Counsel*, a Random House book, published in November, 1976, and written by Samuel Dash, whose job title with the Watergate Committee was the same as J. Lee Rankin's job title had been with the Warren Commission.)

4. DeLoach FBI internal memorandum, December 20, 1963; withheld from public records until January 18, 1978.

5. Olney to Kantor, November 15, 1976.

6. DeLoach memorandum, December 12, 1963; made public by the FBI, January 18, 1978.

7. Specter later became district attorney of Philadelphia.

8. In 1975 Belin served as executive director of President Ford's Commission to Examine Domestic, Clandestine Activities of the CIA. Vice-President Nelson Rockefeller was chairman of the Commission.

9. Ten years later Jenner would become minority counsel for the House Judiciary Committee's historic impeachment proceedings against Richard M. Nixon.

10. Coleman became the only black member of President Ford's cabinet, as Secretary of Transportation.

11. Dr. Goldberg was serving as a chief historian for the Air Force in the Pentagon. He continues in the Pentagon as a widely published military historian.

12. Redlich later would become dean of the New York University's School of Law.

13. A memorandum to FBI Domestic Intelligence Division Director William C. Sullivan, April 3, 1964.

14. October 21, 1975, FBI Deputy Director James B. Adams told a congressional subcommittee that the receptionist in the Dallas FBI offices, to whom Oswald handed the note, recalled it warning Hosty, "I will blow up the FBI and the Dallas police department if you don't stop bothering my wife." Adams said Hosty is supposed to have remembered the note being less specific, with Oswald allegedly warning that "I will take appropriate action and report this to proper authorities."

15. The FBI later maintained that another agent added those remarks more than four years later to the Flynn report on Ruby.

16. Judge Griffin to Kantor, November 5, 1976.

17. Nicholas Katzenbach was in charge of the Justice Department as Robert Kennedy mourned his brother's death.

18. According to senior FBI officials who were questioned privately in 1976 by investigators for the Church Committee's Senate probe into the performance of U.S. intelligence agencies at the time of the Kennedy assassination.

19. DeLoach memorandums, December 12 and 17, 1963; made public by the FBI, January 18, 1978.

20. Conversations with Kantor, July 12, 1976, and April 23, 1977.

21. Hubert to Kantor, August 9, 1976.

22. Helms was CIA director from 1966, during the peak of the CIA's unpopular role in a spreading war in Southeast Asia, into the start of the second term of the Nixon presidency. In 1976, some members of the Senate wanted Helms prosecuted for perjury after he had testi-

fied that he would have opposed any CIA domestic activity—when it later was disclosed that Helms, as CIA director, had known all along about the assistance the CIA gave to convicted Watergate burglar E. Howard Hunt. Helms also became a controversial figure in charges on Capitol Hill concerning CIA participation in the overthrow of the Salvador Allende government in Chile. President Nixon assigned Helms as ambassador to Iran early in 1973 and Helms resigned that post hours before Jimmy Carter's defeat of President Ford, November 2, 1976.

23. The discussion remained classified for 10 years until author Harold Weisberg successfully sued the government to force release of the transcript.

CHAPTER 5   Any Friend Of Needle-Nose Labriola . . .

1. Barney Ross in an interview with the FBI, New York City, June 5, 1964.

2. Jack Ruby's conversation with psychiatrist Dr. Manfred Guttmacher, Dallas county jail, December 21, 1963.

3. In an interview with Sally Quinn, *The Washington Post*, January 7, 1976.

4. Information obtained June 8, 1964, by the FBI from Harry H. Young, assistant foreman, Lissner Paper Grading Co., Chicago.

5. "There is no evidence" was used over and over in the Warren Report, virtually as a "code" to indicate that hard evidence, if not circumstantial evidence, was lacking.

6. The FBI's lengthy interview with Jones, June 26, 1964.

7. Ruby made the statement one night in the fall of 1959 to two people, including Giles Miller, a Dallas businessman with extreme rightwing political connections, who informed the FBI on December 17, 1963, about Ruby's claim that he had been told to live in Dallas.

CHAPTER 6   Put That In Your Pipe And Smoke It

1. Additionally, a Dallas FBI report on July 9, 1964 (not made public until December 6, 1977) said "records made on that date were not completely audible and a detailed transcription could not be obtained."

2. In his interview with the FBI on the subject of Jack Ruby, December 19, 1963, at Birmingham, Alabama, Jones said he first met Ruby early in the fall of 1946, before Jones began to negotiate with Butler and Guthrie.

3. In an interview December 1, 1963, with Secret Service agent Elmer Moore.

4. Ruby to Dr. Manfred Guttmacher, his defense psychiatrist, December 21, 1963.

5. Miles filed his report after witnessing Ruby use explosive language and threaten Vincent Lee, an AGVA official, with violence. Lee, who had been bullied and abused by Bonds, too, was the source of Miles's written report on the associates of Ruby and Bonds.

6. From psychiatric interview notes on Ruby, taken after he shot Oswald.

7. Ruby made the comment to psychiatrist Manfred Guttmacher before the Ruby murder trial.

8. In his interview with FBI agents Hall and Clements, December 21, 1963.

CHAPTER 7   In Search Of Class

1. The FBI suspected Alexander of supplying stolen information to the press—such as excerpts from Oswald's diary and a transcript of Ruby's privately given Warren Commission testimony. In a vituperative handwritten note, revealed December 6, 1977, J. Edgar Hoover referred to Alexander as a "low S.O.B." Another FBI memorandum, written February 8, 1964, quotes Ruby trial judge Joe B. Brown as telling special FBI agent Vince Drain confidentially that Alexander was "a mental case" and that Brown "never could understand District Attorney Wade keeping him as a prosecutor . . ."
2. Page 29 of the book by Kaplan and Waltz: *The Trial of Jack Ruby.*
3. In the July 15, 1976, interview with Tonahill in Jasper.
4. Page 112, *Dallas Justice*, the book written by Melvin M. Belli with Maurice C. Carroll.
5. Tonahill says he accumulated a boxful of Ruby's notes during the trial and later burned them all.
6. Burleson, a Dallas attorney, was an assistant counsel on the Belli-Tonahill defense team.
7. Page 45, *Dallas Justice.*

CHAPTER 8   Cuba

1. Willens to Kantor, September 1, 1976.
2. Ruby never used the box regularly after that. He used it three times in 1960, once in 1961, and never used it again.
3. Judge Griffin in a letter to Kantor, November 5, 1976.
4. She referred to the bodyguard in underworld jargon as a "torpedo" when she talked to FBI agents about McWillie, December 5, 1963, in San Francisco.
5. Ruby to Dr. Guttmacher, the psychiatrist, December 22, 1963.
6. Ruby to Dr. Guttmacher.
7. "And I was bored with the gambling because I don't gamble," Ruby lied to Chief Justice Warren in their June 7, 1964, encounter, when Ruby talked about his stay in Havana.
8. Sorge's relationship with McLane is described in Chapter One.
9. Contraband: a word commonly used by narcotics agents to describe an undercover shipment of dangerous drugs. It also was the word used by Harry Hall, the West Coast criminal who had worked with Jack Ruby in the 1950s in high-stake gambling ventures in Texas. Hall was reported by Secret Service agents Guy H. Spaman and Darwin D. Horn, November 29, 1963, as saying that "one time when he was associating with Ruby he recalls that Ruby said he was going to Florida to buy a load of 'contraband' to send to Israel."
10. From the select Senate Committee to Investigate Intelligence Activities, headed by Senator Frank Church of Idaho.
11. Trafficante was publicly identified as Louis Santos, October 15, 1963, in the Valachi hearings before the McClellan Senate rackets subcommittee.
12. The meeting discussed in Chapter Two.
13. In 1952, a few weeks before he was nominated for vice-president, U.S. Senator Richard M. Nixon of California accompanied Pasadena lawyer Dana C. Smith to Havana. There, Smith lost at the Sans Souci gaming tables and wrote a $4,200 check to cover the losses, giving it to Rothman, who was operating the casino for the syndicate. Once back in the United States, Smith stopped the check. Rothman threatened to sue. Nixon wrote the State Department, August 21, 1952, asking that the U.S. embassy in Havana intervene in Smith's behalf. Nixon already was Dwight Eisenhower's running mate by then. His friend Smith operated the so-called Nixon Fund that provided Nixon with $18,168 until its existence was learned—causing the scandal that led Nixon to offer in a nationally televised speech to resign from the Eisenhower ticket. Eisenhower refused to accept the post-convention offer.
14. The March 19, 1964, memorandum from Hubert and Griffin to members of the Commission.
15. McKeown to Kantor, from his home in Florida, December 13, 1976.
16. These activities by Davis are referred to in Chapter One.
17. When he found out about it, Miss Knight's superior in the State Department's Bureau of Security and Consular Affairs, Abba P. Schwartz, ordered the phone removed. It was a

coded "scrambler" phone that could have allowed the passport chief to talk directly to the CIA on matters she didn't want the State Department to know about.

18. The memorandum was confined to CIA files until July, 1976, when it became partially available to outsiders for the first time through the Freedom of Information Act.

19. Tannenbaum to Kantor, from his home in Gulfport, Mississippi, September 26, 1976.

20. Ruby's trip to New York was an attempt to settle his dispute with AGVA, the entertainers' union. The trip was a failure from Ruby's viewpoint.

21. Could this have been John M. Crawford, employed by the Texas state penitentiary at Huntsville, north of Houston, as the prison system's pilot? Crawford's name was found in Ruby's car by police, the day Ruby shot Oswald, in a list of those who had been given special passes to the Carousel. Crawford subsequently died in a mysterious crash of the prison plane, which he had taken up one night for no specified reason.

22. Many potential witnesses were overlooked by the Warren Commission or did not come forward at the time. Price is in the latter category. Price operates the 525 Club and a taxi messenger service in Houston. On July 19, 1976, Price gave Mark Lane, the attorney and Kennedy assassination specialist, recorded and filmed details of his encounter with Ruby. Price told Kantor on December 13, 1976, he has not yet come up with a corroborating witness to his recalled meeting with the Ruby group. Price says Ruby never directly mentioned Cuba as his destination, since such a flight would be illegal. But the garrulous Ruby made broad references to where they were headed, without using the name.

23. Supplied by Miami FBI source Carlos Villa, December 21, 1963, through a communiqué from Havana. The FBI withheld this from public files until 14 years later.

CHAPTER 9   The Ring Of Bulls

1. Griffin to Kantor, July 12, 1976, Cleveland, Ohio.

2. Notes incorporated into a memorandum to J. Lee Rankin, April 2, 1964.

3. Writing about that system in 1976, persistent Warren Commission critic Mark Lane claimed that "witnesses in Dallas, alive although frightened, know that Charles Batchelor, then assistant chief of the Dallas police department, personally escorted Jack Ruby into the basement via an elevator and that moments later Ruby executed Oswald. Batchelor later was promoted to chief of police." Attorney Lane obviously has talked with present and former Dallas police who are certain Ruby did not enter the police basement by way of the ramp. Lane is obligated to produce at least one reliable witness to swear that the late Chief Batchelor escorted Ruby in an elevator to the basement. Interestingly, Ruby's entrance into the basement either by elevator or by the stairway described in Chapter Three would have led him by the same path he was seen taking by police detectives Cutchshaw and Lowery, about three minutes before the shooting. That path is 90 degrees different from the ramp entrance Ruby later said he took.

4. They were Special Service Bureau lieutenants C. C. Wallace and Jack Revill.

5. The afterthought reports of the three detectives are described in Chapter Three.

6. Page 219 of the Warren Report. Former Warren Commission staffers are quick to point out the use here of the modifying word, *probably*, when Ruby's entry by way of the ramp is cited. But the Commission at all times in its conclusions led the public to think it fully accepted the story of the ramp. For instance a diagram of the police station basement on page 217 of the Warren Report shows Oswald's route and Ruby's route and there is nothing qualifying about the dotted line leading down the ramp and labeled: "Ruby's Route."

7. Page 221 of the Warren Report.

8. Ibid.

9. Desk officer Charles Goolsby's phone call to Harrison is discussed in Chapter Three.

10. Harrison died in June, 1975, a victim of cancer after 27 years on the Dallas police force.

11. The original note is in possession of Penn Jones Jr., Midlothian, Texas.

12. Officer Roy Vaughn was the policeman assigned to guard the top of the ramp and to keep out those without proper credentials.

13. Dean was quoted in *The Dallas Times Herald*, December 8, 1963, by reporter David J. Hughes as saying that he had seen Ruby walk down the Main Street ramp. Dean vehemently denied telling Hughes that in an interview which occurred November 24, the day Ruby shot Oswald.

14. The Warren Commission didn't give polygraph tests. The single exception was the polygraph test administered by the FBI on behalf of the Commission to Jack Ruby, after Ruby made his plea personally to Chief Justice Warren to be given the test.
15. The Ruby trial was over but both the prosecution and defense were preparing for lengthy retrial motions and hearings.

CHAPTER 10   An Amicable Solution

1. A variety of documents from Ruby's childhood and early-adult years show different birth dates for him in the spring of 1911. But March 23 was the date he celebrated during his years in Dallas.
2. In the 1970s Lehrer developed a national reputation as a Washington analyst on national public television.
3. The period in the early 1950s when Wisconsin Senator Joseph R. McCarthy waged an inflammatory and irresponsible crusade against those whom he considered to be subversives in government jobs. His reckless attempts to destroy others led to his own destruction as a viable member of the Senate, and to his deterioration and death.
4. The record shows, with the exception of April 14, Griffin did not reappear in Dallas to resume questioning witnesses for nearly four months after his banishment. None of those he interviewed was connected with the police department. Griffin helped out Leon Hubert on April 14 by conducting four routine interviews in Dallas while Hubert was talking to witnesses in Fort Worth. Otherwise, Griffin's work was confined to Washington between the end of March and mid-July, when he traveled to Dallas and then Chicago to meet with witnesses.
5. Based on the exact measurements of time which could be made through the frame-by-frame studies of "home movies" made by Abraham Zapruder, a spectator at the motorcade murder scene.

CHAPTER 11   May Day

1. The advertisement listed the names of 82 national directors of the organization, which included a number of well-known professors, lawyers and clergymen. The ad appealed for donations and said that the 13-year-old organization, born in the earlier stages of the McCarthy era, had as its purpose the defense of constitutional rights. One of its campaigns, the ad said, was the courtroom defense of three Indiana University students who had been indicted under an Indiana state sedition law for having attended a civil rights meeting. The organization was not alone in its criticisms of the House Un-American Activities Committee (HUAC). Several House members had voted to cut off funds needed to allow HUAC to continue.
2. The Emergency Civil Liberties Committee was not considered to be subversive by the Justice Department in the Truman, Eisenhower, Kennedy or Johnson administrations, which covered the Committee's life span at that time. Redlich had been an outstanding law scholar at Yale and would become dean of law at New York University.
3. The Commission took Wade's testimony nearly a month later. Rankin conducted the questioning. Nothing new came out.
4. The Commission decided it didn't want to interview Howard.
5. On page 66, Book 15, of the Warren Commission hearings, agent C. Ray Hall reported Ruby told him he had entered the police station from the Main Street side but did not say the Main Street ramp. The interview by Hall with Ruby took place before Tom Howard arrived to talk with Ruby at 1:58 p.m. It was after the private Howard-Ruby talk that the ramp story developed.
6. Kantor became the only member of the White House press corps that accompanied President Kennedy to Texas, to be summoned as a Warren Commission witness as a result of the May 14 memorandum. What happened when Griffin and Hubert interviewed Kantor over a two-day period is discussed in Chapter 14.
7. Both institutions later went out of business.
8. The question was if she knew Lawrence Meyers, her brother's friend from Chicago, and knew about any of the Ruby-Meyers contacts in Dallas at the time of the Kennedy trip to Texas.

CHAPTER 12   Man's Best Friend

1. From Ruby's conversations with his defense psychiatrists, Dr. Mannfred S. Guttmacher and Dr. Walter Bromberg, a month after the Oswald murder.
2. In an interview with Kantor, July 26, 1976, in the Oak Cliff section of Dallas where Stevenson is deputy constable.
3. According to notes made by Dr. Bromberg, January 11, 1964, in an analysis of Ruby.
4. In a letter from Ray Pennington to Dr. John K. Lattimer, sent from Duncanville, Texas, May 30, 1967.
5. From diagnostic impressions of Ruby, noted January 7, 1964, by Dr. Guttmacher.
6. From Guttmacher notes, December 27, 1963, filed with the Texas attorney general's investigation of the murder of Oswald.

CHAPTER 13   The Truth, The Whole Truth And Other Fables

1. Appointed by Judge Joe. B. Brown to make an assessment, Dr. Beavers told the judge on April 27, 1964, that Ruby was "acutely mentally ill." Dr. Beavers recommended "immediate psychiatric hospitalization and close observation because of the possibility of a suicide attempt." Ruby could not be executed while determined to be insane and Judge Brown agreed to convene a sanity trial "at the first suitable date." More than two years passed before there was such a trial. It came on June 13, 1966, and both Ruby and his jailers claimed he was sane and very aware of reality. Ruby blasted his own lawyers who said he was mentally sick. A jury agreed with Ruby that he was sane.
2. Ruby entered the testing room at 2:23 p.m. The testing got under way at 3:10 p.m. and concluded at 8:59 p.m.
3. The tempo of the wrangling picked up audibly a week later when Sol Dann flew to Dallas to discharge Fowler and Tonahill. The three had a violent argument. Tonahill publicly accused Dann of trying to make a fast buck off of Ruby, by trying to arrange the sale of the suit Ruby wore on the day he shot Oswald, to a wax museum. Fowler charged Dann was trying to incorporate Ruby as an enterprise. Dann denied all of this and accused the two of threatening him with bodily harm if he remained in Texas on the Ruby case. He threatened both with lawsuits and claimed they called him a "white nigger." Dann gave up plans to sue the Warren Commission for giving Ruby the lie-detector test, but forced Fowler to withdraw from the case. Nearly a year later Texas Judge Louis Holland ordered Tonahill removed from the case, and the parade of defense lawyers continued. Dann suffered a critical heart attack and was forced to withdraw from the Ruby case in November, 1966, just after a new Ruby trial had been ordered by the Texas Court of Criminal Appeals. Dann died in April 1976.

CHAPTER 14   Faster Than A Speeding Magic Bullet

1. Kantor was 37 at the time of his trip back to Texas as a White House correspondent on the Kennedy trip, and had 17 years experience as a reporter.
2. In a 1961 conversation in the news room of *The Dallas Times Herald.*
3. *The Fort Worth Press* was a Scripps-Howard newspaper and Kantor was that paper's special Washington correspondent.
4. Kantor wrote again to Ruby on August 31, 1964, after the trial, after Belli no longer was Ruby's lawyer and after Ruby's lie-detector test. Kantor asked Ruby a number of specific questions about the Parkland Hospital encounter in the August 31 letter—which went unanswered by Ruby after it was intercepted in the Dallas county jail by deputy sheriff J. H. Kitching. Kitching in turn furnished a copy of the letter to the FBI, according to an FBI file made available December 6, 1977. Kitching acted on orders by Dallas Sheriff Bill Decker, according to the FBI.
5. Several months after the Kennedy assassination Mrs. Wilma Tice of Dallas contacted Ruby's sisters and told them she had seen Ruby at Parkland in the early afternoon, November 22, 1963.
6. Mrs. Tice claimed she overheard Ruby, standing outside Parkland, volunteering to donate

a kidney to Governor Connally.

7. Pages 71-96, Volume 15, Warren Commission hearings.

8. Pages 338-426, Volume 20, Commission exhibits.

9. The Warren Report, pages 336-337.

10. Author Jim Bishop utilized some of Kantor's notes in the preparation of his best-selling book, *The Day Kennedy Was Shot*. Another author, Pulitzer Prize-winning reporter Sylvan Fox of *The New York Times*, wrote in his 1965 book, *The Unanswered Questions About President Kennedy's Assassination*, that "Kantor is an experienced and reliable reporter. He gave a coherent account of his meeting with Ruby at the hospital. But the Commission decided that 'Kantor probably did not see Ruby at Parkland Hospital in the few minutes before or after 1:30 p.m., the only time it would have been possible for Kantor to have done so.' Once again, the Commission simply discounts testimony, even from so good a source as this, if such testimony does not fit its conception of the events that took place."

11. He didn't make up his mind quickly enough to make the change in time for the next day's *Morning News*. The Saturday afternoon *Times Herald* carried his "closed" announcement, though.

12. UPI White House reporter Merriman Smith got the quote from Hill, and Smith was beating everybody in sight in covering every aspect of the Kennedy assassination story. It won him the Pulitzer Prize. When it was presented to Smitty the next May, President Johnson said to him, "I'm glad you didn't win it off of me."

13. The false rumor about the slain Secret Service agent spread through Dallas immediately and there probably still are people there who insist the story was true. Several days after the tragedy, Kantor was interviewing a former employer of Oswald who said he believed "those Secret Service people do everything so secretively, they just pulled off that agent and buried him in secret."

14. The Warren Commission reviewed Kantor's notes; never asked about the phone number. The FBI never informed the Commission's Ruby investigators whose phone number that was, according to Judge Griffin, April 23, 1977.

15. Papich to Kantor, October 30, 1975. Papich had become executive director in New Mexico of the governor's Organized Crime Prevention Commission.

CHAPTER 15   A Matter Of Conspiracy

1. In a tape-recorded interview with Kantor, July 27, 1976.

2. "My memory actually is no better, maybe it is as good as the ordinary person's," DeMar told the Warren Commission. His act consisted of having several people in the audience call out the names of objects; then DeMar would have them raise their hands at random and he would recite back to them the objects each had named. He told the Commission the routine was a word-association "gimmick . . . [a] memory stunt, and that is it . . . after it is over, I have forgotten."

3. Filed November 25, 1963, by agents Arthur E. Carter and Charles T. Brown Jr. in Dallas.

4. Jarnagin to FBI agents Ralph E. Rawlings and Bardwell D. Odum, December 6, 1964.

5. Oswald shouted the words at reporters in the Dallas police station.

6. Ruby said this to members of the Warren Commission on June 7, 1964, when he was begging to be taken from his Texas jail cell to Washington.

7. Page 272 in Anson's book, *"They've Killed the President!"*

8. According to prison inmate John Wilson of England, identified by the CIA as "very probably an intelligence agent."

Sources

My own notes were a basic source for this book. I began taking them in Dallas moments after the President was shot, and continued taking them for two more weeks in Dallas. On returning home to the Washington, D.C., area I dictated an additional 10,000 words of impressions and information, and ultimately conducted a series of tape-recorded interviews with people involved with Ruby or the Ruby case. The bulk of the research into government documents was conducted at the National Archives, where Warren Commission exhibits, memoranda and records are maintained, and at the Library of Congress, where numerous writings on the Kennedy assassination are preserved. The most essential of the writings, of course, are the 26 Warren Commission volumes which contain 10.4 million words, based on 26,550 basic interviews. In addition I used the microfilmed newspaper files in the Jefferson Annex of the Library of Congress to extract information from 1963-1964 editions of newspapers in a number of cities, and the private film and videotape files of television stations KXAS (NBC) and KDFW (CBS) in Fort Worth and Dallas. I also regularly used materials in several public libraries in Washington, Dallas and Montgomery County, Md. FBI files—particularly the 98,761 pages made available through the Freedom of Information Act in December, 1977, and January, 1978—provided additional information for this book, as did the following sources:

1. *The Two Assassins.* By Renatus Hartogs and Lucy Freeman. Thomas Y. Crowell Company. 1965.
2. *"They've Killed the President!"* By Robert Sam Anson. Bantam Books, Inc. 1975.
3. *The Trial of Jack Ruby.* By John Kaplan and Jon R. Waltz. The Macmillan Company. 1965.
4. *Accessories After the Fact.* By Sylvia Meagher. The Bobbs-Merrill Company, Inc. 1967.
5. *Jack Ruby's Girls.* By Diana Hunter and Alice Anderson. Hallux, Inc. 1970.
6. *November 22, 1963: You Are the Jury.* By David W. Belin. Quadrangle/The New York Times Book Co. 1973.
7. *The Witnesses.* Prepared by members of *The New York Times* Washington Bureau. McGraw-Hill Book Company, Inc. 1964-65.
8. *Jack Ruby.* By Garry Wills and Ovid Demaris. New American Library. 1967-68.
9. *The Public Papers of President Lyndon B. Johnson.* 1963-64.
10. *Inquest.* By Edward J. Epstein. Viking Press. 1966.
11. *Dallas Justice.* By Melvin M. Belli, with Maurice C. Carroll. David McKay Co., Inc. 1964.
12. *Destiny in Dallas.* Compiled by R. B. Denson. Denco Corp. 1964.
13. *Trauma,* Vol. 6, No. 4, The State vs. Jack Ruby (medical testimony in the Ruby trial). Matthew Bender & Co. December, 1964.
14. *Drew Pearson Diaries, 1949-1959.* Edited by Tyler Abell. Holt, Rinehart and Winston. 1974.
15. *Legacy of Doubt.* By Peter Noyes. Pinnacle Books, Inc. 1973.
16. *The Assassinations, Dallas and Beyond.* Edited by Peter Dale Scott, Paul L. Hoch and Russell Stetler. Vintage Books. 1976.
17. *The Green Felt Jungle.* By Ed Reid and Ovid Demaris. Trident Press. 1963.
18. *The Mobs and the Mafia.* By Hank Messick and Burt Goldblatt. Ballantine Books, Inc. 1973.
19. *The Truth About the Assassination.* By Charles Roberts. Grosset & Dunlap. 1967.
20. *Invitation to Hairsplitting.* By Jacques Zwart. Paris Press. 1970.
21. *Conspiracy Interpretations of the Assassination of President Kennedy: International and Domestic.* By Alfred Goldberg. University of California, Los Angeles. 1968.
22. *Crime Without Punishment.* By John L. McClellan. Duell, Sloan and Pearce. 1962.

23. *Give Us This Day.* By Howard Hunt. Arlington House. 1973.
24. *The Bay of Pigs.* By Haynes Johnson. W. W. Norton & Co., Inc. 1964.
25. *The Death of a President.* By William Manchester. Harper & Row, Publishers. 1967.
26. *The Johnson Eclipse, A President's Vice Presidency.* By Leonard Baker. The Macmillan Company. 1966.
27. *The Day Kennedy Was Shot.* By Jim Bishop. Funk & Wagnalls. 1968.
28. *Lansky.* By Hank Messick. Berkley Publishing Corp. 1971.
29. *Moment of Madness: The People vs. Jack Ruby.* By Elmer Gertz. Follett Publishing Co., Chicago. 1968.
30. *Personal JFK Assassination File.* By Jesse Curry. American Poster and Printing Company, Inc. 1969.
31. *Rush to Judgment.* By Mark Lane. Holt, Rinehart and Winston. 1966.
32. *The President's Commission on the Assassination of President Kennedy.* A report and 26 volumes. Government Printing Office. 1964.
33. *House Government Information and Individual Rights Subcommittee Hearings.* November 11, 1975.
34. *Senate Select Committee on Intelligence Activities.* The interim report on alleged assassination plots involving foreign leaders (November 20, 1975), and the final report on the assassination of President John F. Kennedy (April 23, 1976).
35. *Senate Permanent Subcommittee on Investigations.* Hearings on organized crime and illicit traffic in narcotics. 1963 and 1964.
36. *U.S. Commission on CIA Activities Within the United States* (The Rockefeller Commission). Report to the President. June 6, 1975.
37. *Senate Special Committee to Investigate Organized Crime in Interstate Commerce.* The Illinois Hearings. 1950 and 1951.
38. *Honor Thy Father.* By Gay Talese. World Publishing Co. 1971.
39. *The Grim Reapers.* By Ed Reid. Henry Regnery Co. 1969.
40. *Crime and Coverup.* By Peter Dale Scott. Westworks, Publishers. 1977.
41. *The Unanswered Questions About President Kennedy's Assassination.* By Sylvan Fox. Award Books. 1965.

Index

Aase, Jean (Jean West), 37
Abt, John J., 174
Accardo, Tony (Joe Batters), 31, 32, 101, 104-5
Adams, Francis W. H., 83-84
Albert, Carl, 213
Aleman, José, 136
Alessandri, Jorge, 200
Alexander, William F.: Ruby and, 57, 113-16, 119, 125, 126, 182
Allende, Salvador, 200-1
Anastasia, Albert, 134
Anderson, Jack, 5, 211, 212
Anson, Robert Sam, 14, 210
Archer, Don Ray: Ruby and, 75-76, 113, 114, 144, 145, 160
Armstrong, Andrew, Jr. (Andy): Ruby and, 41-44, 189, 202
Arnett, George C., 24
Arvey, Jake, 98
Attel, Abe, 57

Baker, Robert (Barney): Ruby and, 20, 22, 23, 38, 30-34, 37
Ball, Joseph A., 4, 84
Barbe, Lewis, 30
Barrett, Robert M., 196

Barrett, Sam, 33-35
Batchelor, Charles, 60, 63, 64, 69, 73, 143, 151
Bates, B. A., Jr., 24
Batista, Fulgencio, 13, 133, 134, 137
Beavers, William R.: Ruby's mental state and, 176, 179, 181-84
Beerman, Ralph, 156-58
Belin, David W., 3, 68, 84, 154, 177-78, 204-5, 209
Belli, Melvin M.: in defense of Ruby, 115-20, 122-25, 152, 169, 188, 215, 217
Bentley, Paul L., 61, 74
Bernstein, Leonard, 99
Bierne, Joseph A., 101
Biffle, Kent, 44
Bishop, Morris, 210
Blakey, G. Robert, 214
Blanchard, Allan E., 120
Blankenship, D. L., 148
Bliss, George, 100
Boggs, Hale, 80, 82
Bollman, Mildred, 33
Bosch, Juan, 199
Bowie, Jim, 4
Brading, Eugene Hale (Jim Brading), 32-37, 111
Brantley, Ray, 24

Breen, James, 110
Bringuier, Carlos, 199
Broe, William C., 200
Bromberg, Walter, 42, 43, 47, 119, 169
Brown, Charles W., 67, 72
Brown, Joe B., 120-22, 179
Brown, Morgan H., 34-37
Brumley, Morris, 110
Bruner, Fred (Ed Brunner), 77, 160
Bundy, McGeorge, 132, 164
Burleson, Phil, 123
Butler, George E., 66-67, 104-6, 149, 216

Cabell, Earle, 73
Campbell, Judith Katherine, 33-34
Canfield, Michael, 14
Capone, Al, 98, 101, 137
Carlin, Karen Bennett (Little Lynn), 59, 64, 65, 68, 189
Carlson, Edward E., 77, 148
Carr, Waggoner, 4, 78-79, 90, 162, 163, 203
Carroll, Roger, 35
Carson, E. I., 19
Cash, Ben, 207
Castro, Fidel, 15, 86, 199, 204: CIA plot against, 25, 95, 96, 135-36, 138, 140, 211; and Kennedy's death, 211; mob and, 13, 14, 132, 133, 135-37; Ruby and, 48, 128-30, 140, 141
Central Intelligence Agency (CIA), 93-95, 154: Castro and, 25, 95, 96, 135-36, 140, 211; Davis and, 15, 16, 138; Document No. 150-59 and, 13; Giancana and, 25, 33; in Griffin-Hubert memorandum 161, 162; Hendrix and, 199-201; and Kennedy's death, 211; Olney and, 82; Oswald and, 207, 208, 210; Rosselli and, 131; Ruby and, 11, 127, 128, 132-34, 139, 217-18; Trafficante and, 212; Velásquez and, 217
Church, Frank, 136, 200, 201
Cisco, Riccio R., 20
Civello, Joseph F., 8-9
Clardy, Barnard S., 75-76, 144, 145
Clark, Tom, 31
Clements, Manning C., 187
Cody, Joe, 148
Cohen, Mickey, 21, 22, 116
Coleman, Kay Helen, 48-50
Coleman, William T., 84
Combest, Billy H., 73
Conforto, Janet Adams Bonney Cuffari Smallwood (Jada): Ruby and, 21, 22, 139, 171-72, 174
Connally, John B., 19, 41, 80, 155, 191-94, 206-8
Cooke, Leon R., 99, 100
Cooper, John Sherman, 80
Cornwall, F. E., 216
Cox, William J., 19, 25, 215
Crafard, Curtis LaVerne (Larry), 24, 41-42, 49-53
Crile, George, III, 135-36
Crosby, Bing, 33
Crossland, Taylor, 106, 107
Crowe, William D., Jr. (Bill DeMar), 206
Croy, Kenneth Hudson, 145, 146

Cuban connection, 3, 4, 6, 11, 13-15, 127-41, 160, 210
Curry, Eileen, 110
Curry, Jesse E.: Oswald and, 20, 47, 53, 54, 57-58, 60, 67-68, 71, 73, 74, 202-3; Ruby and, 55-57, 69-70, 75, 114, 145, 150, 216
Cutchshaw, W. J. (Jay): Ruby and, 60, 70, 73-74, 216

Dallas police department: in Griffin-Hubert investigation, 143-51; and lie detector test on Ruby, 180; and removal of Griffin, 153-55; Ruby as informer for, 143; Ruby's relations with, 8, 9, 18, 55-58, 61-62, 109-10, 172, 215-16; and Ruby's presence during transfer of Oswald, 58-61, 63-71, 73-77
Dann, Sol A., 178, 179
Davis, Mrs. T. Eli, 15, 16
Davis, Thomas Eli, III: Ruby and, 14-16, 49, 129, 137, 138
Dean, Patrick T.: in Griffin-Hubert investigation, 2-3, 153, 154, 158, 160-63; Ruby and, 61-62, 73-75, 114-15, 125, 149-50
Decker, J. E. (Bill), 4, 5, 32-33, 36, 53, 60, 124, 166, 178, 187
De Gaulle, Charles, 16
Delgado, Nelson, 205
Denson, Robert B., 126
Dhority, Charles N., 67, 72
Dirksen, Everett M., 78
Dorfman, Paul J., 100-2
Dowe, Ken, 54
Downing, Thomas N., 213
Drain, Vincent E. J., 186
Duclos, Leopoldo Ramos (Leopold Ramos Ducos), 218
Dulles, Allen W., 80, 82, 93, 162
Duncan, Waldon, 106, 107
Dunn, Eddie (Cockeyed), 30

Eastland, James O., 132, 133
Eberhardt, August M. (Mike), 45, 143, 180
Edwards, Sheffield, 25
Egger, Charles, 198
Eichenbaum, Rudy, 21
Eisenhower, Dwight D., 81, 131
Epstein, Edward J., 163, 164
Evans, Sidney, Jr., 63

Faye, Bobby, 23, 24
Federal Bureau of Investigation (FBI), 15, 86-89, 154, 177; Cooke and, 100; coverup by, 87-88; documents withheld by, 197-98, 201; and Griffin-Hubert memorandum, 160-62; Hardee and, 110-11; and H. L. Hunt probe, 112; P. R. Jones and, 101, 106; and lie detector test for Ruby, 181; Oswald-Ruby connection and, 206-7, 209; political pressure by, on Commission, 156-59; and presence of Ruby at hospital, 190-94, 196, 197; Ruby and, 6, 11, 137; Ruby as informer for, 93, 143; Ruby-Weiner and, 29-30; and Ruby's Cuban connections, 127-34, 140; Wise and, 192
Fein, Edward, 29
Fensterwald, Bernard, Jr., 132-33

Ferrell, Mary, 197
Filvaroff, Phil, 83
Fitzgerald, George S., 30
Fleming, Harold J., 63, 64, 66
Flint, Amos C., 29
Flynn, Charles W.: Ruby and, 88, 128-32
Fontana, Carlos, 100
Ford, D. D., 33, 34
Ford, Gerald R., 14-15, 80, 82, 89, 158, 218; and Ruby, 3, 4, 6, 93-94, 178, 182, 189, 190
Foreman, Percy, 152
Fortas, Abe, 79
Fowler, Clayton, 178, 179, 182, 184
Fox, Martin, 11, 13, 14, 130
Fox, Pedro, 11, 13, 14
Frankfurter, Felix, 84
Fritz, J. Will, 44, 47, 148; Oswald and, 53-54, 57, 63, 67-68, 71-73; Ruby and, 57, 76-77, 144, 149, 150

Gerrity, E. J., 200
Giancona, Salvatore Momo (Sam), 25, 32, 33, 135, 136, 211, 212
Gilbert, Daniel, 100
Goldberg, Alfred, 85, 164
Goldstein, Frank, 22
Goldwater, Barry M., 164
Golz, Earl, 35
Gonzales, Henry B., 40-41, 213-14
Goodell, Charles E., 78-79
Goodson, Clyde F., 46
Goolsby (officer), 147
Grant, Eva L., 106, 164, 189; Ruby and, 23, 39-40, 42-44, 77, 98, 107, 179, 193
Graves, L. C., 73
Griffin, Burt W.: CIA, Ruby and, 217; conspiracy question, 215-16; Davis and, 14, 15; Dean, Ruby and, 2-3, 63, 162, 163; and Hoover letter, 88; on lack of investigative staff, 86; memorandum to Rankin by Hubert and, 159-62, 164, 189; Miller and, 61; ordered out of Dallas investigation, 152, 153, 154, 158; Powell questioned by, 196; premeditation question in death of Oswald, 142-43; Redlich and, 159; and Ruby at hospital, 190, 195, 198, 201-2; Ruby investigation under, 6, 29, 51, 82-85, 90-96, 142-51; Ruby and Oswald's transfer, 69; Ruby's Cuban connection and, 127, 128; Mrs. Tice and, 193; and Warren-Rankin, 1-2, 10
Gruber, Alexander Philip, 22, 23, 37, 42, 161
Guglielmo, John (Johnny Williams), 13
Gumbin, Nathan, 102
Guthrie, Steve, 32, 105-6, 149, 155
Guttmacher, Manfred S., 43, 119, 169, 171, 172
Guzik, Jake (Greasy Thumb), 31, 32, 104, 105

Hall, C. Ray, 76, 161, 187
Hall, Harry (Harry Haller; Harry Helfgott; Harry Sinclair, Jr.; Ed Pauley, Jr.), 111
Halley, Randolph, 143
Hallmark, Garnett Claud, 54
Hamilton, Charles, 122-23
Hammett, Art, 187
Hardee, Jack, Jr., 110-11

Harkness, D. V., 54
Harrison, W. J. (Blackie): Ruby and, 60, 61, 67, 70-71, 74, 145-49, 215, 216
Helmick, Wanda Sweatt, 108
Helms, Richard M., 93, 94, 133, 139, 161
Hendrix, Harold V. (Hal), 198-201
Herndon, Bell P., 178-84
Hill, Clint, 195-96
Hintz, Anthony, 30
Hitler, Adolph, 120
Hoeft, W. J., 88
Hoffa, James Riddle, 20, 22, 28, 30, 101, 136, 218
Holman, E. L., 182
Hoover, J. Edgar, 6, 25-26; investigation into Kennedy and Oswald murders under, 79; Oswald and, 88-89; Ragen and, 31; and Ruby, 128, 181; Warren Commission opposed by, 86-88, 93, 156, 158, 159; see also Federal Bureau of Investigation
Hosty, James, 87
Houston, Lawrence, 25
Howard, Tom: Ruby and, 15, 63, 76, 115, 120, 122, 148, 160-61, 187, 217
Howard, William Edward, 23
Howe, Kenneth C., 169
Hubert, Leon D., Jr.: CIA, Ruby and, 217; conspiracy issue and, 215-16; Davis and, 14, 15; Dean, Ruby and, 162, 163; excluded from questioning witnesses, 85; and Hoover letter, 88; memorandum to Rankin by Griffin and, 159-62, 164, 189; profile of Ruby by, 91-94, 96; Redlich and, 159; Ruby investigation under, 51, 82-84, 142-53; Ruby and Oswald transfer, 69; Ruby's Cuban connection and, 127, 128; and Ruby's presence at hospital, 190, 195, 202; Senator interviewed by, 169-71; and Warren-Rankin, 1-2, 10; on Willens, 86
Huffaker, Robert S., Jr., 145
Humphreys, Murray (The Camel), 105
Hunt, Bunker, 35, 37, 39
Hunt, H. L., 35, 37, 111-12, 161-62
Hunt, Lamar, 35, 37

Jackson, John C., 49, 171
Jacobson, Coleman, 29, 42
Jarnagin, Carroll, 206-7, 209
Jaworski, Leon, 4
Jeffrey, Dick, 39, 40
Jenkins, Walter, 78-79, 88-89
Jenner, Albert E., Jr., 84
Johansen, August E., 158, 159
John (prisoner), 122, 123
Johnson, David L., 56
Johnson, Lady Bird, 40
Johnson, Lyndon B., 19, 40, 78-80, 89, 132, 155, 163, 164, 198, 200
Johnson, U. Alexis, 132
Jones, Cal, 148
Jones, O. A., 69
Jones, Paul Rowland: and organized crime interests in Dallas, 104-7; Ruby's connection with, 8, 18, 22, 23, 32, 101, 103, 110, 149, 215, 216

Kaiser, Richard W., 187
Kalinowski, E. S., 20
Kaminsky, Eileen, 29, 42, 43, 175, 193
Kaplan, John, 115-16
Katzenbach, Nicholas deB., 86, 89
Kautt, Laverne, 131
Kefauver, Estes, 143
Kelley, Clarence M., 197
Kelly, Thomas, 99
Kennedy, Caroline, 76
Kennedy, Jacqueline, 38, 51-52, 63, 76, 122, 124
Kennedy, John F., 2, 7, 10, 16-20, 38, 131; Brading and death of, 35-37; and J. K. Campbell, 33-34; CIA documents and death of, 133; CIA-Mafia connection and, 136; conspiracy issue in death of, 203-18; date of Dallas trip fixed for, 33-34; death of, 17, 40-41, 62, 80, 84, 114, 126, 139, 140, 166, 175; death announced, 41, 186, 187, 189, 191, 195, 196; FBI and death of, see Federal Bureau of Investigation; Griffin-Hubert investigation and, see Griffin, Burt W.; Hubert, Leon D., Jr.; Hendrix's Latin American stories and death of, 199-200; Hoover and death of, 89; B. Hunt and death of, 39; H. L. Hunt probe into death of, 111-12; the Hunts and death of, 35; Lane and death of, 90; legislation under, blocked, 117; magic bullet killing, 155, 191-92; mob in conspiracy to kill, 9, 210-13; newspapers fail to investigate death of, 188-89; Oswald charged in death of, 47 (see also Oswald, Lee Harvey); Redlich incident in investigation of death of, 157; Ruby and, 28, 174, 180; Ruby on, 42, 43, 169; and Ruby defense, 119; Ruby at hospital awaiting death of, 161, 184-98, 201-2; Ruby's lie detector test and death of, 179; Ruby's motive and death of, 117; Ruby's movements before death of, 25, 30-32; Ruby's movements after death of, 184-92; Ruby's reaction to, 51-52; Trafficante and, 136, 211-14

Kennedy, Robert F., 25-26, 30, 31, 39, 86, 100-1, 136, 210, 212
Kennedy blood: Marcello and, 136
Kilduff, Malcolm: announces death of Kennedy, 41, 186, 187, 189, 191, 195, 196
King, Martin Luther, Jr., 214
Knight, Frances G., 138
Knight, Russ (Russell Lee Moore), 48
Koch, Graham, R. E., 20, 24, 64-65
Korry, Edward, 200
Korth, Fred, 19
Kutner, Luis, 143

Labriola, Paul (Needle-Nose), 101, 102
Lane, Doyle, 68
Lane, Mark, 90
Lansky, Jake, 13, 14
Lansky, Meyer, 13, 14, 24, 28, 130, 134, 135
Lattimer, John, 168
Law, Ambrose K., 110
Leavello, James R., 72-73
Lee, Ivan D., 196

Lehrer, Jim, 153
Levi, Edward H., 197, 201
Lewis, C. L. (Lummie), 35
Liebeler, Westey J., 84
Lincoln, Abraham, 62, 213
Locurto, Joseph (Joe Bonds), 107, 108
Long, Joe, 46
Love, Robie, 207
Lowery, Roy Lee, 70, 74, 216
Lucas, Jim, 40

McCarthy, Joseph, 154, 158
McClellan, John L., 12, 19, 30, 101
McCloy, John J., 80
McCone, John A., 93-94
McCord, David C., 11-13, 130
McGann, George, 208
McGee, H. L. 148
McKeown, Robert Ray (Dick), 15, 128-29, 137-38
McLane, Alfred E., 12-13, 130, 134
McLean, Bruce, 29
McLendon, Gordon (Weird Beard), 174-75
MacMaster, Ted P., 147
McMillon, T. D., 75-76, 144, 145
McWillie, Lewis J.: Ruby and, 4, 11, 13, 24, 31, 123, 129-32, 138, 211
Maheu, Robert A., 25
Manno, Paul, 105
Marcello, Carlos, 28, 83, 136, 212
Marcus, Stanley, 119
Martin, John, 99, 100, 217
Martin, Mary, 24
Massegee, Beverly Oliver McGann, 207-8
Matte, Arturo, 200
Matula, Frank, 22
Mauldin, Shirley (Robin S. Hood), 207
May, Robert L., Jr., 20
May, Walter, 201
Meany, George, 101
Mearns, Hughes, 56
Merriam, William R., 200
Messick, Hank, 13, 135
Melton, Maurice C., 106, 107
Meyers, Lawrence V., 37
Miles, Ralph J., 108
Miller, Albert B., 187
Miller, L. D.: Ruby and, 60, 61, 146-49, 215, 216
Mitchell, John N., 105
Moore, Elmer W., 4, 58
Moore, Marylin, 172
Moyers, Eldon, 16
Mundt, Karl E., 157-58
Munster, Buddy, 148
Mynier, Elaine, 129-31

Nappi, Jack, 105
Newman, John W., 38-40, 195
Newman, William J., 144-46
Nichols, Alice Reaves, 126, 183
Nixon, Richard M., 105, 200-1, 218
Norman, Earl, 24
Noyes, Peter, 33

O'Leary, Jeremiah A., Jr., (Jerry), 55, 63, 65, 66, 68, 72
Olney, Warren, III, 81-82
Olsen, Harry N., 7, 8, 48-50, 215
Organized crime, see Central Intelligence Agency; Cuban connection; Dallas police department; and specific criminals; for example: Jones, Paul Rowland; Marcello, Carlos; Trafficante, Santo, Jr.
Oswald, Lee Harvey, 20, 34, 189; behavior of, on being arrested, 174, 175; Bishop and, 210; central questions on Ruby and, 215-16; charged with murder, 47; conspiracy issue in death of Kennedy and death of, 69-70, 203-18; conviction of Ruby, 165; expected exoneration of Ruby for death of, 109; fear of a Ruby suicide after death of, 165-67; FBI probe on Ruby, 86 (see also Federal Bureau of Investigation); Fritz and, 53-54, 57, 63, 67-68, 71-73; and Griffin-Hubert investigation of Ruby, 78, 142-55, 160-61; Hendrix on past of, 199; Hoover wanting, as sole assassin, 88-89; as impersonal Nazi image for Ruby, 99; identified as murder suspect, 198; killed by Ruby, 17, 73, 76; Lane and, 90; lie detector test for Ruby and, 176-84; not admitting responsibility for death of Kennedy, 57; plot to kill, by criminals, 9; premeditation question in Ruby's action, 113, 114, 142-43; and prosecution of Ruby, 113-26; prior connection between Ruby and, 203-9; public support for Ruby, 122; Redlich and, 157; Ruby and, 2-5, 8-10, 13, 15, 32, 35, 48, 53, 55, 87, 92, 106, 108-10, 140; Ruby on, 43, 47; Ruby, the mob and, 18; Ruby, Olsen and, 48-49; Ruby, and Oswald's connection with Fair Play for Cuba Committee, 47-48; Ruby in prison for killing, 165-69; Ruby telling Senator of his intentions to kill, 62-63; Ruby and transfer of, 53-54, 58-61, 63-73; Ruby's motive, 18, 19, 168, 215-16; seeks change in undesirable discharge status, 19; trial of Ruby for killing, 115-25; Warren Commission focus in investigation of, 82-84
Oswald, Marguerite, 44
Oswald, Marina, 19-20, 80, 87, 177

Paine, Ruth, 19
Papich, Sam, 133, 201
Pappas, Ike, 48, 65, 66, 68
Patrick, Lenny (Leonard Levine), 22-24, 31-32, 37
Paul, Ralph, 24, 107-8, 189
Pennington, Ray, 167-68
Pereira, Evido, 140, 141
Pereira, Victor Emanuel, 32-34, 37
Pettit, Tom, 74
Pierce, Rio Sam: Oswald and, 61-62, 72, 74-76, 145, 146, 180
Pitts, Elnora, 59-60, 65
Powell, Nancy Monnell (Tammi True), 169, 196
Praskins (Ruby pseudonym), 139, 140
Preston, Bill J., 207
Price, Bob, 139-40
Putnam, J. A., 62

Ragen, James M. (Jack), 31-32
Rankin, John E., 82
Rankin, J. Lee, 84, 85, 155, 203; CIA, Ruby and, 217; Cuba, Ruby and, 127, 139; and Dean testimony, 3, 149-51, 163; FBI and, 86-88; finishing Commission work, 163-64; Griffin and, 153-54; Griffin-Hubert and, 1, 3, 10, 93; Griffin-Hubert memorandum to, 159-62, 189, 202; Hubert and, 82-83; lacks trust in FBI, 86; Miller and, 61; Newman, Ruby and, 145; opinions on, 81; Redlich and, 156, 158; Ruby and, 90, 140; in Ruby interview, 3-4, 6, 10, 11
Redding, Lorraine, 12
Redlich, Norman, 85, 86, 89, 156-59, 163-64, 205
Reid, Ed, 28
Revill, Jack, 71, 216
Rheinstein, Frederic, 55
Rich, Nancy Perrin, 138
Richburg, W. J., 124
Robertson, Victor F., Jr., 46
Rogers, Elaine, 172
Roosevelt, Franklin D., 83
Rose, Earl F., 118
Ross, Barney (Barney Rasofsky), 92, 98
Rosselli, John, 32, 33, 111, 131, 135, 136, 211, 212
Rothermel, Paul M., 112
Rothman, Norman (Roughhouse), 129-30, 137
Rothstein, Arnold (The Brain), 57
Rubenstein, Fanny (Fanny Rokowsky), 88, 96-97
Rubenstein, Joseph, 96-97
Rubenstein, Sam, 98, 102
Ruby, Earl (Earl Rubenstein), 98, 102, 115, 152, 178
Ruby, Hyman (Hyman Rubenstein), 22, 23, 102, 106, 107, 170
Ruby, Jack (Jacob Rubenstein; Sparky): behavior of, on being arrested, 174-75; biographical sketch of, 97-112; cancer, 8; characteristics of, 5-6; Commission investigation of, see Griffin, Burt W.; Hubert, Leon D., Jr.; doodles in prison by, 167-69; financial situation of, 21-25; interest in religion, 167; and J. F. Kennedy, see Kennedy, John F.; and organized crime, see specific criminals; Oswald and, see Oswald, Lee Harvey; and the police, see Central Intelligence Agency; Dallas police department; Federal Bureau of Investigation; sexuality of, 169-74, 183; suicide attempts by, 165-66
Russell, Richard B., 80, 89
Rutledge, John, 45

Sahakian, Juanita Slusher Dale Phillips (Candy Barr), 21-23, 116, 121
Sanders, Barefoot, 143, 151, 153, 164
Saunders, Richard L., 39, 40, 189
Sawyer, J. H., 216
Schafer, Roy, 117
Scheib, Philip Earl, 32
Schweiker, Richard S., 136
Scobey, Alfredda, 80

Senator, George: Ruby and, 50-53, 58-59, 62-65, 169-71, 183, 217
Serur, William G., 173-74
Shanklin, J. Gordon, 87
Sheaver, Buck, 24
Shires, George T., 194
Shires, Tom, 118
Shivers, Alan, 206-7
Siedband, Harry, 111
Silverman, Hillel E., 172-73, 177-78, 183
Simon, Neil, 51
Sims, Richard M., 46
Sisk, B. F., 213
Slaughter, Malcolm, 63
Slawson, W. David, 84
Smalley, Judy, 194
Smith, Howard W., 117
Smith, Hubert Winston, 152-53
Soloman, Elmer Ray, 111
Sorge, Santo, 12, 134, 135
Sorrels, Forrest V.: Ruby and, 2, 72, 75, 76, 114-15, 125
Spaman, Guy H., 111
Specter, Arlen: Ruby and, 4, 62-63, 81, 84, 155, 178, 179, 182
Sprague, Richard A., 136, 210-14
Stanton, Edwin M., 213
Stern, Samuel A., 84
Stevenson, Jess W., Jr.: Ruby and, 7-8, 69, 73, 123-25, 167, 182
Stevenson, M. W., 60, 61
Stokes, Louis, 214
Storey, Robert G., 4
Straeght, Charles, 24
Stuckey, William Kirk, 199
Sucharov, Bert, 133
Sullivan, William C., 87, 89
Swain, Richard E., 72, 74, 148-49
Sweatt, Allan, 36

Talbert, Cecil E., 69
Tankersly, John, 70, 74
Tannenbaum, Harold, 139
Thomas, Albert, 41
Thornton, Thomas P., 138
Tice, James, 194
Tice, Wilma M., 192-93
Timmons, Dave, 70, 74
Tippit, J.D.: Oswald and, 7, 9, 47, 57, 84, 90, 114, 143, 203-5, 209
Todd, James Robert (Jack), 108
Tomlinson, Darrell C., 192
Tonahill, Joe H.: and lie detector test for Ruby, 178-80, 182; Ruby and, 49, 63, 152; in Ruby defense, 116-19, 122, 124, 126; in Ruby interview, 4-6; on Ruby's involvement in conspiracy, 69; on Ruby's movements after Kennedy death, 190; and Ruby's sketches and doodles, 169; and Ruby's suicide attempt, 166
Trafficante, Santo, Jr., (Louis Santos): Cuban interests of, 134-37; and Kennedy murder 136, 211-14; Ruby and, 13, 94, 130, 132, 134, 137, 218
Truly, R. S., 208, 209
Trummell, Connie, 35

Turman, Regan (Buddy), 148
Turner, Jimmy, 65, 70, 145-46

Ulevitch, Dr., 23

Valachi, Joseph M., 5-6, 77
Vaughn, Roy E., 68, 69, 74, 75, 150
Velásquez, Victor, 217

Wade, Henry M., 3, 47, 48; Dean, Ruby and, 149, 153; Griffin-Hubert, Ruby and, 143, 160; Love, Ruby and, 207; Ruby and, 10, 54, 55, 57, 79, 151; in Ruby's trial, 119, 121, 124, 125
Waldo, Thayer, 55, 66, 67
Wallace, Cecil C., 216
Walsh, Gladys, 100
Waltz, Jon R., 115-16
Warner, Doris, 49
Warren, Earl, 50; W. F. Alexander on, 114; Belin Theory and, 205; and CIA witnesses, 94; Commission formed under, 79-81, 84; Davis, Ruby and, 14-15; and Dean as witness, 163; FBI and, 86-88; Hubert-Griffin and, 1, 3, 10; and lie detector test for Ruby, 178; and Olney, 81-82; pressure on, to end Commission work, 155, 159, 160, 163-64; Redlich and, 89, 158; Ruby and, 4-8, 10, 12, 18, 52, 53, 90, 143, 162, 182-3; Ruby on his trial, 120; and teams of lawyers, 85
Warren Commission: formed, 79-81, 84; function and objective of, 82-86
Washington, George T., 83
Weberman, Alan J., 14
Weinberg, Jimmy, 101, 102
Weiner, Irwin S., 28-33, 37
Weinstein, Abe, 22
Weinstein, Barney, 22
Weissman, Bernard, 39, 50, 52, 53, 90
Weston, Wally, 206
Whitten, Les, 211, 212
Wiggins, Woodrow, 69, 72
Wilcox, Howard, 118
Willens, Howard P.: on Commission staff, 3, 85-87, 92, 127, 151, 158, 159, 163-64
Wilson, John (John Wilson-Hudon): Ruby and, 132-33, 134
Wilson, Will R., 105
Winchell, Walter, 48
Wise, Wesley A., 54, 192
Wood (agent), 187
Wood, W. James, 180, 182
Wright, James Skelly, 82

Yaras, David, 31-32, 37
Yarborough, Ralph W., 19, 40

Zwillman, Abner (Longie), 101